Kafka and Wittgenstein

Kafka and Wittgenstein

The Case for an Analytic Modernism

Rebecca Schuman

NORTHWESTERN UNIVERSITY PRESS
EVANSTON, ILLINOIS

Northwestern University Press
www.nupress.northwestern.edu

Printed in the United States of America

10 9 8 7 6 5 4 3 2 1

Library of Congress Cataloging-in-Publication Data

Schuman, Rebecca, author.
Kafka and Wittgenstein : the case for an analytic modernism / Rebecca Schuman.
pages cm.
Based on the author's dissertation—University of California–Irvine, 2010.
Includes bibliographical references and index.
ISBN 978-0-8101-3146-0 (cloth : alk. paper)—ISBN 978-0-8101-3184-2 (pbk. : alk. paper)—ISBN 978-0-8101-3150-7 (ebook)
1. Kafka, Franz, 1883–1924—Criticism and interpretation. 2. Wittgenstein, Ludwig, 1889–1951. 3. Literature—Philosophy. I. Title.
PT2621.A26Z8651716 2015
833'.912—dc23

2015029414

Contents

Acknowledgments *vii*

List of Abbreviations *ix*

Introduction: Why Kafka and Wittgenstein? *3*

Part One: Logical Modernism:
Kafka and the *Tractatus Logico-Philosophicus*

Preface to Part One
Logic, Skepticism, and Mysticism *15*

Chapter 1
The Trial and the Law of Logic *39*

Chapter 2
The Metamorphosis and the Limits of Metaphorical Language *55*

Chapter 3
"The Judgment," Ethics, and the Ineffable *85*

Part Two: Analytic Skepticism:
Kafka and the *Philosophical Investigations*

Preface to Part Two
Wittgenstein's Transition and a More Analytic Kafka *109*

Chapter 4
The Castle and the Paradox of Ostensive Definition *113*

Chapter 5
Rule-Following and Failed Execution: "In the Penal Colony" *137*

Chapter 6
The Private Language Argument and the Undermining of "Josefine the Singer" *167*

Concluding Thoughts: The Problem with (Critical) Progress *193*

Notes *197*

Works Cited *213*

Index *219*

ACKNOWLEDGMENTS

I would like to thank Henry Carrigan at Northwestern University Press for bringing this project under contract and thus into existence as a book, rather than my dissertation, which is how *Kafka and Wittgenstein* began ten years ago in Irvine, California. Speaking of which, my gratitude runs eternal for the rigorous guidance of the University of California–Irvine's Kai Evers, my doctoral adviser, mentor, and friend, and to John H. Smith, David T. Pan, Gail K. Hart, Glenn Levine, and Anke Biendarra.

The second chapter of this book first appeared in *The German Quarterly* as the article "Unerschütterlich: Kafka's *Proceß*, Wittgenstein's *Tractatus* and the Law of Logic," for which I thank James Rolleston and Kata Gellen. My third chapter first appeared in *Modern Austrian Literature* as the article "Kafka's *Verwandlung*, Wittgenstein's *Tractatus*, and the Limits of Metaphorical Language," and its journey into publication was not an easy one. I'd like to thank Craig Decker for championing it through four major revisions, under the nose of an increasingly malcontent reader. Thanks also to Robert E. Norton, Bernie Rhie, Karen Zumhagen-Yekple, Yi-Ping Ong, and Bernhard Malkmus for reading sections of this manuscript, and special thanks to Samuel Frederick for reading the whole thing, and alerting me to any "deal breakers" before I submitted it for review. Finally, I cannot express enough gratitude to the readers who reviewed this book as a manuscript, and recommended it so enthusiastically for publication. I would also like to thank my freelance copy editor, Jason Eversman, who put the manuscript into Chicago style, fixed the hot mess that was my endnotes and bibliography, and masterfully repaired all of the minute textual details at which my impatience and incompetence know no bounds.

This book would not have been possible without the financial support of the following: the University of California-Irvine, which afforded me a Dissertation Year Fellowship in 2009–10; the Austrian Fulbright Commission and the Internationales Forschungszentrum Kulturwissenschaften (IFK), for bringing me to Vienna for 2008–09; and, finally, the American Council of Learned Societies (ACLS), for accepting me into the New Faculty Fellows Program and placing me at the Ohio State University for 2011–13. The ACLS position included a low teaching load and a travel allowance, and enabled me to produce the non-dissertation version of this book, from start to finish, in less than two years.

Finally, I would like to thank my family: Sharon, David, Ben, Lani, Milly, Charlie, and Billy Budd. And most importantly of all, Waldemar Rohloff, my husband and long-suffering companion through every second of this project, and my daughter Halina Schuman-Rohloff, who burst into existence at the very end, and destroyed my scholarly brain in the best possible way.

St. Louis, Missouri, 2015

ABBREVIATIONS

GW Franz Kafka. *Gesammelte Werke* [*Collected Works*] *in Zwölf Bänden*. Edited by Hans-Gerhard Koch and Malcolm Pasley. 12 vols. Frankfurt am Main: Fischer, 1994.

TLP Ludwig Wittgenstein. *Tractatus Logico-Philosophicus/Logisch-philosophische Abhandlung*. Frankfurt am Main: Suhrkamp, 1963.

PI Ludwig Wittgenstein. *Philosophical Investigations* [*Philosphische Untersuchungen: Dritte Auflage, mit englischem und deutschem Register*]. Edited and translated by G. E. M. Anscombe. New York: Macmillan, 1968.

Kafka and Wittgenstein

Introduction

✦

Why Kafka and Wittgenstein?

Franz Kafka's novels and stories have the dubious honor of being often and hastily relegated to the confines of a single adjective that is supposed to evoke both the necessary uniqueness and slippery indescribability of its namesake. Though it may be unfair to the twentieth century's best-known German-language author to relegate him to an "-esque," if I were forced at gunpoint to explain what "Kafkaesque" is supposed to be, I would recite from memory the "Kleine Fabel" ("Little Fable"), a tiny story whose mouse protagonist gives way to an existential cat villain, and in so doing double-crosses us twice:

> "Ach," sagte die Maus, "die Welt wird enger mit jedem Tag. Zuerst war sie so breit, daß ich Angst hatte, ich lief weiter und war glücklich, daß ich endlich rechts und links in der Ferne Mauern sah, aber diese langen Mauern eilen so schnell aufeinander zu, daß ich schon im letzten Zimmer bin, und dort im Winkel steht die Falle, in die ich laufe." – "Du mußt nur die Laufrichtung ändern," sagte die Katze und fraß sie.[1]
>
> "Alas," said the mouse, "the world gets smaller every day. At first it was so wide that I was afraid, and as I ran along I was happy when I finally saw walls appear in the distance at my right and left. But these long walls closed in so fast that I'm already in the last room, and there in the corner is the trap into which I must run." "You've simply got to run the other direction," said the cat, and ate it.

I choose the "Little Fable" because I see it as both a perplexing work on its own and a baffling microcosm of Kafka's fictional universe, partly because the way in which it captivates the reader, even at its tiny length, is the same way in which all of Kafka's most captivating works are captivating. This is an appeal that is surprisingly quantifiable for a writer who himself specialized in the ineffable: that is, "Little Fable" displays three elements now attributed, for better or worse, to the aforementioned Kafkaesque.

The first is the characterization of the mouse, who embodies the Kafkan quasi-protagonist's ability to portray certain doom by way of outside forces that appear to exist precisely to seal that doom—in the fable's case, these forces are depersonified into narrowing walls (representing a slow, oppressive end) and a trap (representing a quick and violent one). This dichotomy appears all over Kafka's canon: we see it in Josef K.'s slowly but inevitably encroaching trial and the quick and gruesome "execution" (or is it murder?) that brings it to an end; we see it in Georg Bendemann's slow, albeit largely symbolic, suffocation via his overbearing father (echoed in the suffocating nature of the Bendemann family flat), itself put to an end by Georg's hastily stipulated suicide. It reappears in the "death" of Gregor Samsa's individuality, freedom, and dreams at the hands of the late-capitalist world, itself brought to an end by his sudden metamorphosis into a monster—which itself brings about yet another suffocating, slow death meant in large part to mirror the one that was taking place before the metamorphosis. And, in its most violent incarnation, we see this dichotomy in the ornamental torture prescribed by the penal colony's officer, one that ends up instead as a quick, grotesque but altogether unvarnished impalement.

The second way in which the "Little Fable" acts as a fitting epigram for the would-be Kafka reader is its double-twisting plot, remarkable in this case, given the story is three sentences long. The first twist comes when the mouse-protagonist realizes (albeit from a shady outside source) that she has been running in the wrong direction; she has been *going about the entire thing the wrong way*. Similar realizations occur once again throughout Kafka's body of work, from Josef K.'s lumberingly slow realization that he has been conducting his trial in precisely the opposite way the Court prefers, to the tiny short story "Die Bäume" ("The Trees"), in which the tree trunks' elegant placement in the snow makes them appear light on its surface and able to be set rolling "mit kleinem Anstoß" ("with a light push"), when in actuality they are "fest mit dem Boden verbunden," or firmly wedded to the ground (*GW* 1:105). But is this even true? The narrator, able to come across in this four-sentence story as both playful and melancholy, twists the tiny plot again, cautioning us: "Aber sieh, sogar das ist nur scheinbar" ("But see, even that is only appearance"). This action is the third and likely most famous element that creates what we broadly call the "Kafkaesque": the second twist, in which despite the important realization of some important wrong in the first twist, the protagonist (or in the case of "The Trees" the reader, wanting some closure on just how movable the trees are) is nevertheless soundly defeated.

In the Kafkan second twist, what had been uncovered as an illusion—in the case of the "Little Fable," the running direction of the mouse—is then *itself* unmasked as an illusion, the uncovering of which finally leads to the *real* problem (which had been well covered up by the illusory problem of direction): the mouse was a mouse in the first place, that is, living cat food, destined to be gobbled up by a larger and more ferocious predator the whole time. This double twist could certainly be classified as a trope reappearing in a large portion of Kafka's writings. Foremost examples of this include "Ein

Landarzt" ("A Country Doctor"), in which the doctor rushes into the night to care for a sick patient, who is actually quite well, but who *really* turns out to be quite ill; or back to "In der Strafkolonie" ("In the Penal Colony"), when the first twist involves the officer choosing to end his own life by way of the torture machine he so loves, and the second coming in said machine impaling him unceremoniously through the head.

And yet, there is at least one more way in which the "Little Fable" resonates with Kafka's work in a larger sense, and it is the impetus for the approach and insights of this book. That is the larger implication of the double twist altogether, or the initial delusion that is actually covering up a larger and more important delusion. For this pattern also occurs in Kafka criticism, from its beginnings in the age of Benjamin to its current incarnation as one of the most prolific subsections of literary studies. As Kafka critics, we are often and understandably under the impression that in the course of our critical exploration, we are going to find out *what his works mean*. The approach I advocate in this book argues instead that in this search we are sorely mistaken. Instead, the problems and illusions we portend to uncover, the important questions we attempt to answer—*Is Josef K. guilty? If so, of what? What does Gregor Samsa's transformed body mean? Is Land Surveyor K. a real land surveyor or not?*—themselves presuppose a bigger delusion: that such questions can be asked in the first place.

The story of this approach is one that veers away from Kafka and then back to him, by way of one of his contemporaries, Ludwig Wittgenstein. Though Wittgenstein is widely considered the most important philosopher of the first half of the twentieth century, his influence in the literary world is limited. And although the many points of intersection between Wittgenstein's philosophy and Kafka's prose are too complex to distill into a single sentence, and indeed occupy the entirety of this book, the first similarity I would like to put forth is rather indirect but quite fitting. That is the way in which Wittgenstein's own epigram to his second major published work (second of two), the *Philosophische Untersuchungen* (*Philosophical Investigations*), relates to Kafka's "Little Fable." The motto of the *Investigations* is a line that Wittgenstein didn't write. It comes from a little-known Viennese satirist of the mid-nineteenth century, Johann Nepomuk Nestroy, and his play *Der Schützling* (*The Protégé*). Taken from the words of the hapless rags-to-riches-to-rags protagonist Gottlieb Herb, it reads: "Überhaupt hat der Fortschritt das an sich, dass er viel größer ausschaut, als er wirklich ist" ("But overall, the thing about progress is that it always appears greater than it really is").[2]

This apparent truism is ambiguous in a very perplexing way. Is the "thing about progress" that it is actually insignificant, but *looks* great, and thus we should be thinking about how insignificant it is and possibly try to make it "truly great" by progressing some other way? Or, is the "thing" about progress the very fact *that* it appears great to us—that we are prone to view it as either great or small at all?[3] This funny, frustrating ambiguity points back toward Kafka's fable: is the trouble with the mouse's "progress" in a certain direction that it *wasn't* correct—or is it *that* she was under the misguided impression *of* a correct direction? This points again to the daunting task of the Kafka critic: is the problem with our critical "progress" that it is not nearly as significant as we think it is—or that we were under the misguided impression that such progress was possible to make?

It is this question that provides the impetus for *Kafka and Wittgenstein*, and for the subsequent case for what I have decided to call "analytic modernism," a literary modernism that shares the ideology—intentionally or not—of the early analytic tradition in philosophy, which is usually not viewed in conjunction with literature. But the impetus to view Kafka and Wittgenstein together is both deceptively clear—each is, after all, a foremost exemplar of the twentieth century in his respective field—and highly complex. For example, first I must explain that *Kafka and Wittgenstein* might actually be called *Kafka and Wittgensteins*. This is because the majority of scholars who study Wittgenstein separate his work into two periods, the "early" period (1912–23), wherein he was primarily interested in refining the logical philosophy of Gottlob Frege and Bertrand Russell, and the "late" period (1933 to his death in 1951), wherein Wittgenstein found tremendous fault in not only his own early work, but the entire concept of a "philosophy of logic" altogether. While the late period contains reams of posthumously published notes and lectures, including the works now known as *The Blue and Brown Books*, *Vermischte Bemerkungen* (*Culture and Value*), *Über Gewißheit* (*On Certainty*), and the *Investigations*, the early period is characterized by a single book, the *Tractatus Logico-Philosophicus*, and an ensuing decade of silence.[4] Although several prominent philosophers, coalescing in the early 1990s and calling their approach the "New Wittgenstein" (foremost of whom are Cora Diamond and James Conant), present compelling reasons for a unified Wittgenstein, and although I address and work with the "new reading" in some detail in later chapters, I have chosen nonetheless to relate Wittgenstein's work to Kafka's in two parts. The first concentrates exclusively on Kafka and the *Tractatus*; the second on Kafka and the *Investigations* and, to a much lesser extent, *Culture and Value*.

There are two important reasons for my decision to frame my own investigation within the "two Wittgensteins" paradigm. The first is that there is a tremendous amount to be gained by looking at particular problems of language, logic, communicability, and referentiality in several of Kafka's most famous texts, specifically from a perspective that takes into account only Wittgenstein's early work. This is in part because if I were to view the early work from the perspective of the later work, I would have to keep acknowledging that in Wittgenstein's (later) eyes the early work was "wrong," or misguided, and thus could not treat any of its important developments in formal logic as if they meant or said anything. I believe this approach would preclude an entire oeuvre of potential Kafka scholarship, one that takes into account a vital scientific development that was underway at exactly the same time Kafka wrote all of these works, that of "the New Logic."[5] As I will argue in the first half of this book, Wittgenstein's early goal in the *Tractatus*—composed while its author was a soldier and then a prisoner during the First World War—was to delineate the limits of a logically ideal language. This is very much a modernist project, one that sought to pare down the concept of "linguistic sense" into a set of rules as elegant, clean, and functional as the house Wittgenstein designed for his sister in 1925.[6]

This is both because and in spite of the apparent contentiousness of Wittgenstein's position within modernism, one Michael LeMahieu points out that Wittgenstein created himself by apparently dismissing any self-placement within the philosophical canon in the *Tractatus*'s introduction: "Wieweit meine Bestrebungen mit denen anderer Philosophen zusammenfallen, will ich nicht beurteilen" ("To what extent my endeavors concur with those of other philosophers I do not wish to judge") (*TLP* 2).[7] Indeed, in the exact gesture of refusing to reconcile the logical and what many describe as the later aphoristic elements of the *Tractatus*, Wittgenstein expresses, in LeMahieu's conception, a "bad" modernism—as opposed to a "good" modernism that reconciles art and life.[8] All that said, the *Tractatus*'s stated goal, what it does hope to elucidate and reconcile, is the uncovering of illusory, misguided philosophy.

But is this goal even realized? Only, it turns out, in its self-immolation and the complex recognition of its own impossibility at the *Tractatus*'s conclusion, an end that brought about first a decade in which Wittgenstein left philosophy altogether, and then a return that signaled a radical departure from modernist "ideal language" philosophy.[9] So, why should we even concentrate on the *Tractatus* for a minute, much less a hundred pages, if it fails (and, indeed, I will have more to say about the relative importance of said "failure")? Because in order to see how Wittgenstein got to this failure, it is vital to concentrate first on the *Tractatus* in isolation, so that we can see how Kafka's own works reflect both the language skepticism of early modernism and accompanying idealism of the New Logic—a tension that happens to be exemplified in the *Tractatus*.[10] Only by understanding this relationship to the fullest possible extent will we then appreciate Kafka's relationship to the later Wittgenstein—to, as it were, the breakdown of formalist modernism and the advent of the expressionistic, and eventually postmodern.

The second reason I chose to address the early Wittgenstein in isolation is that I envision this as a truly interdisciplinary piece of scholarship: that is, one that does not seek to incorporate philosophical texts into the literary methodology, but instead considers the philosophy on its own terms, using its own canon and its own approaches. To that end, the majority of philosophical approaches to the *Tractatus* do consider it to contain valuable insight into logic and language, and consider it distinct from the later work, and so for the most part I would like to as well. Further, by and large the discipline of philosophy views the *Tractatus* as one of the founding documents of analytic philosophy; hence, the "analytic" in the "analytic modernism" I hope to uncover here.[11]

In connecting Kafka's work to the earlier Wittgenstein, I reapproach from a logical perspective three common questions we ask ourselves and each other about three of Kafka's most famous works, questions to which I have alluded above. In *Der Proceß* (*The Trial*), is protagonist Josef K. guilty—and if so, of what? In *Die Verwandlung* (*The Metamorphosis*), what does Gregor Samsa's transformed body represent? And, finally, in "Das Urteil" ("The Judgment"), why does Georg Bendemann take that fated jump to his death off the bridge? Each of these questions, I find, actually unearths a larger problem that can be elucidated by an analysis of the logical structure of each story's interior world.[12]

In the case of *The Trial*, it is the unexpected discovery that the apparently senseless proceedings against Josef K. are actually quite valid in a logical sense, a discovery made possible by a close analysis of Wittgenstein's conception of the functions of tautology (something true under all conditions) and contradiction (something true under none) in logical symbolism. In *The Metamorphosis*, I use Wittgenstein's famous assertion in *TLP* 4.1212 that "Was gezeigt werden *kann, kann nicht* gesagt werden" ("What *can* be shown, *cannot* be said") to facilitate a dramatic and transformative expansion of the common assertion (most commonly attributed to Stanley Corngold) that Gregor Samsa is a literal truth metamorphosing into his metaphorical self. Finally, in the case of "The Judgment," I use one of the revelations at the *Tractatus*'s conclusion (that ethical judgment is nonsensical) to undermine the titular judgment of the story.

Because the *Tractatus* is so seldom used in literary analysis—and because, in fact, the very idea of logical analysis of literature seems on the surface impossible—this book's first half begins with an extensive preface that offers both an accessible distillation of the *Tractatus*, and an exploration of its wider contextualization within Austrian modernism, and within the milieu of other specialized "modernisms" that have come out of decades of critical study: Marxist, Zionist, fascist, structuralist, post-structuralist, and so on. The preface for the book's second half, which deals entirely with Kafka's relationship to the *Investigations*, the primary text of the so-called later Wittgenstein, is quite a bit shorter, due to the ease of introducing the *Investigations* directly alongside the Kafka criticism. Additionally, Wittgenstein's transition from the *Tractatus* to the *Investigations* is so interesting and so crucial, that it is worthwhile to jump far ahead of ourselves and discuss it briefly here—another reason the preface to part 2 is able to get away with such brevity.

The "late Wittgenstein" is a period that began after the decade of silence into which Wittgenstein entered after the publication of the *Tractatus* and its apparent goal to end all philosophy by proving philosophical propositions impossible. Wittgenstein spent his premature retirement from philosophy as a village schoolmaster in Puchberg am Schneeberg outside of Vienna, and as an architect, designing the aforementioned sleek house for his sister Margarete, which still stands today in Vienna's third district. When he finally returned to philosophy in the early 1930s, it was as a changed man: first, as Wittgenstein began the *Investigations*, he was in the process of transitioning to what Ray Monk aptly terms "a new life" in Cambridge.[13] And he was philosophically changed as well, no longer satisfied with logical philosophy. Instead, he was quite convinced that not only was philosophical logic insufficient at explaining how our language did and did not work, but that the entire conceit of a philosophy of logic was mistaken. As Wittgenstein remarked in *Culture and Value*, even (and especially) the *Tractatus*'s very famous notion—and one that will be discussed in this book in a tremendous amount of detail—of ascending and then discarding a ladder (*TLP* 6.54) was misguided:

> Ich könnte sagen: Wenn der Ort, zu dem ich gelangen will, nur auf einer Leiter ersteigen wäre, gäbe ich es auf, dahin zu gelangen. Denn dort, wo ich wirklich hin muß, dort muß ich eigentlich schon sein.
>
> Was auf einer Leiter erreichbar ist, interessiert mich nicht.[14]

> I could say: if the place I am trying to get to could only be reached by a ladder, I would give up trying to get there. Because the place where I really want to get to must be the place where I already am.
>
> What is reachable by a ladder does not interest me.

This massive shift was in stark contrast to the views of the logical positivists (Rudolf Carnap, Moritz Schlick, and others in the well-known Wiener Kreis, or Vienna Circle), who treated the *Tractatus* like a founding document, much to Wittgenstein's annoyance. For he, true to his word, sought to discard it altogether, or rather, as the remark above suggests, to simply disengage entirely. There is a lively and interesting debate in the philosophical community, one that the second half of this book visits in more detail, surrounding just how interconnected the early and late Wittgensteins are, but again, even if one were to take the view of the so-called New Reading and argue for a unified Wittgenstein, one must understand the early Wittgenstein on its own terms.

The structural differences are vast and apparent between the two representative texts of Wittgenstein's canon, books that have granted him the place in the philosophical community of the early twentieth century's most important philosophical mind.[15] The *Tractatus* is a scant eighty pages long, full of white space between enumerated propositions that are for the most part quite pithy. And these propositions number only seven in total, with the rest of the text made up of their sub- and sub-sub-remarks. The *Investigations*, on the other hand, are both voluminous in pages and inconsistent in format. The first half consists once again of numbered remarks, though this time no sub-remarks exist, and although the remarks often coalesce around what appear to be main points—three of which I address in great detail in this book's second half—just as often they do not, and their intricate system of cross-reference extends even to their highly challenging writing style (and the second half of the *Investigations*, meanwhile, is written in largely uninterrupted prose). Further, while the German of both the *Tractatus* and the *Investigations* is remarkably clear and contains not a single superfluous word, the *Investigations* complicate matters immensely by being "narrated" by at least two (probably more) interlocutory voices, one of whom seems to be a Platonist "straw man," and the rest of whom seem to be setting that straw man straight.[16] The two texts' structural differences also seem to highlight their differences in focus and approach: while the *Tractatus* sought, via rigorous logical analysis and the refinement of a logically perfect notation, to define as clearly and irrevocably as possible the "limits of language," the *Investigations* sought to dethrone the conceits of philosophy (including logical philosophy) by undermining one alleged philosophical "problem" after the next. Both texts were primarily concerned with language, but while the *Tractatus* sought to formalize all language that could be used (and relegate the rest to nonsense, or *Unsinn*), the Wittgenstein of the *Investigations* delighted in returning words "from their metaphysical back to their everyday use," which is why the later Wittgenstein is often associated with ordinary language philosophy.[17] These complex issues, and their relationship both to Kafka and to the deconstructionist critical canon, are all approached in great detail in the second half of this book.

Another difference between the "two Wittgensteins" is one of use in the literary canon. As we will see, the *Investigations* are quite a bit more popular in conjunction with literary studies—and, further, unlike the sparse, enumerated *Tractatus*, the *Investigations*, though vast, can be waded into with, as I have just mentioned, a far briefer preface. Instead, the section of this book devoted to what I call "analytic skepticism"—that is, Kafka's textual relationship with the *Investigations* and the later Wittgenstein, one that is quite similar to his relationship to later deconstructionist movements—begins as the *Investigations* do, with an investigation of a particular delusion under which language users often labor: that of ostensive definition, or the idea that one can learn the referent of a word by another person pointing to the object that word "stands for" and saying the word.

It turns out that an excellent way to demonstrate why this understanding of language is flawed is by looking at the way Kafka plays with the "referents" of the word *Landvermesser* (land surveyor) in *The Castle*; I have placed the term in scare quotes because, as we will see, what Kafka actually succeeds in doing is undermining the gesture of ostension in a way that would make Wittgenstein proud, despite the latter's alleged distaste for the writings of the former.[18] It is also highly appropriate to begin the late-Wittgenstein section of this book with a look at a land surveyor (or at any rate the word for "land surveyor," since K. does not actually survey land), given Wittgenstein's own introduction to the *Investigations*, which insists that rather than philosophical theses, what he presents to us in this book is an album of "Landschaftsskizze," or "landscape sketches."[19]

If we return once again to the *Investigations'* motto ("But see, the problem with progress is that it always looks greater than it really is"), we can see how it works together with Wittgenstein's "landscape sketches" mentality, and with his later assertion that he is no longer concerned with getting anywhere a ladder goes. And, further, we can see the expansion of such a mentality in the final two chapters of this book, which examine later developments in the *Investigations* alongside Kafka's "In the Penal Colony" and "Josefine the Singer." Again, my reading of the motto is that the real "problem with progress" is neither its direction, its destination, nor the perceived amount thereof, but rather that by being preoccupied with measuring said progress (in degree, in direction), we have been ignoring the real problem that has been staring us in the face: the problem of determining and orienting our actual location.

In this view, which is the position taken by what philosophers call the "Pyrrhonian" approach to Wittgenstein, the *Investigations* do not, then, *advance* philosophical theses. Countering the Pyrrhonian argument is the "positive," "ordinary language philosophy," or anti-Pyrrhonian argument, which posits instead that Wittgenstein has unmasked the old, failed ways of doing philosophy to show us how to do philosophy better.[20] The Pyrrhonian view, on the other hand, insists that Wittgenstein is trying to show us that philosophers have been misguided all along.[21] The Pyrrhonians, as with the *Tractatus*, are most concerned with taking Wittgenstein as literally as possible, in which case, as Robert Fogelin argues, Pyrrhonians see "his aim [as] not to supply a new and better pair of glasses, but, instead, to convince us that none is needed."[22] The conundrum for Wittgenstein readers is, then, this: do the *Investigations* reject bad philosophical progress in favor of better philosophical progress, or do they reject the entire notion of philosophical progress altogether? It is precisely this debate, and its development around two more fascinating paradoxes—rule following and private language—that allows us to see the way in which Kafka undermines several pretenses about prose narration in much the same way Wittgenstein undermines the pretense of philosophical progress.

In this book's discussion of "In the Penal Colony," I pick up where the exploration of *The Castle* left off—with Wittgenstein's apparent assertion that while referential theories of linguistic meaning are misguided, our language can have meaning in its use (§43). The trouble with this assertion, however, is the highly problematic need to have a universal understanding of what "use" means—that is, to have rules for how language works. Instead, there is no such thing as following a rule, only single instances of individual behavior; as such, there is also no way to tell if someone or something has followed a rule—such as, for example, whether or not a bloodthirsty officer's suicide on the torture apparatus he has spent the entire narrative space praising "malfunctions."

This book's seventh and final chapter visits Kafka's last story, "Josefine die Sängerin, oder das Volk der Mäuse" ("Josefine the Singer, or the Mouse Folk"), and once again uses the *Philosophical Investigations* to uncover not one, but two instances of radical skepticism in disguise. Both of these skeptical moments come in the exploration of the *Investigations*' Private Language Argument. I will first uncover a potential reason behind the apparent failure of Josefine's "singing" to captivate its audience. But it will then be Wittgenstein's subsequent undermining of the illusion of philosophical progress *altogether*—the so-called Pyrrhonian project many philosophers attribute to the *Investigations*, and especially the Private Language Argument—that allows me to draw the final and most dramatic parallel between Kafka and Wittgenstein. That is, I argue that with "Josefine," Kafka finishes what he started with "In the Penal Colony": namely, just as Wittgenstein undermines the conceit of philosophical progress with the Private Language Argument, Kafka's "Josefine" also displays a complete and radically skeptical undermining of the conceit of prose narration.

Both Wittgenstein texts are from the modernist canon—indeed, both are exemplary of modernist spirits, though different variations thereof. The *Tractatus*'s "logical modernism" showcases its radical rejection of idealism and realism by isolating the few elements of our world that can display a "truth"—true/false propositions, as we will momentarily see—and paring them down to their unadorned general form. The "analytic skepticism" of the *Investigations* showcases what was most interesting and radically skeptical about late-modernist movements—namely, the full breakdown of the conceit of "truth" altogether; indeed, what some might be inclined to call the nascent moments of deconstruction, several years before the term was coined. It is my intention in the pages that follow to demonstrate the relevance to Kafka studies—to literary studies in general—of viewing these two philosophical modernisms as philosophical companions to modernist literature. As I have endeavored to demonstrate in this introduction, the primary trajectory of this book is not to pose new questions about Kafka, but rather to show that what would serve us best is to dismantle the old ones, and in doing so unearth a preexisting but largely unexplored avenue in literary inquiry, one that contains the kernel of deconstruction but predates it by several decades, and one that should, in its undermining of the most important questions we ask about Kafka, free us from the illusions that often undergird them.

Part One

✦

Logical Modernism

Kafka and the *Tractatus Logico-Philosophicus*

Preface to Part One

✦

Logic, Skepticism, and Mysticism

The *Tractatus Logico-Philosophicus* (also rarely called *Logisch-philosophische Abhandlung* in German), fewer than ninety pages long, is the only book Wittgenstein published in his lifetime. And yet, as P. M. S. Hacker has put it, this "masterpiece" is responsible for nothing less than "chang[ing] the face of philosophy in the second quarter of the [twentieth] century," and, according to Hans Sluga, has "baffled and fascinated" readers since its publication.[1] This brief synopsis can by no means stand alone as an authoritative exegetic source on one of the most difficult books in the history of philosophy; for that, I direct readers to the classic introduction by H. O. Mounce, the thorough and accessible criticism of David Stern, and the superlative recent book by Ray Monk, *How to Read Wittgenstein*.[2] What I will provide here instead is, in effect, the bare minimum one might want to review about the so-called Early Wittgenstein to contextualize the arguments that I later present, as well as the *Tractatus*'s place in Austrian intellectual history and the history of analytic philosophy, and, finally, the *Tractatus*'s brief appearances in, and larger relevance to, literary criticism.

Issue 1: How the *Tractatus* Works

The title of Wittgenstein's first book was suggested by G. E. Moore as a play on Baruch Spinoza's *Tractatus Theologico-Politicus*; the book was published in 1921 after a considerable struggle, largely because publishers simply did not know what to make of it. This is likely because the so-called treatise consists of a two-page prose preface, followed by seven numbered propositions and a multitude of sub- and sub-sub-propositions that, as LeMahieu has elegantly described them, "oscillate between logical propositions and enigmatic aphorisms."[3] What results is a masterfully complex web of cross-referenced and allusive declarations ranging from the logical structure of facts to the ineffability of the ethical, all rendered in prose that Sluga aptly describes as "dauntingly severe and compressed."[4] And yet, the *Tractatus*'s stated goals are nothing less than to chart out as clearly as possible *exactly* what our language can and cannot express. The book ends with a highly debated self-negation, one that implores us to "throw away the ladder" once we have climbed it:

> 6.54 Meine Sätze erläutern dadurch, daß sie der, welcher mich versteht, am Ende als unsinnig erkennt, wenn er durch sie – auf ihnen – über sie hinaufgestiegen ist. (Er muß sozusagen die Leiter wegwerfen, nachdem er auf ihr hinaufgestiegen ist.) Er muß diese Sätze überwinden, dann sieht er die Welt richtig.
>
> My propositions elucidate in the following way: that he who understands me finally recognizes them as nonsensical, when he has climbed through them—on them—over them. (He must, so to speak, throw away the ladder, after he has climbed up on it.) He must conquer these propositions; then he sees the world correctly.

How did Wittgenstein get to this place? More than a decade earlier, he had begun his twenties consumed with a more accurate rendering of symbolic logic after reading Russell and Whitehead's *Principia Mathematica* and Frege's *Begriffsschrift.* Indeed, his early adulthood is marked by insistent pilgrimages first to Frege in Jena and then to Russell in Cambridge, where his demands to know whether he was a philosophical genius were answered in the affirmative after several months of unique haranguing.[5] What both captivated and challenged the young Wittgenstein was the development of "the New Logic," what is now taught in classrooms around the world as first-order logic. Wittgenstein was consumed with refining, among others, the following two ideas: Frege's insistence that a logically perspicuous "conceptual notation" (*Begriffsschrift*) could be developed in order to express any scientific or mathematical proposition on earth; and Russell's theory of descriptions and logical atomism, themselves vehement rebuttals to Hegelian monism in which Russell insisted that the world did indeed consist of smaller "simples" in relation to one another, rather than what he saw to be Hegel's hackish conception of an ideal Reality that, as a whole, was only (un-)reachable through dialectic motion.[6]

Further, Wittgenstein's ascent into the vernacular of every prominent philosopher of logic in the twentieth century was a result of his uniquely insistent personality and his Rockefeller-level wealth; he was able to charter entire trains to take his friends on ultimately disappointing "vacations," and finance studies and living wherever he chose.[7] (Interestingly, before giving up his fortune to his sister shortly after the First World War, Wittgenstein financed and thus effectively birthed the careers of many of Austria's literary greats around the turn of the century, including Georg Trakl and Stephan Zweig.)[8] Wittgenstein also chose to enlist in the Austrian Army four days after Austria-Hungary's entry into the First World War, serving with what we can characterize as either extraordinary bravery or wanton recklessness. On the Vistula in the river fighter *Goplana*, and later behind enemy lines imprisoned in Italy, Wittgenstein refined the logical-philosophical treatise he had begun before the war's outset. The result is what Monk aptly calls a hybrid document that "had at its very heart a mystical paradox," one that not only contains a comprehensive analysis of formal logic, but also sections about ethics, aesthetics, and how to live.[9]

The spare, severe prose of the *Tractatus*'s seven primary propositions helps them seem simple—especially the first: "Die Welt is alles, was der Fall ist," or "The world is all that is the case"; and the last: "Wovon man nicht sprechen kann, darüber muß man schweigen," or "What we cannot speak about we must be silent about."[10] Despite the book's deserved reputation for difficulty, in a way these propositions *are* simple, as each section develops directly out of the section before it, and deals with a very specific and clear element of how the world is set up, how logic works or how language works. And yet, thousands of pages have been and continue to be devoted to parsing these seven sparse propositions and their sub-remarks. The following summary is, thus, in no way exhaustive, but should serve as a minimalist foundation to the more in-depth analysis in the chapters that follow.

TLP *1–3: Facts, Not Things*

The *Tractatus*'s first section describes the logical structure of the world by asserting that it is divided into "facts, not things," and by introducing the idea of logical independence, an important and decisive break from key parts of Russell's theory of logical atomism. It also begins to detail the logical structure of these facts, the charting of which represents Wittgenstein's major break from Russell. Wittgenstein sets up this break by following *TLP* 1 with a line that at first seems to echo Russell's theory: "Die Welt ist die Gesamtheit der Tatsachen, nicht der Dinge" ("The world is the totality of facts, not of things").[11] There is nothing in this single line that seems inherently different from Russell's logical atomism.[12] That is, the world, rather than being a single unified Reality or a collection of things, is instead a state of all objects that exist *in their factual, spatiotemporal relationship* to one another. However, the breakthrough in the first section comes with Wittgenstein insisting that these facts exist in logical space, but are not themselves determined by logic; that is, the logical "relations" of which Russell speaks are not *logical objects in* the "atom," but rather the space in which the atom resides, and the force that binds them together. Thus, even though the world is determined by the facts (1.11: "Die Welt ist durch die Tatsachen bestimmt und dadurch, dass es alle Tatsachen sind" ["The world is determined by the facts, and by these being *all* the facts"]), these facts do not themselves *contain* logic. Rather, logic contains them: "Die Tatsachen im logischen Raum sind die Welt" ("The facts in logical space are the world") (1.13).

The first set of remarks leaves us with several unanswered questions: What is logical space? What is a fact, and why is it different from a thing? Pieces of answers emerge in the second section, with the introduction of the word *Sachverhalt* (translated, with some contention, as "state of affairs") in remark 2, followed by this refinement:

> 2.01 Der Sachverhalt ist eine Verbindung von Gegenständen (Sachen, Dingen).
>
> A state of affairs is a union of objects (matter, things).

This is why the world must be the totality of facts, and not things—what makes it "the world" is *how* these things relate *to each other* in logical space, not the things themselves. The reason "the world" consists of a totality of facts in logical space is, Wittgenstein explains, because with a thing comes all of its possible *Sachverhalt* arrangements, so although it is possible to think of a logical space with nothing in it, it is impossible to think of a thing without its logical space, which includes *all* of its possibilities (2.013). A thing must have its logical possibilities just as a fleck must have a color (not a *particular* color, but *a* color) and a tone must have a pitch (2.0131). But how, then, does a *Tatsache*—this thing in relation to other things—really work? Simple *Gegenstände* (objects) hang together in logical space like links on a chain (2.03) in a specific way to form a *Sachverhalt*, which is a logical arrangement; the existence of that *Sachverhalt* is the *Tatsache* (fact). Logic again is the binding force of this arrangement, but does not *determine* it.

The early remarks of the second section conclude with Wittgenstein's answer to the question: what, then, must language be in order to represent these logical arrangements of facts—this reality, "die Wirklichkeit," which is, according to 2.06, "das Bestehen und Nichtbestehen von Sachverhalten" ("the existence and nonexistence of states of affairs")? It must directly correspond to the facts we picture to ourselves: "Wir machen uns Bilder der Gedanken" (2.1). This is the so-called picture theory of language, which biographical legend has it that Wittgenstein developed after being inspired by a famous court case in which an automobile accident was recreated in the courtroom using models.[13] Facts in our minds, Wittgenstein decided, should work along similar lines, their *logical form* mirroring the way the actual "things" they refer to in the world are arranged. Therefore:

> 2.16 Die Tatsache muß, um Bild zu sein, etwas mit dem Abgebildeten gemeinsam haben.
>
> In order to be a picture a fact must have something in common with what it pictures.

And thus we have in *TLP* 2.18 one of the *Tractatus*'s most crucial distinctions:

> 2.18 Was jedes Bild, welcher Form immer, mit der Wirklichkeit gemein haben muß, um sie überhaupt—richtig oder falsch—abbilden zu können, ist die logische Form, das ist die Form der Wirklichkeit.
>
> What every picture, of whatever form, must have in common with reality in order to be able to represent it at all—rightly or falsely—is the logical form, that is, the form of reality.

In this way the second set of remarks account for the "picture" part of the picture theory of language, and the third and fourth the linguistic aspect. The picture theory is generally agreed to be a three-element arrangement of reality, thought, and language: the way the *reality* is expressed in *language* through the verbalization of a *thought*, which is a logical mental arrangement of the *Tatsache* in reality (*TLP* 3), whose own syntactical/logical form mirrors the logical form of whatever it is in reality that language would ostensibly like to express. The end result of this is that a picture of the whole world is a totality of all of the "true" thoughts in it (3.01).

TLP 4–7: *Sense and Nonsense*

The relationship of language to thought—that which takes up the remaining pages of the *Tractatus*—is on the surface quite simple: "Der Gedanke ist der sinnvolle Satz" ("A thought is a sensical proposition"), with "proposition" standing in for the German *Satz* to mean "declarative sentence" (*TLP* 4).[14] Indeed, the primary concern of the fourth, fifth, and sixth sections of the *Tractatus* is how language that makes sense manages to do this. Early in the fourth section, Wittgenstein claims that we can understand that propositions make sense without having that fact explained to us (4.02). And this is because a proposition *shows* its sense:

> 4.022 Der Satz *zeigt* seinen Sinn.
> Der Satz *zeigt*, wie es sich verhält, wenn er wahr ist. Und er *sagt, daß* es sich so verhält.
>
> The proposition *shows* its sense.
> The proposition *shows* how things stand, if it is true. And it *says*, that they do so stand.

The picture theory of language thus comes together to work like this: the fact that a proposition depicts is compared with reality (4.05) and then judged on whether it matches or does not match what is really there. Thus, although a proposition is the expression of a fact, its sense is independent of what that fact actually *is*. This brings us to 4.12 and 4.1212, the most succinct expression of Wittgenstein's distinction between saying and showing, to which I return several times in this book:

> 4.12 Der Satz kann die gesamte Wirklichkeit darstellen, aber er kann nicht das darstellen, was er mit der Wirklichkeit gemein haben muß, um sie darstellen zu können—die logische Form.
>
> Propositions can represent the whole reality, but they cannot represent what they must have in common with reality in order to be able to represent it—the logical form.
>
> 4.1212 Was gezeigt werden *kann*, *kann* nicht gesagt werden.
>
> What *can* be shown *cannot* be said.

Wittgenstein's major illustration of this distinction comes in his elucidation of how the tautologies and contradictions of logic can be *sinnlos*, "senseless," but not all the way nonsensical (*unsinnig*). What separates them from utter nonsense is that they display logical form, which Wittgenstein illustrates, literally, using the construction of a truth table (4.31). Because tautologies and contradictions *can* be put into a truth table, the way in which they tell us nothing has been divined using logical symbolism; therefore, the logical form of a tautology or a contradiction still exists. And this is possible because logical form *shows* itself in the form of a sentence and has nothing to do with the content of it.

Wittgenstein continues to elucidate how language makes sense in the fifth and sixth sets of remarks, when he charts out the general form of proposition. This formula—which to most of us is little more than a literal and figurative jumble of Greek—is what every sensical proposition has in common. This is not simply that it is truth functional, but that it *always*, in order to be a sensical proposition, consists of a combination of simpler propositions (*Tatsachen*, *Sachverhalte*, "pictures") connected with some combination of the "neither-nor" operator (which can, in its combinations, equal "both" or "and" or "not" or "neither" or any combination of them). Thus the general form amounts to a quantification of every possible way to express "Es verhält sich so und so," or "such and such is the case," and thus, since the limits of language are also the "Grenzen [der] Welt" ("limits of the world"), whatever the limits are of "Es verhält sich so und so" *are* the limits of language and the world (6, 5.6).

Wittgenstein purportedly runs up against these limits in the sixth section of the *Tractatus* when he elucidates what *cannot* be said. This includes riddles, enigmas, aesthetics, and ethics—in short, what many at the time considered (and still consider) to be philosophy. In the case of ethics and aesthetics (6.42–6.43), Wittgenstein dismisses them as non-truth-functional because whether or not one is happy, sad, "good," or "evil" does not change the facts in logical space—and since the expressible world is only the totality of facts in logical space, anything involving *feelings* about these facts is not part of language, and thus not part of the world. In the case of enigmas, the dismissal is fairly simple (and again, this remark will reappear later once its context and relevance to Kafka have been fleshed out):

> 6.5 Zu einer Antwort, die man nicht aussprechen kann, kann man auch die Frage nicht aussprechen.
>
> *Das Rätsel* gibt es nicht.
>
> Wenn sich eine Frage überhaupt stellen läßt, so *kann* sie auch beantwortet werden.
>
> For an answer which cannot be expressed the question too cannot be expressed.
>
> *The riddle* does not exist.
>
> If the question can be put at all, then it can also be answered.

What, then, remains of philosophy? It is a briefly asserted call to "dissolve" (*verschwinden*) rather than solve its own problems—

> 6.521 Die Lösung des Problems des Lebens merkt man am Verschwinden dieses Problems.
>
> The solution of the problem of life is seen in the vanishing of this problem.

—that then shortly follows its own advice:

> 6.53 Die richtige Methode der Philosophie wäre eigentlich die: Nichts zu sagen, als was sich sagen läßt, also Sätze der Naturwissenschaft—also etwas, was mit Philosophie nichts zu tun hat—, und dann immer, wenn ein andere etwas Metaphysisches sagen wollte, ihm nachzuweisen, daß er gewissen Zeichen in seinen Sätzen keine Bedeutung gegeben hat. Diese Methode wäre für den anderen unbefriedigend—er hätte nicht das Gefühl, daß wir ihn Philosophie lehrten—aber sie wäre die einzig streng richtige.
>
> The right method of philosophy would be this: To say nothing except what can be said, *i.e.*, the propositions of natural

> science, i.e., something that has nothing to do with philosophy: and then always, when someone else wished to say something metaphysical, to demonstrate to him that he had given no meaning to certain signs in his propositions. This method would be unsatisfying to the other—he would not have the feeling that we were teaching him philosophy—but it would be the only strictly correct method.

Thus: *all* philosophy is *unsinnig* (6.54). This especially applies to every proposition in the *Tractatus*, including the end of 6.54, when Wittgenstein implores us to throw away the ladder and "see the world aright." Throwing away the ladder in this way results in only one option: that of which we cannot speak we must pass over in silence (7). According to most philosophically mainstream (or "metaphysical" readings) of Wittgenstein, what is left of the *Tractatus* in a world of self-imposed philosophical "silence" is a set of pseudo-propositions that have been revealed as nonsensical but which nevertheless gesture at some immutable truth concerning the logical form of language and reality.[15] With the ladder thrown away, we are supposed to be "free" from the illusion that philosophy *could* say something meaningful, but we can still see that it has *shown* us what is most meaningful of all (that it cannot say something meaningful).

The effect of the *Tractatus* on the philosophy of the twentieth century cannot be understated—even if that effect was completely different than Wittgenstein expected or wished. Wittgenstein meant for the *Tractatus* to end philosophy as people knew it, but instead it sparked more interest in what he considered a poor interpretation of his work and a misuse of the term philosophy: logical positivism. Out of this, much to Wittgenstein's apparent dismay, came the work of Rudolf Carnap, the Vienna Circle, and logical positivism, and thereby the building blocks of analytic philosophy as we now recognize it—and, thus, in the Anglo-American tradition, in large part the discipline of philosophy itself. The effect of the *Tractatus* on literature is markedly smaller—or rather, as we are about to see, it *appears* to be smaller than it really is. We will return shortly to the content of the *Tractatus* in much greater depth as the chapters in this section progress. For now, the aim is to have charted out this unique text's deceptively simple trajectory and primary skeptical project, for which I will now offer a brief historical contextualization—a contextualization that extends to Kafka.

Issue 2: Linking Wittgenstein, Language Skepticism, and Kafka

As Karen Zumhagen-Yekplé has also pointed out recently, there is no record of awareness on Kafka's part of Wittgenstein's work, nor should there be, as Wittgenstein did not really gain fame outside of Russell's cohort until after

Kafka's death, and Kafka did not gain fame until after his own. The sole mention of Kafka in Wittgenstein biographical lore comes from Monk, who relates an occasion on which Elizabeth Anscombe recommended *The Trial*, and Wittgenstein dismissed it with this telling remark: "This man gives himself a great deal of trouble not writing about his trouble."[16] In examining this lack of a genetic link, Zumhagen-Yekplé has argued, quite rightly, that instead of a genetic connection, what really connects these two authors is that they are both "men who go to quite a lot of trouble not writing (at least not directly) about their troubles, the problems they grapple with and prompt their readers to grapple with in turn."[17] Zumhagen-Yekplé is here talking about both Kafka's and Wittgenstein's participation in the larger modernist current of radical skepticism of idealistic subjectivity, which dates back at least as far as Nietzsche's "Über Wahrheit und Lüge im außermoralischen Sinn" ("On Truth and Lying in the Extramoral Sense"), wherein he excoriates the illusion of "truth" as simply "ein bewegliches Heer Metaphern, Metonymien, [und] Anthropomorphismen" ("a moving army of metaphors, metonyms, and anthropomorphisms").[18]

Indeed, the *Tractatus* emerged on the tail end of what we now call the *Sprachkrise* (language crisis) in Austrian modernism. This phrase, "language crisis," chiefly refers to Hugo von Hofmannsthal's Lord Chandos character in the short story "Ein Brief" ("A Letter"), who, in his fictional letter to Francis Bacon, laments: "Mein Fall ist, in Kürze, dieser: Es ist mir völlig die Fähigkeit abhanden gekommen, über irgend etwas zusammenhängend zu denken oder zu sprechen" ("My case, in short, is this: I have completely lost the ability to think or speak about anything coherently").[19] The crisis Hofmannsthal portrays is not the realization that he can't say anything at all (for the letter itself is written), but that he can no longer say anything important. This is, then, very close to a narrative playing out of Wittgenstein's ultimate proclamation in the *Tractatus*, as the only things Chandos is capable of expressing concern facts (specifically, facts about the renovation to his home), and nothing "higher" or emotionally significant. Chandos's only mistake, from a Tractarian perspective, is that he does not know when to shut up.

This sort of linguistic skepticism seems to reject referential expression of the "higher" things on a purely linguistic level: these things (feelings, ethical expression, philosophical expression) are somehow themselves preclusive of language; it is *language's fault* for being inadequate. This is, to be sure, an important—if not the most easily understood—conception of language skepticism. But from the philosophical viewpoints of the two main critical figures in language skepticism, Fritz Mauthner and to a much more excoriating extent Karl Kraus, it is equally (if not more) the language *user's fault* that linguistic expression doesn't "work." And this goes beyond the expression of the most important things: in Mauthner's case, and especially in Kraus's, all language is vulnerable to misuse and misunderstanding by its human purveyors, and not merely because of its intrinsic inadequacies.

Mauthner, like Wittgenstein after him, saw all philosophy as language philosophy, or "Sprachkritik," though Wittgenstein hastened to add in *TLP* 4.0031 that *his* is "nicht allerdings im Sinne Mauthners" ("certainly not in the sense of Mauthner")—this despite reference to the "throwing away the ladder" metaphor, which appears in Mauthner's *Beiträge zu einer Kritik der Sprache* (*Contributions to a Critique of Language*, see below). And Mauthner, to a different extent but with similar skeptical passion as Kraus after him, faults not the elements of language themselves for causing human miscommunication to flourish, but rather man's hasty assumptions *about* language's ability to convey meaning, which Mauthner dismisses as *Sprachaberglaube*, language superstition. Indeed, Mauthner insists that we gain no knowledge of the world through language: "Die einfachste Antwort wäre: 'die Sprache' gibt es nicht; das Wort ist ein so blasses Abstraktum, dass ihm kaum mehr etwas Wirkliches entspricht." ("The simplest answer would be: there is no such thing as 'language'; that word is a mere abstraction, one that hardly corresponds to something real.")[20] This is because how every person conceives of the meaning of his language is dependent entirely upon his own experience, and since no two people's experiences are identical, no two people's meaning systems of language can be either. Wittgenstein's take on this is starkly different—that, per 6.43, the world of a happy man is different than that of a sad one, though the facts remain the same—though, despite his protestations to the contrary, Mauthner's influence remains clear. That is, Wittgenstein's conclusion is simply that certain "higher" things cannot be said; Mauthner's is rather more sweeping, insisting instead that *any* communication between two people—even two people knowing each other—is impossible:

> Kein Mensch kennt den andern. Geschwister, Eltern und Kinder kennen einander nicht. Ein Hauptmittel des Nichtverstehens ist die Sprache. Wir wissen voneinander bei den einfachsten Begriffen nicht, ob wir bei einem gleichen Worte die gleiche Vorstellung haben. Wenn ich grün sage, meint der Hörer vielleicht blaugrün oder gelbgrün oder gar rot. . . . Das abstrakteste Wort ist das vielseitigste[:] Mut, Liebe, Wissen, Freiheit sind ebenso zerfahrene Worte. Durch die Sprache haben es sich die Menschen für immer unmöglich gemacht, einander kennen zu lernen.[21]
>
> No one knows anyone else. Siblings, parents and children do not know each other. A primary medium of lack of understanding is language. We have no idea, even regarding the simplest expressions, whether any of us has the same conception of the same word. When I say green, perhaps the hearer thinks of blue-green, or yellow-green, or even red. . . . The most abstract word is the most multivalent: courage, love, knowledge, freedom and other such scatter-brained words. Through language humankind has always ensured that it is impossible to get to know one another.

Above we can see more clearly why Wittgenstein's "Sprachkritik" departs from Mauthner's; this, however, does not mean they don't also converge. For Mauthner, to reach any sort of truth, we must somehow *transcend* language:

> Will ich emporklimmen in der Sprachkritik, die gegenwärtig das wichtigste Geschäft der denkenden Menschheit ist, so muss ich die Sprache hinter mir und vor mir und in mir vernichten von Schritt zu Schritt, so muss ich jede Sprosse der Leiter zertrümmern, indem ich sie betrete. Wer folgen will, der zimmere die Sprossen wieder, um sie abermals zu zertrümmern.[22]

> If I want to ascend in the critique of language, which at present is the most important business of thinking mankind, then I will have to annihilate the language behind me and in front of me, step by step; so must I destroy every rung of the ladder on which I am climbing. Anyone who wants to follow me secures the rungs further, but only in order to destroy them once again.

Despite Wittgenstein's protestations, each of these ideas reemerges in either the *Tractatus* or his later work. It is also important to note that one particular element of Mauthner's philosophy—a marked disapproval for those who are "language superstitious" (that is, who insist on a referential theory of meaning)—also reemerges in Kraus's work on language which, like Mauthner's, consumed much of his writing life.

Kraus filled hundreds of issues of *Die Fackel* (*The Torch*)—the magazine he edited and, increasingly, wrote in its entirety, of which Wittgenstein was a vocal and devoted fan—with biting, and often outrageous and hilarious excoriations of the casual Austrian speaker's inability to perceive (and in most cases, use) German: after all, "Die Sprache ist die Mutter, nicht die Magd des Gedankens" ("Language is the mother of thought, not its handmaiden").[23] As J. P. Stern has described it, Kraus's "ever-repeated contention" is that "the very last thing he and his readers have in common is the German language, that their use of it is so sloppy and imprecise, so pretentious and corrupted, that they will not understand exactly what he is saying." Furthermore, since to Kraus, precision is "the very essence of language, he claims that, in not understanding exactly, his readers will not understand at all."[24]

Kraus demonstrates the ramifications of the seemingly trivial misuse contained in the Austrianism "Wieso kommt es," which idiomatically means "why is it . . ." but literally, to Kraus, means "why is it that it is . . ." and is thus hopelessly redundant.[25] And this is precisely *not* a triviality—for Kraus, the very mistaking of a linguistic choice *for* a triviality is an offense ("Die Verantwortung der Wortwahl—die schwierigste, die es geben sollte, die leichteste, die es gibt . . ." ["The responsibility of word choice—which should be the most difficult task there is, but actually is the easiest . . ."])—and presents a legitimate philosophical problem, for, as Stern puts it, the "fuller—or perhaps one may be allowed to say deeper—meaning and usage of 'wieso' is inaccessible to him who had misused the word in the first place."[26]

However, one of Kraus's chief complaints about language users' grievous misuse of language is that, as leveled in "Die Sprache" ("Language") the average intellectual simply fails to understand that the "language" of journalism and banal expression—as Wittgenstein would say, the expression of facts—is simply not the same thing as the "language" of poetic figuration. This should seem obvious:

> Der Versuch: der Sprache als Gestaltung, und der Versuch: ihr als Mitteilung den Wert des Wortes zu bestimmen — beide an der Materie durch das Mittel der Untersuchung beteiligt — scheinen sich in keinem Punkt einer gemeinsamen Erkenntnis zu begegnen.
>
> The attempt to define language as *poesis*, and the attempt to define it as mere communication of the value of a word—both, as a matter of fact, engaged through the medium of analysis—appear to result in exactly no point of mutual insight.[27]

And yet, how can one not conflate them? After all, in an apparent (perhaps inadvertent) dig at Gottlob Frege:

> [D]och ist es dieselbe Beziehung zum Organismus der Sprache, was da und dort Lebendiges und Totes unterscheidet; denn dieselbe Naturgesetzlichkeit ist es, die in jeder Region der Sprache, vom Psalm bis zum Lokalbericht, den Sinn dem Sinn vermittelt.[28]
>
> Yet it is the same relationship to the organism of language that here and there separates the living from the dead; for it is the same adherence to the laws of nature, which in every sphere of language, from psalm to the local news, that imparts meaning to meaning.

And yet: "Nichts wäre törichter, als zu vermuten, es sei ein ästhetisches Bedürfnis, das mit der Erstrebung sprachlicher Vollkommenheit geweckt oder befriedigt werden will." ("Nothing would be more foolhardy than to presume some sort of aesthetic need be awakened [or pacified] through striving for linguistic perfection.")[29] This is, according to Kraus, the chief mistake many so-called philosophers of language or literature make: they attempt to use language in a way it simply cannot be—as Wittgenstein would say, they are operating under the illusion that they are making sense when instead they are talking nonsense.

Thus Kraus's skepticism relates quite pointedly to the *Tractatus*—Wittgenstein, after all, faults *philosophers* for assuming their language can express and not recognizing its own nonsense. In fact, Wittgenstein so considered himself a kindred spirit of Kraus that when he first searched for a publisher for the *Tractatus*, he sent it to Kraus's press, Jahoda, with no commentary, assuming that it would be sent along to Kraus, who would immediately understand it as a truth-tabled expression of his own skeptical vision.[30] This, was not to be the case—in fact, the *Tractatus* was only to be published in 1921, and then only with an introduction from Bertrand Russell that primed it to be, largely against Wittgenstein's wishes, a foundational document for logical positivism. Philosophers would largely ignore the linguistic skepticism in the *Tractatus* until the publication of the even more radically skeptical *Philosophical Investigations* after Wittgenstein's death. It is in many ways a substantial shame that Kraus's publisher did not have the sort of telepathic abilities of Wittgenstein's assumption (nor the recognition of Wittgenstein's book as "mainly literary"), for publishing the *Tractatus* both with Kraus's blessing and in a more literary context might have brought its skeptical aspect into sharper relief against the backdrop of other skeptical literary texts—including those by Franz Kafka.

The only thing Karl Kraus seemed to hate more than the misunderstanding of language's purpose and limits—one loathed hallmark of the Viennese—was another loathed hallmark of the Viennese: psychoanalysis. It was, after all, "jene Geisteskrankheit, für deren Therapie sie sich hält" ("that mental disease which holds itself as the cure"), and to be reviled above almost all else.[31] Kraus must have loathed, then, that a key aspect of early psychoanalysis—specifically that particular to Dr. Freud and his compatriots—dealt in its own way with the limits of language. Namely, none other than Freud's most famous early case, Dora, centered on the mysterious acquisition of both aphasia and the ability to speak in a foreign language. Indeed, the connection between Freud's studies of the limits of language (as conceived, that is, by the language-producing ego; as terminally inaccessible by that insatiable id) is crucial to the study of modernism. Kraus would never admit it, but even Viennese psychoanalysis participated in the *Sprachkrise* ("crisis of language").

All of this linguistic skepticism—logical, philosophical, literary, and even psychological—overlaps with views on language Kafka expressed in both his fictional and autobiographical writing, views that were varying and often aphoristically expressed, but which consumed what appears to be his entire writing life. Consider, for example, his first preserved attempt at literary writing, made at seventeen, in which he bemoaned words as neither an adequate means to the end he sought, nor that adequate end itself: "Denn Worte sind schlechte Bergsteiger und schlechte Bergmänner. Sie holen nicht die Schätze von den Bergshöhn und nicht die von den Bergstiefen" ("For words are poor mountain climbers as well as poor mountain men. They do not retrieve treasures from the mountaintop, nor do they from the mountain core") (*GW* 10:5). Bookend this with the final entry in his journal, written at forty-one, which beheld, after two decades of unfinished novels and stories composed in fits and starts, an awe of words, but this time of their penchant for self-destruction:

> Jedes Wort, gewendet in der Hand der Geister—dieser Schwung der Hand ist ihre charakteristische Bewegung—wird zum Spieß, gekehrt gegen den Sprecher. Eine Bemerkung wie diese ganz besonders. (*GW* 11:236)
>
> Every word wielded in the hand of the spirits—this sweep of the hand is their characteristic movement—becomes a spear, turned back toward the speaker. Especially a remark like this one.

The skepticism in this final entry, though focused on the unexpected abilities of language still, is something far more complex than the more direct language skepticism not only of Kafka's youth, but also of, for example, Hofmannsthal's "Letter." Kafka's metaphorical use of "jedes Wort" here, which turns the "word" into an instrument of violence, of reverse overcoming (of self-succumbing), shows that certain aspects of language—for example, metaphor—are not merely metaphorically destructive to the descriptive impulse, but literally so to the describer. And, further, that it is not a higher truth or form of experience that self-destructs, but the basest levels of self-expression.

In the intervening decades he also continued to express language skepticism both directly and indirectly. In several of his floating aphorisms, he alludes to problems we often associate with language, problems about what it can and cannot express. For example, in number 57 he writes that language is only capable of expressing objects from the sensory world (*die sinnliche Welt*):

> Die Sprache kann für alles außerhalb der sinnlichen Welt nur andeutungsweise, aber niemals auch nur annähernd vergleichsweise gebraucht werden, da sie entsprechend der sinnlichen Welt nur vom Besitz und seinen Beziehungen handelt. (*GW* 6:237).
>
> For anything outside the sensory world, language can be used only allusively, but never, not even approximately, by way of analogies, since it, in correspondence to the sensory world, only deals with possession and its relationships.[32]

This would not be a problem were it not also the case that, as put forth in aphorism 54, the sensory (or sensical) world (*sinnliche Welt*) is an evil pest in the spiritual world (*geistliche Welt*), which is the only world there really is

(*GW* 6:237). Therefore, as Walter Sokel extrapolates, because "language only refers to the sensory world, it can never be the instrument of truth," since truth is only to be found in the spiritual world.[33]

This would seem to reinforce Kraus's directive in "Die Sprache" that the language of the physical world (journalism, ordinary conversation, scientific inquiry—where some philosophy is based) cannot transfer to the language of the poetic world (where literature resides, as does other philosophy), especially for those, like Corngold, who see a metaphysical drive in Kafka's mature prose.[34] Complicating matters is an aphorism Kafka once wrote about truth, namely that "Die Wahrheit ist unteilbar, kann sich also selbst nicht erkennen; wer sie erkennen will, muß Lüge sein" ("Truth is indivisible, and thus cannot recognize itself; anyone who recognizes it must be a lie") (*GW* 6:241). The truth, even if it were to be expressible in language, would by its nature be precluded from being recognized as such—in effect, in the spirit of the *Tractatus*, the sense of the world must lie outside it.

But here is the problem with judging the content of the "Wahrheit" aphorism: we cannot really understand the content unless we define the aphorism's form, which the content *itself* proscribes (this will be a problem that returns in Kafka's work, again and again). That is: are we meant to take this aphorism as *itself* a revelation of a truth? If we have understood it correctly, then that act of recognition means that *we* are "a lie," for if we ourselves were privy to the truth, we wouldn't require the act of recognition. If we are "a lie," then we are not to be trusted in rendering something the truth. But if we do not recognize the aphorism to be the truth, then that saves us from being "a lie," but it also invalidates the content of the aphorism. This collapsing movement, in which a piece of writing seems to express an opinion or thesis that destroys the validity of the very piece of writing that brought it about, is almost identical in gesture to the end of the *Tractatus* (and it appears again in Kafka in "The Judgment"; see chapter 3).

More compelling than Kafka's diary entries and aphoristic explorations of the complicated relationship between language and truth are the representations of this complicated relationship in his small stories. These stories many refer to as parables, a designation most famously made by Theodor W. Adorno, who reminds us that we are trained to expect symbols in literature to evoke certain higher meanings, but that nothing is less apt for Kafka. Kafka's works are, instead, outcasts, neither symbolic nor traditionally allegorical; the best distinction Adorno makes is that Kafka's works can be looked at as parables without keys.[35]

In using this confounding form, then, Kafka especially struggles with language difficulties in the small stories. Take, for example, the climactic moment of "Die Brücke" ("The Bridge"), which Kafka begins by writing "Ich war steif und kalt, ich war eine Brücke" ("I was stiff and cold; I was a bridge"). It is precisely this act of self-naming that brings about the death of the narrator-bridge: when an unfamiliar stranger jumps on top of the narrator and he succumbs to his curiosity and turns to see who it could be ("Ein Kind? Ein Turner? Ein Waghalsiger? Ein Selbstmörder?" ["A child? An acrobat? A daredevil? A suicide?]"), the situation ends badly for the simple reason that bridges can't turn around ("Brücke dreht sich um!" ["A bridge turning around!"] [*GW* 6:39]). Here the narrator does not die because of his essence *as* a bridge, he dies because he has *called* himself a bridge.

And perhaps most characteristic of how Kafka's work approaches the troubles of language (by way of language's troubles) is in his parable on parables, "Von den Gleichnissen," in which he once again allows the short narration to fold back in on itself—allows its characters to discover the contradictions within it, the contradictions that *make* it—not once, but twice. This little story offers a sort of trickster's take on the "words of the wise" that hide their "real" meanings, that point instead toward some fabulous beyond, something unknown ("sagenhaftes Drüben, etwas was wir nicht kennen")—or, rather, at the fact that many complain "Viele beklagten sich," that this is the case (*GW* 8:131). The problem, the narrator finds, is that "Gleichnisse wollen eigentlich nur sagen, daß das Unfaßbare unfaßbar ist und das haben wir gewußt. Aber das womit wir uns eigentlich jeden Tag abmühn, sind andere Dinge" ("Parables only want to say that the unreachable is unreachable, and we knew that already. But what we actually struggle with every day is other things"). That parables can only express a tautology (the only kind of "truth" there is, at least according to Nietzsche) would seem to strengthen the separation instinct between words that express something "wise" and words that express something everyday. But that is where Kafka surprises us, by introducing dialogue into a story that was up until now almost purely aphoristic, and by having that dialogue "transition" the text to self-immolation. There would be no problem, says the first character, only referred to as "einer," if everyone just followed the parables: "Dann wäret Ihr selbst Gleichnisse geworden und damit schon der täglichen Mühe frei" ("Then you would be made into parables yourselves, and thereby free of everyday struggle"). But someone new ("ein anderer") answers him that he bets this "solution" is itself just a parable ("Ich wette daß auch das ein Gleichnis ist"); his friend replies: "Du hast gewonnen" ("You have won"). And Kafka inverts the arc again: the skeptic (who guessed that the advice to become a parable was a parable) has "won." But the skeptic is too clever for that, and points out: "Aber leider nur im Gleichnis" ("But only in the parable"). To which his friend replies: "Nein, in Wirklichkeit; im Gleichnis hast Du verloren" ("No, in reality; in the parable you have lost") (*GW* 8:131–32). Thus apparently a parable can only be understood in the following ways: it can express its special, unreachable "truth" (that, being unreachable, is useless in the everyday realm), or it can be exposed as a parable (that only points toward an unreachable yonder), in which case its interpreter receives a small amount of literal satisfaction at identifying a parable, but comes no closer to the "truth," since parables can only express the unsatisfying truth of the tautology that the ineffable remains ineffable.

But the question remains: what form is "Von den Gleichnissen"? Is "On Parables" meant itself as a parable? If so, as with the "Wahrheit" aphorism, we should be reading it as one; that is, understanding that whatever "Drüben" it points to cannot be of everyday use—but what if we do "understand" it (if, for example, the interpretation I have just offered has any merit)? If we "understand" what it is saying about the inexpressibility of the "words of the wise" in ordinary language, then we must ourselves be "wise"—or, more likely, we must realize that "On Parables," because we do understand it, is *not* a parable. By this rationale, whatever problem or complaint about parables "On Parables" details is merely a fictional invention, and, further, one expressed in language that seems more ordinary than parabolic, especially given the end of the dialogue, in which "einer" insists that his friend has "won" (i.e., understood) only in the ordinary world. Thus, by seemingly presenting a poetic affirmation of a view on poetic language similar to Kraus's, but then undermining that view in the process of its own figuration, or "Gestaltung," "On Parables" brings the relevance of ordinary language—and thus of the philosophy that purports to deal with it—into question. Therefore, what may actually be most important about "On Parables" is what it does with its own form: how it challenges the form of the parable by defeating it.

Zumhagen-Yekplé explores the connection between "On Parables" and the *Tractatus* in great depth, pointing out quite correctly that both texts consist, in effect, of two parts, the written part, and the part that is not written, the present absence of the part that is most important—in Wittgenstein's case, his unstated and unstatable ethical corpus, and in Kafka's, the ostensible punch line that would reveal "On Parables" as itself a parable and thus also a clearer conclusion as to what, if anything, parables can teach us.[36] The Wittgenstein text she views, after Diamond, in a "resolute" fashion, characterizing it as an "an elaborate two-part puzzle text that functions as an aesthetic medium for its author's own unique brand of indirect instruction."[37] Although I certainly view the *Tractatus* as more than her characterization as "mock doctrine," I find Zumhagen-Yekplé's characterization of the similar gestures in each text—gestures that both create and depend upon an absence and a silence, that teach by way of withholding or demanding that exactly the most important lesson is the one that cannot be said—to be quite a compelling description of the basic and enduring similarity between Kafka and Wittgenstein as authors, and the reason that a concurrent study of their work is indeed so fruitful. This study is, further, only just begun in the revelation of points of confluence between the *Tractatus* and some of Kafka's emblematic shorter work; this is a small fraction of what is possible when examining Kafka and the *Tractatus* together.

Issue 3: The Limits of the "Literary *Tractatus*"

While my choice of primary text is not unique, my methodology—the rest of the "analytic" in "analytic modernism"—is.[38] The pairing of literary modernism (and Kafka's modernism in particular) with a philosophical approach has been standard practice for almost a century. What follows is by no means an exhaustive list of "turns" and vogues in modernist criticism, but it is a healthy sampling that demonstrates just how prevalent the pairing of philosophy and modernism are. Every Kafka scholar has, for example, studied carefully the many variations of Marxist modernism (most notably Theodor W. Adorno's *Aufzeichungen zu Kafka* [*Notes on Kafka*], and anything influenced by it); Walter Benjamin's historical-materialist literary scholarship remains among the most influential of the modernist period. The postwar decades brought a somber reflection on the relationship between modernism and the Shoah (Adorno and Horkheimer, etc.); the final quarter of the twentieth century brought surges in, for example, psychoanalytic modernism (especially in Kafka studies, with Walter Sokel and Stanley Corngold being among the foremost figures in this subgenre), and postcolonial modernism (John Zilkosky's work, for example). And the turn of the new millennium ushered in, among other fascinating representations, Michael LeMahieu's multi-philosopher approach to "bad" and "good" modernisms, and Kai Evers's very recent and highly engrossing *Violent Modernists*.[39] Several of these current or past "modernisms" even incorporate, as LeMahieu's does, Wittgenstein and the *Tractatus*—but none of them, not one, focuses on the *Tractatus*'s revolutionary developments in the philosophy of logic, thus leaving a massive contemporaneous aspect of modernism, as it relates to the literature of its own time period, all but unexplored.

What is instead often the case in the world of literary scholars working with the *Tractatus* is that we approach it using literary methodologies; that is, we mine the words and turns of phrase in his spare, haunting lines for literary device, we examine its form and its alleged purpose (put forth in Wittgenstein's more prosaic introduction), we ponder over the multiple possible meanings of a phrase like "alles, was der Fall ist" ("All that is the case") (*TLP* 1). This comes from what LeMahieu has wisely called the "split personality" of critical reception engendered by the very oscillation between proposition and aphorism that characterizes the book. Those in the discipline of analytic philosophy "describe a foundationalist text that initiated the tradition of logical positivism," while scholars who focus entirely on the later propositions about ethics and aesthetics—almost exclusively literary scholars—"tend to describe a work closer in spirit to Nietzsche and Heidegger . . . than to Frege and Russell."[40]

Much of the work on Wittgenstein and Kafka, including Sussman's groundbreaking formal critique (1990), as well as recent and emerging work by Yi-Ping Ong and Zumhagen-Yekplé, seems to do the latter.[41] And the

Tractatus has much to offer the interpreter who chooses this approach: Marjorie Perloff has used the language of the *Tractatus* (and, to a lesser extent, the *Tractatus*'s treatment of language) to reorient the notion of "poetic translatability," for example.[42] Further, this view seems substantiated by Wittgenstein's own characterization of the *Tractatus* as "literary" in his initial (and largely unsuccessful) search for a publisher: to Ludwig von Ficker of *Der Brenner*, he explained that the work was "strictly philosophical and at the same time literary, but there is no babbling in it."[43] Ficker rejected it nonetheless, and as we have seen, Wittgenstein's early work was embraced by exactly the kind of logical positivists he deplored, literariness seemingly forgotten. However, Wittgenstein persisted in characterizing his (and all) philosophy in poetic terminology at different times throughout his career, most notably late in his career and life, in *Culture and Value*, when he wrote the passage that has likely encouraged the *Tractatus*-as-poetry approach more than any other:

> Ich glaube meine Stellung zur Philosophie dadurch zusammengefaßt zu haben, indem ich sagte: Philosophie dürfte man eigentlich nur dichten. Daraus muß sich, scheint mir, ergeben, wie weit mein Denken der Gegenwart, Zukunft, oder der Vergangenheit angehört. Denn ich habe mich damit auch als einen bekannt, der nicht ganz kann, was er zu können wünscht.[44]
>
> I believe I summarized my position on philosophy when I said: one may only do philosophy as poetry. For this it seems to me it must be clear to what extent my thinking belongs to the present, future, or past. Because I have thereby also made myself known as someone who cannot really do what he wishes.

This oft-cited insistence on "poetizing" philosophy, combined with the *Tractatus*'s own apparent self-immolation at its conclusion, enable literary scholars (when they ignore the fact that Wittgenstein may have actually meant that pejoratively) to concentrate on a very small percentage—the "poetic parts," as opposed to the "logic parts"—of an already sparse text: the introduction; some references to Mauthner (for example, the aforementioned *TLP* 4.0031); the first few enigmatic lines; the final call to silence. This approach allows us to leave the *Tractatus*'s viscera, its internal developments in logic (with their tangle of truth tables and formulae) largely in peace: to "pass [them] over in silence," as most English translations of the *Tractatus*'s final remark have it—and on the surface this *should* be fine, because Wittgenstein himself has just said they are nonsensical anyhow (6.53). But even a so-called resolute approach to the *Tractatus* requires that one reckon with all of its "nonsensical" contents *first*, as the pioneers of this approach, Cora Diamond and James Conant remind us.[45]

I certainly do not deny any loftier, metaphorical (even metaphysical) meanings some lines of the *Tractatus* have—after all, according to Wittgenstein himself, that may be the only meaning there is to be found: something transcendental and necessarily ineffable.[46] However, the desire to read the *Tractatus* as literature when using it to interpret literature becomes problematic the moment one decides to progress beyond its opening line. For *TLP* 1 as poetry may relate to *TLP* 7, its corresponding line at the end calling for silence, but without a literal understanding of what Wittgenstein means by the totality of true facts, we are forced to ignore the intricate progression of eighty-six pages of text in between them. This is why Wittgenstein, poaching Mauthner, refers to the propositions of the *Tractatus* as a ladder—that, lest we forget, we actually have to climb before we are qualified to throw it away.

It should thus come as no surprise that here I endeavor to read neither the *Tractatus*'s opening sentence nor the text that follows it with a particularly literary methodology: until I am explicitly told not to at the conclusion (6.53), I read the remarks of the only book Wittgenstein published during his lifetime as declarative propositions. For example, "Die Welt ist alles, was der Fall ist," whatever its rewarding poetic implications, is shorthand for Wittgenstein's early conception of the actual world we literally, physically inhabit *as the totality of all true facts at once*. And yet this may itself be problematic, because such an approach in literary study teeters on the brink of anathema—why not focus on the poetic implications? Is there a "correct" way to use the *Tractatus* in literary studies?

As an example, J. P. Stern gives a decidedly literary interpretation to Wittgenstein's assertion in *TLP* 6.42 that "Der Sinn der Welt muss außerhalb ihrer liegen. In der Welt ist alles, wie es ist, und geschieht alles, wie es geschieht; es gibt in ihr keinen Wert - und wenn es ihn gäbe, so hätte er keinen Wert." ("The sense of the world must lie outside it. In the world everything is how it is, and happens how it happens; there is no value in it—and if there were, it would have no value.") Whereas logicians view this proposition to mean that the *logical form* of language—how grammar, syntax, and structure bind the parts of a sentence together—must be precluded from linguistic expression, literary theorists seem to grant it more far-reaching significance. But in his argument, Stern definitely takes this proposition broadly, that is, to refer to the "sense of the world" in a larger, more metaphysical way that has more to do with personal satisfaction with language and less to do with logical form.

But if, as I argue, a more analytic reading of Wittgenstein's philosophy, especially the *Tractatus*, is the richest approach to it, then why would such a rich approach be precluded from the study of literature? The easy answer to this is the idea that logical language and literary language are not the same entity (something with which Karl Kraus would certainly agree), and the *Tractatus* as a work of analytic language theory deals with logical and not literary language. Literary language, we are told, is literary precisely because it does not really "mean" what it means, pointing instead to larger metaphorical, allegorical, or otherwise extratextual truths, truths Wittgenstein would surely deem "outside the world."

But is this really the case? While many of us in literary studies, and Kafka studies in particular, may assume that the real "truths" of his fiction lie outside the texts, it should not be forgotten that the stories themselves contain plots, characters, and (ostensible, if invisible and morphing) rules, all of which constitute what John Searle has, in discussing logical truth in literature and fiction, called a "horizontal" system of referentiality, and Michael Rifarterre refers to in *Fictional Truths* as the internal-meaning-granting power of "verisimilitude."[47] It is possible, Searle says, "for an author to use words literally and yet not be committed in accordance with the rules that attach to the literal meaning [in the actual, as opposed to fictional world] of those words."[48] This is, according to Searle, made possible through *pretend illocutionary acts*—through "actually performing utterance acts with the intention of invoking the horizontal conventions that suspend the normal illocutionary commitments of the utterances."[49] Josef K.'s arrest, Gregor Samsa's life and death as an *Ungeziefer*, a "vermin," the Penal Colony's officer committing "ironic" suicide—these gestures in Kafka's fiction cannot even begin to have extratextual "meaning" without the preunderstood condition that they are, in some way, taking place in the fictional space.

To presuppose a metaphorical meaning without a literal meaning with which to contrast it is just to presuppose a single (and thus literal) meaning. So to say that all but the most deliberately surrealist fiction has no literal truth is to say that all fiction is complete gibberish—or, rather, that there should be no way to distinguish between fictional acts that make sense in the context of that fiction (such as Gregor Samsa waking up) and those that do not (such as Gregor Samsa waking up an *ungeheures Ungeziefer*, or monstrous vermin). And yet most readers of fiction can tell this difference, because they are able to discern—in most cases, sometimes after a protracted amount of labor—the various "horizontal conventions" of a given narrative (as Searle reminds us, "what counts as coherence for a work of science fiction will not count as coherence in a work of naturalism").[50] Thus, there is indeed some sort of "fictional truth": there is, as Currie puts it, what is "true in the story."[51] Thus, as the discoveries about logical form and the limits of language in the *Tractatus* deal entirely with facts, states of affairs, and possible states of affairs, although it would seem counterintuitive to examine the facts, states of affairs, and possible states of affairs in literary fiction, because even Kafka presents things that are (varying degrees of) "true in the story," this is not actually the case.

Simple category error, then, is not sufficient to preclude an analytic approach to Kafka's literature—but ideology may be. It is unwise to forget the motivations for the original schism in the philosophical discipline just before the turn of the twentieth century. Michael Lackey, in a brief but lively study of what he calls "the Modernist rejection of philosophy," attributes the analytic break as a reaction to the anthropomorphism of the discipline—the rejection of absolute ideas in favor of pure narrative creations of the philosophers themselves. This would explain, at least partially, the Continental embrace of literary studies—the shared acknowledgement of the creation of "concepts" through narrative, as opposed to the expression of pure concepts already existing.[52]

Lackey refers to Wittgenstein in this debate as well, but, interestingly enough, does not fully place him into the analytic tradition—instead he is an example of the other modernist "choice" with regard to confronting the anthropomorphism of philosophy: his mid-career rejection of philosophy altogether. "While Wittgenstein may have broken his post-*Tractatus* silence," Lackey reminds us, "he never gave philosophy back the ladder it had once used to ascend into the metaphysical heaven of Ideas."[53] Furthermore, any assumption that philosophy is "an intellectual discipline with a pre-given nature that we can define" makes the assumer behave "as an analytic philosopher."[54] It is precisely this proverbial line in the sand that causes us to believe, over a century after this alleged schism, that analytic philosophy and literature preclude each other: just as Continental philosophy rejects the idea of an immutability of concepts, analytic philosophy is so wedded to that idea that it refuses to acknowledge the *possibility* of the creation of concepts.

And yet, in the better part of a decade I have now spent with Wittgenstein and Kafka together, I have found far too many common frustrations with language and expressibility in their work to preclude a costudy that still views Wittgenstein from the dominant philosophical—by which I most certainly mean "analytic"—paradigm. Does this make Kafka in my mind an "analytic writer"? Does it make Wittgenstein, as Lackey or the "New" group might characterize him, antiphilosopher *ne plus ultra*? Both of these are equally possible, but why I have decided to make a case for Kafka's "analytic modernism" has not a small amount to do with the content of the *Tractatus* itself, but equally as much to do with how I approach it in conjunction with the literary. That is, for this half of the project at least, I do read the *Tractatus*—and, to a certain extent, the "fictional truths" of the Kafka universes—as if *indeed* "immutable concepts" in them exist, as if each author's work *is* capable of presenting specific problems which I can then tackle in an equally specific and precisely circumscribed way—that is, a bit like a philosopher.

The "literary *Tractatus*" has certainly offered a substantial amount to the canon, but in the world of philosophy it is the (from our paradigm's perspective) "nonliterary" Wittgenstein that is the "real" one. This Wittgenstein presents substantial and important advances about logic and language, even *if* they are later allegedly rendered invalid by their own rules—for to know this, one still has to learn those rules. Ironically, without an analytic approach, the full realization of the relevance of the *Tractatus* to literature remains unavailable. For to understand how dramatic the *Tractatus* is at its conclusion, to understand what it has really done to circumscribe the "limits of the world," one must understand precisely how Wittgenstein has charted out the logic to work as an ineffable structural force that holds, shapes, and binds a proposition, that gives it its sense. None of this would be possible without an approach to the *Tractatus* that is more analytic and thus allegedly less literary than we are used to.

Logical modernism seems at last, then, like a perfectly acceptable and long-overdue companion to Kafka's works—so long, one might suppose, as it results in a workable thesis. But what if it doesn't? What if Wittgenstein was *wrong*?[55] This is especially pressing, given that Wittgenstein himself didn't end up believing he was "right" about the logical form of reality—indeed, the second half of this book explains this turnaround in some detail. But here is a rather uncomfortable thesis, upon which I am willing to insist, and to which I will return several times: reading Kafka and Wittgenstein together—and finding Wittgenstein's logical rules and their paradoxical consequences everywhere—does not at all depend upon Wittgenstein being "right." All I seek to do is unearth a larger preoccupation with language, one that led both Kafka *and* Wittgenstein to grapple with inexpressibility in markedly similar ways that have nevertheless rarely, if ever, been examined in concert.

Just as I am not here to show what Kafka's works mean (but rather *how*, or even *if*), I am not here to show *that* Wittgenstein is right, but how his argument fits together. And part of that argument's mechanism is the dismantling of questions exactly like "Is Wittgenstein right?" As we will see, the way in which Wittgenstein dismantles misguided questions changes throughout his career, but the act of dismantling the "wrong" questions remains his focus for his entire life. He always says, in effect*: I'm not going to solve this problem, I am going to prove that you are looking at the wrong problem.* I believe that when we ask whether the early Wittgenstein was "right" and use that relative correctness as a measure of whether the *Tractatus* is worthy of study alongside Kafka, we are committing exactly that kind of understandable misstep, one that both the early and late Wittgenstein would call identifying *the wrong problem*.

The remaining fruits of this approach are, then, as follows: I have found that three of Kafka's most famous stories—*The Trial, The Metamorphosis*, and "The Judgment"—do nothing less than dramatize Wittgenstein's most important findings about logic and language on the fictional plane, in a fictional reality, with fictional facts whose alleged "problems" actually merit what Wittgenstein would call dis-solving (*das Verschwinden*) by way of pointing out their logical and linguistic issues. And, furthermore, I find that these real issues hide behind the "fake issues" we already know too well.

Chapter 1

✦

The Trial and the Law of Logic

If I am to make a case that logical modernism belongs with modernist studies as much as, for example, psychoanalytic modernism, postcolonial modernism, or Marxist modernism does, the primary case I must make is one on behalf of the relevance to literary study, and to Kafka's work in particular, of symbolic or formal logic—"the New Logic" to Kafka's contemporaries.[1] Wittgenstein's early work, taking after Frege and Russell, insisted that all language that made any sense whatsoever did so because it could be pared down to its symbolic equivalent. But how does this relate in any way to Kafka's most famous novel, *Der Proceß* (*The Trial*), one that has been held to hundreds of standards in the near century since its publication, but never—and for seemingly good reason—this particular standard? After all, as a work of fiction, and of nonrealist fiction at that, it hardly seems that such a concern would at all be relevant to the search for an answer to the novel's primary and most pressing question: is protagonist Josef K. guilty despite never having a formal charge leveled against him? And, if so (and, as we will soon see, most critics tend toward "yes"), what is his crime? Or, from a more psychoanalytic perspective: what is the origin of his *inherent* guilt? It is precisely by applying for the first time a new logical standard to this text that we can make a rather astounding discovery: that is, that all these previous questions are not necessarily the right ones to be asking.

This is not to say that they are not interesting or worthwhile, or that the fruits of the labor of ninety-plus years of criticism are not compelling. Indeed, by the time K. allows his executioners to twist the knife twice in his heart, his death seems to be a foregone conclusion ("Sie sind also für mich bestimmt?" he greets them ["You're meant for me?"] [*GW* 3:236]), and critical interpretations of *The Trial* largely seek to "solve" why this can possibly come to be, especially given the cause for K.'s arrest and trial, which is never made satisfactorily clear. Historical analyses have focused on K.'s behavior in both his urban and social surroundings; for Rolf J. Goebel, K. is a sort of anti-flâneur whose subjectivity "mirrors" the reality of the city, the "petty-bourgeois conventionality of his lodging house, the strict hierarchy in operation at his bank, the many sexualized scenarios, the crowded proletarian streets in the suburb, and the court's labyrinthine corridors and overcrowded chambers" all counting as "outward manifestations of K.'s inner world," specifically and especially his "narrowmindedness and social pretensions."[2]

Further, for Mark Anderson, K.'s rebellion against the Court is an expression of Kafka's own rebellion against the "typing" of the "born criminal" that was in vogue at the time of Kafka's law studies.[3] Structural approaches have pointed to the opacity of K.'s trial as a literal expression of the novel's textual function: as an expression of the necessary opacity of the text in general. David I. Grossvogel, for example, has called *The Trial* simply "a text about the confusion of critics and other readers that shortly confuses critics and other readers."[4] Psychological approaches such as Walter Sokel's have focused, understandably, on the notion of guilt (he argues, "The existence of guilt—some guilt—is assumed, but its nature is left undefined and remains unknown both to the protagonist and to the reader").[5] K.'s guilt in *The Trial* has no obvious juridical or literal source within the narrative; thus, what is left for the psychoanalytic critic is to determine whether his guilt—and he must be guilty, for he accepts his execution—is predestined (i.e., "Oedipal") or self-inflicted ("existential").[6] For "the unknown guilt in K.'s trial is identical with his being, not in the sense of original sin, but as a consequence of the silence of the Court as to what constitutes guilt."[7] Sokel also reminds us that "in the absence of any standard definition of guilt and non-guilt, what might appear most innocent to [K.'s] examiner might be precisely the root of his guilt if viewed from another perspective."[8]

The purpose of this chapter is to demonstrate that the seemingly opaque proceedings of *The Trial*—especially Sokel's crucial revelation about the absence of either guilt or "non-guilt"—do actually adhere to at least one straightforward and rigid internal system, though likely not the one we expect.[9] While the Law (*das Gesetz*) of the mysterious Court (*das Gericht*) remains necessarily undiscoverable, there is another sort of law at work in the novel, one that governs perfectly and without exception. This is the law of formal logic, which, as I have mentioned, at the time of Kafka's writing career would have been called "the New Logic." This "new" formal system, a self-contained language of symbols, rules, and formulae, was invented by Gottlob Frege in 1879 to express and assess the validity of arguments in mathematics and the sciences.[10] Forty years later and not quite as new, formal logic then came under Wittgenstein's philosophical scrutiny in the *Tractatus*, a text that actually offers a surprisingly significant amount of heretofore-unexplored insight to the inner workings of *The Trial*, despite their obvious differences in form and content.

It first becomes inviting to search for convergence of the texts because of historical confluence: while *The Trial*, written from 1914–15, details a man's yearlong detainment by an inscrutable authority, the *Tractatus* was composed between 1914 and 1918, partly while Wittgenstein was himself actually detained by the Italians as a prisoner of war.[11] Along more strictly textual lines, as I have previously mentioned, a more general relationship between Kafka and Wittgenstein has certainly not gone unnoticed in the critical canon, the most canonical examples of which include work by Henry Sussman and Stephen Mulhall.[12] However, this presents only a fraction of what the early Wittgenstein has to offer Kafka's work, and *The Trial* in particular.[13]

For whereas the mysterious juridical Law in K.'s case seems designed entirely to preclude him from understanding it, and serves to make the action of *The Trial* seem to diminish in validity as it progresses, the "unshakable" laws of logic deliver an entirely different verdict (*GW* 3:241). This is due in large part to the unique logical status of what Wittgenstein will call one of the two "extreme cases" of logical proposition: the contradiction, which we will recognize in *The Trial* at vital junctures in the story. Wittgenstein, as we will also see, grants a special status to the contradiction and its logical partner the tautology: these are without sense (*sinnlos*) but not nonsensical (*unsinnig*); they tell us nothing while still belonging seamlessly to the larger system of formal language (*TLP* 4.461). Here I will use Wittgenstein's logic to show that K.'s chargeless arrest, quest for tautological innocence, contradiction-filled trial, and perplexingly expected death actually comprise a progression that is, at least according to one law—that of formal logic—wholly valid.

"How True It All Is": Truth Conditions in a Fictional World

The clearest way to introduce a logico-philosophical inquiry into *The Trial* is to unearth a common thread between the foundational element of Kafka's novel, K.'s arrest, and the foundational concept of logical argument: truth conditions. During K.'s arrest, the warder Franz tells K., "Sie werden bald sehen, wie wahr es alles ist" ("You'll soon see just how true all of this is") (3:11). The remarkable thing about this statement is not its ominousness but its ambiguity. This is not just because *wahr* can be read as, among other things, "true," "real," "verifiable," and, fittingly, "just," but also because it is entirely possible to quantify how true, or how real or how just something is—only to conclude that the answer to this investigation is: not true, real, or just at all. This interaction underscores a fundamental issue not only in this scene, but also in logical analysis: in order to proclaim a judgment to be the opposite of *wahr*—be that "unjust," "unreal," or "false"—the ability to judge "wie wahr" is necessary. After all, at the climax of K.'s interaction with the Priest, as K. is proclaimed "thought guilty," he rebuts: "Wie kann denn ein Mensch überhaupt schuldig sein" ("How can a person be generally guilty?") (3:223). It is, as Jean-François Lyotard has expressed in *The Differend*, "impossible to establish one's innocence, in and of itself. It is a nothingness."[14] Therefore, in order to see "wie wahr" his situation is, K. must have the ability—the conditions present—to judge "wie wahr" altogether. This is apparently the premise inherent in Franz's threat, but its power as both a threat and a promise remains in question because of the very absence of the condition necessary to judge the (juridical) justness of the situation: a named charge.

This ability to judge "wie wahr" once again signals the necessity of truth conditions (*Wahrheitsbedingungen* or *Wahrheitsmöglichkeiten* [*TLP* 4.41]). In a logical sense, we might thus begin to recognize Franz's apparent threat as empty because the truth conditions necessary to make such a judgment never materialize. Instead the "threat" tells K. nothing threatening, because it tells him nothing at all—rather it simply misleads him into expecting the presence of truth conditions (this never-materializing named charge) down the road. But this is only part of the exceedingly complex state of affairs.[15] As *The Trial* progresses we realize that Franz's statement was simultaneously empty and prophetic, depending on how one reads *wahr*: if it is "true" or "just" then the statement is (perhaps intentionally) misleading, because K. never does learn how true or just his arrest is, since for that to happen the truth conditions of his charge would have to have been named. If we read *wahr* as "real" or "actual," however, then Franz was indeed making a threat, and a true one at that: the outcome of K.'s trial is an actual, rather than metaphorical, death.

However, most disputes concerning *The Trial* are not about the actuality of K.'s death, but rather about its justice. Thus, using the more juridical meaning of *wahr*, the fact remains that because K. is not charged, he is also not provided with the truth conditions necessary to pronounce said charge "true" or "false." This in effect means that K.'s trial does not take place in a system in which he can be found guilty or not guilty of something. This system either lacks truth conditions altogether or they are hidden. Though in the end it does not really matter—if there was ever a charge, it remains "hidden" the whole time and thus might as well not exist—at the early stage of K.'s trial he seems to presume a system that can and will offer him a charge if only he unearths it: after his disastrous first interrogation, he professes "kein[en] Zweifel, daß hinter allen Äußerungen dieses Gerichtes, in meinem Fall also hinter der Verhaftung und der heutigen Untersuchung eine große Organisation sich befindet" ("There is no doubt that behind all appearances of this court—in my case, behind my arrest an the investigation today—there is a massive organization") (3:56). This may be true, but it is not the sort of organization whose criteria for innocence and guilt are manifest. For example, inside the books he presumes contain the Law he may or may not have flouted, K. instead finds amateurish pornography:

> Ein Mann und eine Frau saßen nackt auf einem Kanapee, die gemeine Absicht des Zeichners war deutlich zu erkennen, aber seine Ungeschicklichkeit war so groß gewesen, daß schließlich doch nur ein Mann und eine Frau zu sehen waren, die allzu körperlich aus dem Bilde hervorragten, übermäßig aufrecht dasaßen und infolge falscher Perspektive nur mühsam sich einander zuwendeten. (62–63)

> A man and a woman sat naked on a sofa, the crude intention of the artist easy to discern; however, so substantial was his lack of skill that in the end one could only make out a man and woman dominating the picture, sitting exaggeratedly upright and, due to the artist's false perspective, merely leaning toward each other in a belabored fashion.

The crude picture K. encounters presents a poor but nevertheless recognizable approximation of the actual state of affairs of a man and woman in coitus, and it offers us our next opportunity to gain insight from the *Tractatus*. The ability this picture has to represent an actual "state of affairs" also happens to be the sole criterion Wittgenstein presents in the *Tractatus* for how our language makes sense to us. In Wittgenstein's theory, a proposition (*Satz*) creates a logical picture that can be compared with the totality of possible actual states of affairs (*Sachverhalten*) in reality—with all possible truth conditions (*TLP* 2). A proposition thus presents a relationship between objects in logical space, and the hearer or reader compares that state of affairs with the true state of affairs in the world ("was der Fall ist," or "what the case is" [*TLP* 1]). If the picture in the proposition matches reality, the proposition is "true"; if not, it is "false" (3.24). However, what if neither is possible, because the conditions are not present in either the picture or reality to make that comparison? This seems to be the state of affairs K. finds himself in, a world—pornography aside—whose sacred texts either do not exist or do not present a logical picture with which he can compare the state of affairs around him. It is a scheme whose conditions he cannot discern, and thus cannot deem *wahr* (true, just) or its opposite.

K.'s Contradictory State of Affairs

Instead, what we see is a juridical system where there seems to be no need for a formal criminal charge. This K. has no way of understanding, however, so one of his earliest reactions to the arrest is to ask why ("Und warum denn?"), and then for the "Legitimationspapiere . . . und vor allem den Verhaftungsbefehl" ("identification papers . . . and most importantly your arrest warrant") (3:11, 14). When K. learns that a warrant is not necessary, he attempts to impugn such an alleged law: "Dieses Gesetz kenne ich nicht," he informs Franz and Willem ("I don't know this law") (3:14). To this Franz makes a succinct and perceptive (if peremptory) point: "Sieh Willem er gibt zu, er kenne das Gesetz nicht und behauptet gleichzeitig schuldlos zu sein" ("Look here Willem, he claims he doesn't know the law and the same time claims he's innocent") (3:15). To maintain innocence but not know the law that defines it is to be neither guilty nor not guilty.[16]

K.'s new presumed state of affairs can be thus expressed in formal logic as follows: if the situation "guilty" is G, the act of negation the symbol "~", and the state of conjunction "&" then Josef K. is: ~G & ~~G.[17] This is a logical contradiction, one of the extreme cases ("extreme Fälle") of propositions whose characterization the analytic philosopher of language Max Black argues is "of decisive importance for Wittgenstein's philosophy of logic," and which Black described in 1964 as "original and illuminating, even for those who cannot accept [Wittgenstein's] analysis of the essence of representation and symbolism."[18] Contradictions, "unter keinen Bedingungen wahr" (true under no conditions), are one extreme, and their partner, tautologies (true under all conditions), the other (*TLP* 4.461).

To illustrate this extremity, Wittgenstein calls to mind the simple tautology "It is raining or not raining." This tells us nothing, for after hearing it, we have no idea whether we need an umbrella (4.461). And because the tautology imparts no information that matches (or fails to match) with the real world (tautologies and contradictions are not pictures of reality [4.462]), in Wittgenstein's terminology it is senseless (*sinnlos*). This is because, as with the aforementioned pornography, a linguistic "picture" makes sense only when it can be compared with, and judged to match or not match, a real state of affairs (4.461). The contradiction also tells us nothing (fails to represent a picture), but in the opposite way: if someone were to tell us "It is raining and not raining," that would be utterly useless to us no matter the actual situation outside.

In *The Trial*, Franz recognizes that the assertion that one is both ignorant of the law and innocent under it is laughable, that it does no good to impugn the Law or exonerate K. To Wittgenstein, this situation would thus be *sinnlos*, as K. has correctly, albeit inadvertently, attested (3:21). There are many reasons why K. is patently unaware of the structure and power of the contradiction that has just been attributed to him (as well as the many to come), and most of these will not be able to come to light until Wittgenstein's philosophy of logic and language is unfurled in far greater detail, but I would like to digress slightly to finesse—and, it is hoped, offset—a point of possible confusion with this approach before I progress. What I'd like to keep in mind is that although logical contradictions exist in the narrative, its protagonist (and likely its author) do not need to be consciously aware of them for them to exist. Mine is what we could call a literarily logocentric exploration, one that echoes Wittgenstein's insistence that logical relationships have always existed in both language and the world, that our charting out of them does not bring them into existence but rather reveals them as having been there the whole time. In the textual analysis of this and the following contradictions in *The Trial* I am not superimposing upon its protagonist a metatextual awareness of a system it is highly unlikely he would know, but rather pointing out a logical structure that would be there regardless of the novel's content.[19]

Returning to *The Trial*, then, Franz's assertion is but one of the numerous contradictions that together make up the larger narrative progression. Although K. himself begins to recognize and name (and register disapproval of) contradictions as his case progresses, at first he seems either unaware of or unbothered by them. When, for example, he threatens to phone the attorney Hasterer, he is told that of course he may call the lawyer, but that he will not receive the help he expects: strictly speaking, K. may and may not call for help (3:21). Even more contradictory is the discovery that although he is technically "being held" (*gefangen*), K. is not literally being confined, as he remains allowed and encouraged to go to work (3:23). Although the purported contradiction here seems easily explained away by the designation of one *gefangen* as literal and the other as metaphorical, a contradiction still remains, for while K. is arrested—an extraordinary situation—he is also compelled to go on with his ordinary life. K.'s process of locating his first interrogation is also, in its own way, contradictory: by not asking directly where the Court is but being addressed by the court usher's wife as if he has indeed asked where the Court is, K. in effect both refuses to ask and asks a question (3:47). As he goes deeper into his case, K. even attempts to defend himself against a contradiction (a statement that is "false" under all conditions) by producing its opposite: a tautology, a general defense brief whose proclamation of innocence is instead "true" under all conditions: "Er wollte darin eine kurze Lebensbeschreibung vorlegen und bei jedem irgendwie wichtigeren Ereignis erklären, aus welchen Gründen er so gehandelt hatte" ("He wanted to offer a short description of his life, and explain why he had handled himself in every situation that could possibly be determined important") (3:118). Here we see a brief appearance of the other "extreme case" of the proposition: the tautology, true under all conditions. In attempting to exonerate himself of all possible wrongdoing (of the specifics of which he remains necessarily unaware), K. will have to craft a *pro se* brief that proves innocence under all possible conditions. And, as we might expect, the problem that arises with this attempt is that just as the contradiction that is K.'s legal predicament is impossible to defeat because it itself says nothing, this all-encompassing defense, were it even possible to compose, would also, in its attempt to defend against everything, actually say nothing (*TLP* 4.461).

As K. continues to interact with his legal defense, the contradictions continue as well, and he even begins to recognize them more clearly. Contemplating the dismissal of Huld, for example, K. views his case thusly: "Immer gab es Fortschritte, niemals aber könne die Art dieser Fortschritte mitgeteilt werden" ("There was always progress, but this sort of progress could never really be called progress as such") (3:129)—that is, the case both progresses and does not progress. But it is when he is introduced to the painter Titorelli that the contradictions in his predicament become most egregious. In the squalid "atelier," K. notices something odd about a figure the painter has incorporated into the portrait of an influential judge: he has painted Justice and the Goddess of Victory in one (3:153). This is, after K.'s arrest itself, the most major contradiction we have as of yet encountered, as well as the most symbolically powerful. And, as K. looks closer, the contradiction becomes threefold: she is actually Justice, Victory, and the Goddess of the Hunt (3:154).[20] This is crucial, because it shows the contradiction in the logic of the Court's law: Justice, who should be impartial, instead is always the victor, and even ensures this state of affairs by active pursuit of her prey. In order to understand how the law works, we must primarily (and most importantly of all) understand that the Court's victory, merciless pursuit, and Justice are the same thing. All maneuvering within the system somehow must acknowledge and work with or around this contradiction.

Again, K. does not realize this—he will not until he leaves the cathedral several scenes later—and instead prompts Titorelli to expound on the methods of acquittal. These, in turn, are all contradictions in terms simply by naming themselves "acquittals," but since K. has not yet accepted that contradiction is an inherent part of the Law, he still protests their alleged nonsensicality. Titorelli's explanation of "die wirkliche Freisprechung," which none, to his knowledge, has ever received, K. finds simply astounding (3:160). K. specifically points out that Titorelli's description of the Court as both impervious to petitions of evidence and "open," followed by the assertion that the innocent need no help from the Court ("der Unschuldige [braucht] vor dem Gericht keine Hilfe") is a contradiction ("Widerspruch") (3:160). And, further, that Titorelli has claimed that one can influence the judges personally, but denied that actual acquittal ("wirkliche Freisprechung") can ever be reached through personal influence: another contradiction (3:160). Titorelli responds that these contradictions are easy to clear up—with another contradiction: "Es ist hier von zwei verschiedenen Dingen die Rede, von dem was im Gesetz steht und von dem was ich persönlich erfahren habe, das dürfen Sie nicht verwechseln" ("We're talking about two different things: what's in the law and what I have personally experienced. You can't confuse them") (3:161). K.'s next course of action is to fire his attorney—who, in a contradictory action, refuses to stop working for him (3:195).

These contradictions—and, more crucially, the Court's relationship to contradiction altogether—coalesce during K.'s encounter with the prison chaplain and attempt at exegesis of "Vor dem Gesetz" ("Before the Law"). It is here that the priest reveals that K. has been approaching the contradictions he's encountered all wrong; effectively, the priest must spell out what others have been showing K. for the entire novel. There is, claims the priest, no contradiction where K. claims to see one (K. has claimed that because the door was meant for the man from the country alone, that it is contradictory for him not to be granted admittance to it). The door has, instead, been created uniquely for the man from the country to be barred from entrance (3:228). There is still, however, a contradiction in the exegesis of the parable altogether, and this is the contradiction whose acceptance might have allowed K. a better outcome of his trial; it is this contradiction that lies at the center of the Law in both its parabolic and "literal" form. It is the priest's assurance—one Sussman has rightly said "sets the stage for the parable's unsettling open-endedness"—that "Richtiges auffassen einer Sache und mißverstehen der gleichen Sache schließen einander nicht vollständig aus" ("Correctly understanding something and misunderstanding the same thing are not mutually exclusive") (3:229).[21]

K.'s "misunderstanding" of the parable (that the door meant for the man should have let him in and the doorkeeper deceived the man) and the "correct" understanding of it (that the door meant for the man should have kept him out and thus the doorkeeper never deceived him and instead just performed his job admirably) are not mutually exclusive. In effect, a simultaneous "right" and "wrong" understanding are necessary to grasp the full import of the Law, to see what it is capable of doing or not doing and why it "wants nothing" from its defendants and instead just greets them when they arrive and bids them goodbye when they leave (3:235). This assertion also conjures up later sections of the *Tractatus*, wherein Wittgenstein writes that ethical propositions are not part of the factual world because one's opinion on a matter does not change its facts: "Die Welt ist unabhängig von meinen Willen," he writes in 6.373 ("The world is independent of my will"). Just as, as Wittgenstein says, one's opinions do not change the facts (the world), it seems one's feelings toward the Law do not change its facts. This includes one's feelings toward the contradiction inherent in the demand that both the power and the irrelevance of an inaccessible Law be acknowledged simultaneously.

Ex Falso Quodlibet and K.'s Valid Conclusion

It is after this defining moment that K. begins to understand how his trial must end, and indeed in the next scene he dies. The proclamation that one must accept such a dramatic and seemingly ridiculous contradiction in a sovereign Law is what seems, frankly, senseless, and what lends the Court its reputation among critics for complete opacity and obtuseness. And as a contradiction it is necessarily senseless (*sinnlos*)—again, because it does not tell us anything (*TLP* 4.461). However, Wittgenstein does help us to make two vital discoveries about this senselessness, both of which, unlike the contradiction itself, tell us a tremendous amount about K.'s plight. The first distinction we must understand is that to Wittgenstein, contradiction, while *sinnlos*, is not nonsensical ("unsinnig" [4.4611]). The second distinction we must understand is that this unique standing preserves the contradiction's place within the system of formal logic and thus also its place within wholly valid arguments. It is these distinctions together that will allow us to see both the logic and the validity in the outcome of K.'s case.

K. complains that in the Priest's interpretation of "Before the Law," one must take the Doorkeeper's proclamations for true, and the Priest responds: "[M]an muß nicht alles für wahr halten, man muß es nur für notwendig halten" ("One must not hold all of this for true, one must only deem it necessary"). This K. finds to be a depressing opinion ("trübselige Meinung"), for then the lie establishes the world order ("[die] Lüge wird zur Weltordnung gemacht" [233]). From a logical standpoint, K. is wrong once again, in that the Priest has not stated an opinion ("Meinung") but a fact—in logic, a step in an argument does not need to be true, but only needs to conform to the necessary criteria in the logical symbolism. Our first task here is to recognize why, exactly, contradictions and tautologies remain part of the logical symbolism and thus conform to these necessary criteria (*TLP* 4.461). To demonstrate this, Wittgenstein constructs a truth table that lays out all possible truth conditions and results for a particular proposition (see below). For example, if we wanted to determine the conditions under which "Today is the first of December" is true, we would use the letter "p" to stand in for the date, and create a table with two columns, one for each possibility. We then fill out the table with the totality of all possibilities; that is, if the actual date is December 1, then "p" is true and "~p" is false; if the actual date is any other date, "p" is false and "~p" true, etc.

The usefulness of the truth table becomes clearer, however, when we are dealing with more complicated propositions, such as "Today is not the first of December, and it is raining," with the second elementary proposition (*Elementarsatz*) now represented by r. In this more complicated case, the above proposition is only true when the ~p column has a T and the **r** column also has a T, and perusing the table allows us to determine easily and quickly exactly the conditions necessary for that to happen (see bold text at bottom right):

p	~p	r	~r	~p & r
T	F	T	F	F
F	T	F	T	F
T	F	F	T	F
F	T	T	F	**T**

It is also possible to use the same structure to discern the truth and falsity of propositions that are never true in the actual, physical world—or, alternately, always are. Take, for example, "It is raining or not raining," and "It is raining and not raining." Wittgenstein knows unequivocally that tautologies are true under all conditions while contradictions are true under no conditions precisely *because* he has used the truth-table method to determine this much. Because of this, these extreme cases still belong to the structure, the symbolism. Thus, while they tell us nothing (are *sinnlos*), they are not nonsensical in the way "octopus is a verily" is nonsensical, in that "octopus is a verily" cannot be truth tabled due to the very category errors that make it appear nonsensical in the first place. In Wittgenstein's parlance, a piece of complete gibberish does not have the form of reality (4.18)—the logical form of reality, expressible in a truth table (below). "It is raining and not raining," however, does—as does "Josef K. is neither guilty nor not guilty":

G	~G	~G & ~~G ~(G v ~G)
T	F	F
F	T	F

This is why a logical contradiction, (also called "the False"), can, as contemporary logicians Jon Barweise and John Etchemendy put it, "act[] just like any other sentence in a proof"—why, as Wittgenstein put it before them, a contradiction still belongs to the logical symbolism.[22] However, more important for our purposes than the fact that a contradiction still belongs to the logical symbolism is the philosophy behind why a logical problem can remain valid with a contradiction still in it. This is the heart of why K.'s predicament is valid despite the many contradictions in the Law. When a logician is attempting to solve an argument, in the course of her proof she may come upon (or, more often, intentionally create) a contradiction. Here is the remarkable part: after a contradiction, the logician may continue the argument any way she chooses, presumably to reach a "true" conclusion but often to reach a "false" but still valid one, thanks to the rule of *ex falso quodlibet*, or "after a contradiction comes anything."[23]

Barweise and Etchemendy describe this rule as an effective way to find a solution to a tricky proof by, in many instances, deriving a contradiction on purpose in a subproof, counseling the beginning logician: "If in a proof, or more importantly in some subproof, you are able to establish a contradiction, then you are entitled to assert any [first-order logic] sentence P whatsoever."[24] So it is not just that the contradiction belongs to the symbolism and "acts just like any other sentence in a proof," though that is what enables *ex falso quodlibet*. The complex philosophical origin of this rule in the *Tractatus* comes in remark 5.12, when Wittgenstein argues, "Insbesondere folgt die Wahrheit eines Satzes 'p' aus der Wahrheit eines anderen 'q', wenn alle Wahrheitsgründe des zweiten Wahrheitsgründe des ersten sind." That is, for the truth of a conclusion p to follow out of the truth of a premise q, this is only possible when all of the truth conditions of p are also truth conditions of q. Let's say one of the premises (q) of a long argument is "That man is wearing shoes." And let's say that after several other premises whose details we won't go into yet (r, s, t, etc.), the true conclusion (p) of this argument is "Today is the first of December." What this means is that the truth conditions of p (today's date) must contain the truth conditions of q (whether or not a particular man is wearing shoes).[25] Now let's say that one of the aforementioned premises r is "That man is not wearing shoes." This means that r is actually the negation of q: r=~q. Now, things get interesting. If r=~q and we've already established in the argument that q and r are both premises in the same argument, then we are faced with a contradiction. Now let's say after many more complex lines in our proof, our true conclusion is still p: "Today is the first of December." Wittgenstein has claimed that p still contains the truth conditions of q & r: p still contains the truth conditions of the contradiction.

This is possible because the contradiction, though it is allowed to participate in an argument owing to it belonging to the logical symbolism, is true under no conditions and thus effectively has no truth conditions (4.461). This, in turn, is possible because a contradiction works, as Wittgenstein says, like the zero in mathematics: everything is capable of containing "nothing" within it, in addition to whatever else it has—that is, if I have seven apples, I have nothing plus seven apples. Thus, to say that if a conclusion p follows out of a premise q but q is part of a contradiction, p—whatever p is—can obviously contain those truth conditions, since those truth conditions are null, and everything can contain "nothing." Wittgenstein describes this quite beautifully by allowing that in 5.143 that "die Kontradiktion verschwindet sozusagen außerhalb der Sätze. [Sie] ist die äußere Grenze der Sätze" ("the contradiction disappears, so to speak, outside the proposition. She is the outermost border of the proposition").

Ex falso quodlibet (or the rule of "False Elimination") applies to Josef K.'s predicament in much the same way. Many—or rather most, if not all—of the premises leading up to K.'s conclusion (as it were) are contradictory: "Josef K. is not guilty and not not guilty"; "Victory and justice are the same thing"; "An arrested person is also free"; "An acquitted person is actually just pre-arrested"; "Correctly understanding something and misunderstanding the same thing are not mutually exclusive"; and so on (3:153, 229). After each contradiction, Kafka may put anything he wants, so long as it is grammatically put together in such a way that it belongs to the logical symbolism. And that thing, whether true or false, will be valid, because the only definition of logical validity is that it is invalid for all of the premises of an argument to be true but the conclusion false.[26] Thus, *The Trial*'s own conclusion can be interpreted as "Therefore, Josef K. is executed," or "Therefore, Josef K. is murdered," or "Therefore, Josef K. commits assisted suicide," and all are equally valid. Thanks to the complete lack of truth conditions the Court has presented us—in both K.'s foundational predicament where he is denied a named charge, and in the contradictions that follow—we will never know whether any of these interpretations of K.'s death is *wahr* (true or just). But according to the law of logic, anything that happens to K., so long as it can be phrased in a German declarative sentence with the correct logical form (*TLP* 4.18), is, as the Priest says, "notwendig," because it conforms to the criteria necessary to obey the law of logic. Depending upon our views of K.'s inherent, existential, or self-created guilt, we may call what has happened to him fair, we may call it unfair, we may call it predestined, we may call it a shock—but thanks to 5.12, we may not call it illogical, nonsensical, or invalid. And this is the case purely due to the internal logic of his situation, and possible to see even without the aid of extratextual markers such as the bestowing of original or, as Sokel has argued, "existential" guilt upon K. to make his predicament make sense.[27]

Conclusion: K.'s False Elimination and the Ineffable

And yet, saying that K.'s death makes perfect sense does not really make the end of *The Trial* more satisfying. If his chief crime during the trial was failing to recognize the power of contradictions in logic, can he really be blamed for that? Can any of us? Leaving aside the fact that most of us do not reduce juridical quandaries into first-order logic as a matter of course, it still would have been impossible for K. to understand this about his trial. This is because, in addition to including tautologies and contradictions in the valid symbolism, logic as Wittgenstein conceives it contains another caveat: its structure—that which makes it logical, that which makes language logical—cannot be uttered in language. Therefore, the fact that K.'s case makes sense logically, is logically valid, does not help him at all, because nobody can explain this to him and he cannot explain it to himself.

The problem is that according to Wittgenstein, logical structure shows itself with language, but cannot be uttered in language. It is in fact logic, rather than any metaphysical "truth," that is the subject of Wittgenstein's famous utterance from *TLP* 4.1212: "Was gezeigt werden *kann*, *kann* nicht gesagt werden" ("What *can* be shown, *cannot* be said"). Since what is happening to K. is a matter of logical rather than juridical necessity, it follows that it is beyond K.'s language to conceive what is happening to him altogether.[28] However, that K. cannot utter the essence of his predicament—the form of a logical contradiction—is not merely a result of all logical form being unsayable. As we have discussed before, though contradictions can be put into a truth table—though they have the form of reality—they do not present an actual picture that can be compared with the real state of affairs (4.462). Wittgenstein points out that because we cannot picture what we cannot picture to ourselves, we also cannot say what we cannot picture: "Was wir nicht denken können, das können wir nicht denken; wir können also nicht sagen, was wir nicht denken können" ("We cannot think what we cannot think; accordingly, we cannot *say* what we cannot think either"). Accordingly, logic fulfills the world ("die Logik erfüllt die Welt"), and the limits of the world are also its limits ("die Grenzen der Welt sind auch ihre Grenzen" [5.61]). What we cannot picture to ourselves—a tautology, a contradiction, or even real nonsense—we also cannot say; thus, although logically valid, the nature of

K.'s predicament cannot be said clearly, and thus, according to Wittgenstein, cannot be said at all (*TLP* introduction). Since, as has now been established from multiple angles, one cannot defend oneself against nothing—despite the inclusion of that "nothing" in a valid argument—K. still has no chance to speak this truth to himself, since he has no possibility of doing so.

As K. is being led to his death, Kafka's narrator makes the following claim, one that at first appears to be the basis for K.'s last struggle for life: "Die Logik ist zwar unerschütterlich, aber einem Menschen der leben will, widersteht sie nicht" ("Logic is no doubt unshakable, but it cannot withstand a man who wants to live") (3:241). K. likely means one or more lay appropriations of Aristotelian logic here—though nothing is to stop the reader with a vivid imagination from arguing that he read Frege and Russell outside the narrative space—so assuming that when K. thinks about "die Logik" he means formal logic may seem like a stretch. However, Wittgenstein's entire conception of logic—adapted from Frege's before him—is that all language, and therefore all thought, is logic, whether we see it there or not (*TLP* 5.61). Therefore, even though K. might not explicitly be talking about formal logic when he claims "die Logik ist . . . unerschütterlich," it is the force that binds together the form of his reality and of the thoughts and spoken language that have attempted to express it.

Thus, if we indeed think of "die Logik" as actual formal logic, then we can see that only the first part of K.'s pre-death assessment is true, at least according to Wittgenstein: logic is, indeed, unshakable, its structure not contained or containable within language and thus impervious to its malfeasant content, including the contradiction. The second part, however—that logic, though unshakable, cannot withstand a man who wants to live—makes Kafka's sentence, and thus also K.'s juridical sentence, into yet another contradiction. For if something is both unshakable and cannot withstand a certain force, it is the false. And, further, had K. decided to fight for his life and win, this "conclusion" would have been as valid as any other—the logic would actually have withstood a "man who wants to live," making the second half of the statement false and thus once again proving both the arbitrariness of K.'s death and the unshakability of logic itself.

Logic is, indeed, unshakable, and its law provides an unshakably clear and present, if ineffable, consistency to a narrative progression many of us mistakenly assume to be opaque. For being opaque is not the same as being ineffable but clearly present in form and structure; Wittgenstein's "what *can* be shown, *cannot* be said" is supposed to clarify, rather than obscure, our understanding of the logical form of language and reality. Furthermore, K.'s trial is certainly rife with contradiction many of us would call paradox, but rather than simply accept the alleged canceling out of a paradox, we might notice instead that viewed formally, contradiction presupposes neither an illogical nor an invalid state of affairs. The unmasking of that contradiction instead offers a novel interpretation of K.'s situation on a metalevel, while reaffirming that the essence of what K. actually needs to know to help himself can never be known to him because he cannot utter it and thus cannot think it. It is my hope that this exploration has offered a convincing point of departure in my quest to connect formal logic and literature, especially during the explosive time in literary history when *The Trial* was written, when language skepticism was a powerful current in Austrian literature and thought, and rigorous analysis of logic was just coming into importance. And finally, I also hope that my initial excavation of a preexisting "logical turn" in modernism will stand together with the various other currents in analysis of *The Trial*, as well as, so to speak, on its own validity.

Chapter 2

✦

The Metamorphosis and the Limits of Metaphorical Language

In *The Trial*, what seemed to be a nonsensical persecution actually revealed a truly unshakable law: that of symbolic logic.[1] Not that this helped K. at all, for instead of proving himself innocent, he ends up chastised for *not* understanding that a bipolar innocence/guilt structure is irrelevant to his situation—that, instead, contradiction rules: one should be able to view something "correctly" while simultaneously misunderstanding it (3:223). The wages of K.'s refusal—or failure—to take part in a world that contradiction dominates is death. This poses a question: if, as in *The Trial*, the very questions "Is Josef K. guilty?" and "What is he guilty of?" are illusory, what other major questions of Kafkology might also be?

There is most certainly a second alleged problem in Kafka studies that requires a dissolution rather than a solution: namely, what appears by all accounts to be the central issue in Kafka's most widely read work, *Die Verwandlung* (*The Metamorphosis*). Whereas the undoing of the guilt/innocence issue in *The Trial* is a fine example of the logical universalism of an unrealistic fictional situation—a man being simultaneously guilty and innocent with no charge to prove or disprove—*The Metamorphosis* presents us with a different sort of logically related issue, one that is perhaps even more unique to the literary world. That is, Kafka's most famous story, famous for what appears to be its central and incontrovertible metaphor, Gregor Samsa's monstrous body, actually offers a fascinating skepticism of the metaphor altogether. This skepticism goes far beyond even the "metamorphosis of metaphor" Corngold introduced into the discipline some decades ago. Although I agree with Corngold that the structure with which Kafka has written Gregor Samsa's body makes it impossible for it to be a metaphor *for* anything, I take Corngold's classic analysis further and argue that Gregor as he is written utterly fails as a metaphor altogether. I will argue that this failure is only possible to see alongside Wittgenstein's crucial remark in the *Tractatus* that "what *can* be shown, *cannot* be said" (4.1212), a remark I believe applies indeed to the form of all language—including metaphorical language.

The Form of Literal-Metaphorical Storytelling

Kafka's depiction of Gregor's body will lead us to a vitally important realization about the structure, purpose, and (lack of) meaning of metaphor itself. This task Kafka accomplishes in large part by narrating Gregor's story using that hallmark of what many term, somewhat dismissively, the "Kafkaesque": the paradoxical but compelling act of literal-metaphorical storytelling. Literal-metaphorical storytelling characterizes the technique of creating narrative elements—some more blatant than others—that *cannot* make literal "sense" in the universe we know, or in any realistically narrated universe: the half-man/half-ape of "Ein Bericht für eine Akademie" ("A Report to an Academy"); the sentient burrow-creature out of "Der Bau" ("The Burrow"); the mouse-people of "Josefine die Sängerin" ("Josefine the Singer"); the talking jackals of "Schakale und Araber" ("Jackals and Arabs"); a team of horses that appear, as if conjured by magic, in a vacant pig stall in "Ein Landarzt" ("A Country Doctor"). And yet, despite their metaphorical necessity, despite nonliteral elements that span from the fantastical to the absurd, the narrative language surrounding these scientific impossibilities proceeds in a matter-of-fact literal fashion.

Martin Greenberg offers a compelling characterization of Kafka's narrative prose as literal-metaphorical; this trait, he argues, is evident in both Kafka's writing process itself and his reflections about it. Greenberg reminds us that Kafka did not typically revise, that instead "his hand moved as if possessed across the page, sentences flowing with uncanny smoothness," and, further, that "his mode of creativity was inspiration rather than making. He was the inspired poet rather than the poet as maker. He did not make or construct so much as he transmitted, even though what he transmitted was shaped at every point by the pressure of his conscious art."[2] As Greenberg sees it, what Kafka "abominated" was

> "constructions," the deliberate contrivances of the calculating consciousness. When his confidence deserts him, then he cries out that *Alles erscheint mir als Konstruktion*—that everything looks like an artificial construction to him, false and dead, as opposed to the "power of life" that he feels. Inspiration meant the spontaneous expression of his more intuitive, more unconscious side, with its truer grasp of reality, with its grasp of the hidden living rather than the mentally constructed reality.[3]

This Greenberg sees substantiated by the following entry in the *Oktavhefte* (*Octavo Notebooks*), wherein Kafka distinguishes between two kinds of truth, the "eternal" truth from the Tree of (a priori) Knowledge, and the transient, manufactured truth from the Tree of Life (that is, experience).

> Es gibt für uns zweierlei Wahrheit, so wie sie dargestellt wird durch den Baum der Erkenntnis und den Baum des Lebens. Die Wahrheit des Tätigen und die Wahrheit des Ruhenden, in der ersten teilt sich das Gute vom Bösen, die zweite ist nichts anderes als das Gute selbst, sie weiß weder vom Guten noch vom Bösen. Die erste Wahrheit ist uns wirklich gegeben, die zweite ahnungsweise. Das ist der traurige Anblick. Der fröhliche ist, daß die erste Wahrheit dem Augenblick, die zweite der Ewigkeit gehört, deshalb verlöscht auch die erste Wahrheit im Licht der zweiten. (*GW* 6:204)

> For there exist for us two kinds of truth, as given to us in the Tree of Knowledge and the Tree of Life, the truth of the active principle and the truth of the static principle. In the first good separates itself from evil; the second is nothing other than the good itself, and it knows no difference between good and evil. The first truth is given to us really, the second only intuitively. That is what is so sad to see. The cheerful thing is that the first truth belongs to the present moment, and the second to eternity; thus the first fades out in the light of the second.

For Kafka, it seems as if inspired writing that is necessarily thus free of construction reveals the "truth" from the Tree of Life, which is a more authentic and eternal truth than the constructed "truth" from the Tree of Knowledge. Thus it would follow that to get at this more eternal and unconstructed truth, there has to be some sort of nonconstructed sense of meaning as well. The misguided notion of eternal referential meaning must thus be dismissed as construction, a version of the Nietzschean dismissal of truth as a series of metaphors that have, after generations of unquestioning use, finally died.[4] Kafka, it seems, in addition to the Nietzschean language-skeptical undertones so easily attributed to him, embodies a sort of twentieth-century version of Schiller's naive/sentimental dichotomy—the idea that *true* great literature was not created, it just was, just came, and with it there was no need for flourishes or "construction"—artificialities such as simile, overbearing narrative voice, or overt metaphor in descriptive language. Greenberg refers to this as Kafka's "renunciation of metaphors," dismissed because they are "embellishments that obscured rather than revealed the clear lines of things; they were not 'true.' "[5]

But just because "constructed" language (and thus overt metaphor) is inauthentic does not mean all metaphor must go: Kafka just made metaphor *into* his literal narration. As Greenberg explains it, Kafka aimed for a "strict truthfulness" in his prose, and he went about that aim by making metaphor "the very basis of his narrative art. Most of his stories are founded squarely on a single metaphor; they are the literal enactment of an abstraction, the embodiment in a concrete image of an idea."[6] The result being, of course, that Kafka's narratives depict single, large metaphors described as if they were literal truth. Take, for example, "Description of a Struggle" ("Beschreibung eines Kampfes") where only being able to speak in metaphor is the Fat Man's disease; metaphor is the form and the content of his ailment (*GW* 5:74); it is the form and the content of Georg Bendemann's leap to his death in "The Judgment" (*GW* 1:52); it is the form and the content of the titular structure that exists only in perception and not in "reality" in *The Castle*.[7] Indeed, metaphor in the place of "straight" expression is everywhere in Kafka; as Adorno or Anders has extrapolated (or, in their own way, Deleuze and Guattari have)—Kafka's prose *is* metaphor in form and content. For Kafka, the metaphor is not a way to *convey* the narration or a "point" to the reader, but rather it *is* the narrative, in both form and spirit.

Critical reactions to the literal-metaphorical narrative generally come from two polarized camps, both of which have found much to extrapolate from Kafka's journal entry in 1921 in which he listed metaphor along with insufficient heat in his flat as "eines der Vielen, die mich am Schreiben verzweifeln läßt" ("one of the many things that make me despair of writing") (*GW* 11:196). One, which includes the still-compelling work of Anthony Thorlby and J. P. Stern from several decades ago, argues that by literalizing metaphor, Kafka has made *everything* into metaphor. Thorlby, as we will see momentarily in more detail, argues on behalf of Kafka wrestling with the impossibility of literal expression and emerging victorious by creating "a self-contained metaphorical world."[8] There is certainly something to be said for the argument that Kafka thus slips into a totally metaphorical universe where literal meaning does not exist (and this seems strengthened by the attack on literal meaning in *The Trial*). In this popular view, his works are absolved of making literal "sense," or really any sort of "sense" at all within the narrative. But how, then, does one explain that the vast majority of Kafka's narration—that is, the drily reported events that take place around the metaphorical set pieces and characters—is not in the least fantastical? That is where the other argument comes in: one that we will see advocated by not just Greenberg, but Corngold, Anders, and Deleuze and Guattari: that Kafka has instead "killed" all metaphor, made *all* metaphor literal. The fact that "killing" metaphor is itself a metaphorical gesture notwithstanding, the consternating element in the scorched-earth approach is that this metaphor obliteration acts itself as a larger metaphor for the (or Kafka's) writing process and difficulties (along the vein of, for example, Clayton Koelb's "Kafka and the Scene of Reading" or Corngold's reading of "In the Penal Colony" as an authorial fight with the composition of *The Trial*).[9]

Though the points each side presents are convincing, each leaves at least one disturbing bit of obscurity. If, for example, we are to adhere to the "self-contained metaphorical universe" approach, what should we make of the literal narration in Kafka's work? In "Als Gregor Samsa eines Morgens aus unruhigen Träumen erwachte" ("As Gregor Samsa awoke one morning out of unsettling dreams") does no literal entity Gregor Samsa exist, and does this nonentity not actually wake (*GW* 1:93)? On the other hand, if we are to believe, really, that Kafka has "killed all metaphor," then how are we to treat the fact that this gesture can only be expressed in metaphor—and how are we to treat the fact that this approach altogether works largely as a metaphor for the writing process itself? Is the literal approach useless when it itself cannot be metaphorized? It is a highly worthwhile endeavor to peer into the dark spots that both of these approaches either deliberately or accidentally obscure, by examining not the result or the "point" of Kafka's literal-metaphorical narration, but rather the structure and form itself.

All this is to say that the argument that Kafka has something at stake in the creation and portrayal of metaphor in *The Metamorphosis* is not particularly novel; what is exciting (in both its literary and philosophical implications) is the charting of why the literal metaphors in *The Metamorphosis* work—and why, more importantly, at times they do *not* work. This in turn provokes us to ask what the parameters for a "successful" metaphor in this story's context are and what, if anything, a "failed" metaphor means or does. First: what does it mean to say that some of Kafka's metaphors "succeed"? Widely discussed movements such as Gregor Samsa's odd protection of the framed portrait of the lady in fur (*GW* 1:131), or Herr Samsa's reverse-inverse-Oedipal pummeling of his son's exo-shell with apples (*GW* 1:135), are what a critic in the vein of I. A. Richards (and after him Corngold) or the analytic philosopher of language Max Black would probably deem live, functioning, or "interactive" metaphors: that is, certain (some, *but not all*) characteristics of one thing (or action) are supplanted onto another. And what does it mean to say that some of Kafka's metaphors "fail"? A failed metaphor is a "metaphor" that looks and acts like a metaphor but is actually the expression of its literal self: it takes the *structure* of one thing evoking the characteristics of another, but evokes a metaphorical "meaning" that is the same as its literal meaning. I will argue that Kafka evokes exactly such a failed metaphor when he creates Gregor Samsa's body as an *Ungeziefer*, an untranslatable word choice that I will argue cannot lead to any other reasonable conclusion. Kafka's rendering of Gregor's body as a metaphor for itself reveals the essence of Kafka's conception, in this story at least, *of* metaphor itself. What metaphor is, it will emerge, is not a *thing* but a form, an assertion already somewhat common with critics, Corngold foremost among them, but rarely paralleled with Wittgenstein's *Tractatus Logico-Philosophicus*.[10]

The Metamorphosis and Metaphorical Sense

While the argument that Kafka has something at stake in the creation and portrayal of metaphor in *The Metamorphosis* is not particularly novel, what is exciting is the charting of why—or, more precisely, if—the literal metaphors in *The Metamorphosis* actually do make metaphorical sense (if not literal sense). For a metaphor makes sense as such when it is easily understood that what has just been described is neither a magical entity nor a lie, but rather a creative use of language that is understood to add richness to the thing described. A nonsensical metaphor, on the other hand, is an alleged metaphor whose context or rendering signals to us that it ought to be taken metaphorically, but which, despite appearances, is actually just something expressing its literal self. The nonsensical metaphor takes the structure of one thing evoking the characteristics of another, but evokes a metaphorical "meaning" that is the same as its literal meaning. Kafka's rendering of nonsensical metaphors in *The Metamorphosis*, rather than his depiction of sensical ones, will in the end reveal the essence of his conception, in this story at least, of metaphor itself.

In *The Metamorphosis*, the "successful" narrated metaphors are the least remarkable: they are those events or objects that, portrayed in the way Kafka has portrayed them within the story, evoke extraliteral (theoretical, emotional, philosophical) consequences without much incident. They are the metaphors whose definition as "metaphors" is perhaps least objectionable (though at times they beg to be explained away as allegory): a framed portrait of a lady in fur, whose animal/sexual appointments evoke the instincts Gregor's rigid lifestyle seems to have precluded (1:93); three boarders at the Samsa flat that look exactly alike, and whose replication itself replicates the encroachment of capitalist necessity (1:143); a relationship with his sister whose gestures are almost overripe for psychoanalysis; an apple that is "really" both a phallus and a weapon (1:135).[11] But at the same time they are metaphors that in their successful evocation—in the complete eclipsing of their literal meaning by their bevy of metaphorical interpretations, in their very vulnerability to the "solution" of allegory—say the least about how metaphor "works." This is because, unlike the far more interesting "unsuccessful" metaphors we will discuss shortly, the successful metaphor provokes no confrontation of the limits of metaphor, because in its very nature (of being well-contained within those limits) it does not have to.

Justifiably, much of the theoretical debate surrounding metaphor in *The Metamorphosis* centers not only on *what* Kafka's metaphors mean, but on *how* they mean, how they "work" (or do not work). The initial impulse—one many critics indulge but just as many refute—is to treat the story as some amalgam of a dream narrative and allegory for something specific, usually for either Kafka's fraught relationship with his father, the destructive alienating power of late capitalism, or both.[12] It seems gratifying at first to treat *The Metamorphosis*'s more puzzling narrative elements as dream-allegory symbols that only need to be decoded and analyzed. This is not particularly egregious, especially given the exegetic power granted to Kafka's oft-cited assertion that his work was an attempt to communicate his "traumhaft inneres Leben" ("dreamlike inner life").[13] As we have just seen, Greenberg has made a strong case that the literal-metaphorical hybrid is the embodiment of dream logic, that "Kafka's kind of metaphor—the literal expression in a concrete image of an abstraction—works essentially like dream metaphors.

Embarrassment, in a dream, is not a long word with two r's and two s's; it is being naked in public."[14] That is: repulsiveness *is* waking up transformed into an "ungeheures Ungeziefer" (usually translated "monstrous vermin"). This is straightforward enough.

But what about the early assertion in the story that it was no dream ("Es war kein Traum" [1:93])? And what about the minor detail that, aside from the transformation itself (which takes place outside of the narrative space), the ninety-odd pages of narrative contain, peppered by a few predominantly metaphorical (or possibly allegorical) gestures, a largely literal and causally plausible narrative, one in which the characters do not morph and their actions are consistent with their initial characterizations? This would seem to undermine the designation of *The Metamorphosis* as a pure dream narrative. And what about Adorno's reminder that it is fine (facetiously) to call Kafka's work allegory so long as one recognizes that said allegory has no key—that is, that the corresponding real-life narrative has either been lost or never existed in the first place, a distinction that seems particularly fruitless to pursue?[15] This would seem to undermine the allegorical pursuits of the story as well.

If allegory and dream symbol are too easily undermined in interpretation of *The Metamorphosis*'s (purportedly) nonliteral or extraliteral moments, and metaphor is the most accurate designation, then that still leaves the question: (how) do Kafka's metaphors work? For Sussman, they are indications and parts of Kafka's "linguistic theology experiment," one that "displac[es]" the "metaphoric substrate of literary figuration" to "a setting of . . . antipodal alienation and marginality, as in 'The Metamorphosis,' " and thus grants literary metaphor "an acrobatic extension and prolongation."[16] That is, Kafka uses metaphor to stretch and test its own limits, an assertion that will be revisited and revealed as most plausible during the discussion of "unsuccessful" metaphor, but that applies to the "successful" metaphors we are about to discuss as well. Thorlby's conception of Kafka's metaphor is, in complement but not contrast to Sussman's, that for Kafka metaphor and (all) language are one and the same, that metaphor *is* language, is what is both powerful and despair-provoking about it. The "one and the same" approach (which echoes the Nietzschean) Kafka expresses, unsurprisingly, with a metaphor, the spear remark we have already discussed, from the diary entry from June 1923, his last (see preface).

As Thorlby sees it, what Kafka is doing here is "summing up . . . his most fundamental insight into language," that being "its metaphorical capacity not only to transform the experience from which it arises in life into something beyond itself, but actually to reverse what was lived as one thing into what is 'thought of' in an infinitely regressing series of reflections." Language, to Kafka, "presents itself . . . as a problem to be overcome. How can he solve it? The passage itself demonstrates the answer."[17] Thorlby is certainly accurate about the transformational capacity of metaphor—to make language, *through itself*, more powerful, to make words into spears while at the same time claiming that that is what they always were. He is also right in claiming that the passage itself demonstrates *an* answer—that language can be both powerful and self-destructive, that metaphor might be the source of this trait, and that the best or only way to express this idea is with a metaphor. But I am not sure about his assertion that Kafka sees metaphorical language as a "problem" to be overcome. I see the diary entry instead as the expression of a phenomenon, as a manifested impossibility, the claim (*through* the form of metaphor) that something was always a certain way, a claim that nevertheless only becomes that "certain way" in the moment it is claimed. The assertion that metaphorical language is a "problem to be overcome," however, is a necessary precondition to Thorlby's larger conception of Kafka's use of metaphor, which is that it is all-encompassing: that Kafka transformed whatever his stories' "real impulse[s]" were "entirely into the language of metaphor—indeed, into a self-contained metaphorical world."[18]

The question still remains, however: how does Kafka's successful metaphor really "work"? In my conception—one culled from several compelling metaphor theories from the analytic tradition in philosophy—and in the broadest possible terms, the working metaphor functions by successfully employing what I call *metaphorical form*: a description of one entity (Y) in a way that applies selected characteristics of that entity onto another entity (X), so that the Y entity is presumed to be understood in scare quotes: X is a "Y." To begin to explore this, I will concentrate on the analytic philosopher (and early Wittgenstein critic) Max Black's conception, one that seems to echo (by coincidence rather than design) I. A. Richards's "tenor/vehicle" model (and thus also Corngold's).[19] I believe Black's schematization of metaphor is an accurate depiction of what Kafka evokes with and about metaphor, which he (Black) accomplishes by being simultaneously highly technical and recognizing, in the end, that even with (or possibly because of) a schematization, there is no rational reason why some metaphors "work" and some do not. Such arbitrariness is, we will see, due to something that is both true and ultimately inexpressible about metaphor: that it is a *structure* whose essence precludes it from being expressible in literal language. This is why so many philosophers—even analytic philosophers such as Black and Davidson—only seem to be able to explain metaphor, even while deriding it, in metaphor.

Black's problem with metaphor is not the simple scourge of its use in philosophy, though he does begin his study by pointing out that "to draw attention to a philosopher's metaphors is to belittle him—like praising a logician for his beautiful handwriting."[20] Black's problem is that its critics simply assume metaphor is "doing" something far less complicated than it really is. This he breaks down by explaining two erroneous views of metaphor, the "substitution view" and the "comparison view."[21] The substitution view he sees as facile and, furthermore, not actually "working" as metaphor at all. In the substitution view, "when we speak of a relatively simple metaphor, we are referring to a sentence . . . in which some words are used metaphorically, while the remainder are used non-metaphorically."[22] An easy example of a metaphor it would be natural to view "substitutionally" would be something like "Mein Vater ist noch immer ein Riese" ("My father is still a giant of a man," from "The Judgment"), wherein everything but "Riese" is meant to be taken literally (*GW* 1:44). What, in the substitution view, we are then to do with "Riese" (given that the speaker's father is a human of slightly larger than average size) is to recognize that the "word or expression having a distinctively metaphorical use within a literal frame" is being "used to communicate a meaning that might have been expressed literally."[23] Further, "it is the reader's task to invert the substitution, by using the literal meaning of M[etaphor-expression] as a clue to the intended literal meaning of L[iteral sentence]. Understanding a metaphor," then, "is like deciphering a code or unraveling a riddle."[24] This hits upon what I believe is the very nature of Kafka's work with metaphor—why it made him "despair of writing" and, at the same time, why so many of his readers oversimplify his use of it. The "substitution view" of metaphor presupposes a "solution" to the riddle or a "key" to the allegory—but, lest Adorno remind us again, that is not possible.[25]

Black's analysis deserves further exploration yet: in the substitution view, metaphor is supposed to "plug the gaps in the literal vocabulary."[26] The problem with this, with viewing metaphor as "a species of catachresis," is that the substitution view of metaphor simply calls for the "putting of new senses into old words." The problem here is that if the catachresis actually "serves a genuine need, the new sense introduced will quickly become part of the literal sense," and the metaphor will kill itself: therefore if viewing one's father as a "giant" is actually apt, "giant" will somehow take upon itself a new meaning of "larger than average father" that is just as denotative (rather than connotative) as the word "orange" (as a color, taken from the fruit) is to us now.[27] An example of an otherwise "successful" metaphor that in the "substitution view" causes more problems than its solves in *The Metamorphosis* comes when Gregor is struggling to leave his bedroom on the first morning of his transformation, an act he seems to think will resolve the conflict with his boss and family but instead results in unsurprising horror (1:110–11). As Gregor struggles to turn the key in his bedroom door with his mouth, he injures it, and a brown liquid comes out of his mouth (1:106). This provokes an understandable but in the end misguided use of the "substitution view" of metaphor. An easy metaphorical designation for the brown liquid would be as a physically repulsive representation of Gregor's loss of language—as a literally impossible concretization of Gregor's metamorphosis from allegedly successful language user to vermin animal, as the brown liquid both takes the place of words and is physically alarming and repulsive. In the vein of Deleuze and Guattari, one could potentially argue that this moment seems to indicate a de- (or re-)territorializing of the mouth and teeth, from language organs to their primal function as eating organs, or, in this case, the unappetizing reversal of that, excreting organs.[28]

But this interpretation, in the "substitution view," is too simple (and we will view it again in the more complex "interaction view" in a moment) and too harshly relegates some elements of the moment to the literal realm and some to the metaphorical: that is, in order for the metaphor of the "braune Flüssigkeit" to "work" substitutionally, as an indication of de- or reterritorialization or anything else, the rest of the moment—that is, of *Gregor Samsa in his literally impossible metamorphosed new form* attempting to open his door—must be read literally. But the choice to take Gregor's body (especially this early in the story) at face value but the brown liquid it excretes as something "special" is arbitrary—it would seem far more logical to say that either both things, the body and its secretions, are metaphorical *or* literal. But with this choice made the moment becomes even more complicated: if Gregor's body must also be metaphorical in this moment, then the "special" designation of the brown liquid is lost—as is, somewhat ironically, the metaphorical expository power it purportedly has in underscoring both the aphasia and the repulsiveness of Gregor's new condition. If the brown liquid must also be literal in this moment, then there is no metaphor at all. And yet this moment, in its suspense and vivid imagery, does have a metaphor to express (one that may even be the hypothetical one about aphasia)—it is simply that it cannot be schematized with the more common "substitution" view of metaphor.

Gregor's struggle with the door comes during a period of narrative focus in the beginning of the story on Gregor's mouth and its obviously shifting capabilities—another indicator that Gregor's mouth and everything it is purported to interact with (food, language, objects) has a role in the story that we should not ignore and a metaphor (or metaphors) that, though elusive, will prove to be vital in both the development of the narrative and Kafka's confrontation with metaphor's limits. Before Gregor opens the door he attempts to shout excuses through it at both his family and, later, his supervisor. He is shocked and repulsed at the sound of his new voice, one that Deleuze and Guattari have argued that, as the indicator of the movement (and not the evocation of an archetype or any other recognizable referent) of the "becoming-insect," comes out as "a mournful whining that carries along the voice and blurs the resonance of the words."[29] This, in context, is actually somewhat of an understatement:

> "Gregor," rief es—es war die Mutter—"es ist dreiviertel sieben. Wolltest du nicht wegfahren?" Die sanfte Stimme! Gregor erschrak, als er seine antwortete Stimme hörte, die wohl unverkennbar seine frühere war, in die sich aber, wie von unten her, ein nicht zu unterdrückendes, schmerzliches Piepsen mischte, das die Worte förmlich nur im ersten Augenblick in ihrer Deutlichkeit beließ, um sie im Nachklang derart zu zerstören, dass man nicht wusste, ob man recht gehört hatte. (1:96)

> "Gregor," came the voice—it was his mother—"it's a quarter to seven. Didn't you want to leave?" That gentle voice! Gregor was shocked as he heard the voice in which he answered. It was nearly unrecognizable compared to his earlier voice, which nevertheless remained barely present like an undertone as it mixed with an irrepressible, painful squeaking that made the words audible only in their first moments, so that it wasn't clear if one had heard them correctly.

The gentle voice of Frau Samsa seems to make Gregor's painful squeaking all the more terrifying to him—most shocking of all seems to be the labored, silenced version of Gregor's previous voice the new shrieking has all but eclipsed. Gregor's supervisor seems shocked as well; from the other side of the door, he decries it as an animal's voice, a "Tierstimme" (1:105). This sentence of dialogue, "Das war eine Tierstimme" ("That was an animal's voice"), provokes the exposure via Black of another tempting but ultimately erroneous conception of metaphor, the "comparison view."

The comparison view is the idea that metaphor is just a compressed simile. Black's chief example of this is the sentence "Richard is a lion," which Black takes as "really" meaning "Richard is like a lion (by being brave)."[30] The problem with the comparison view is that it suffers from a "vagueness that borders on vacuity," because the implied simile is *also* allegedly attempting to say something about the literal qualities of the metaphorically evoked subject. What qualities of a lion are supposed to be invoked in Richard? Carnivorousness? A mane? Without the simile there to explicitly refer to bravery, nobody can really be sure.[31] Therefore, in Black's view, it would actually "be more illuminating in some of these cases to say that the metaphor creates the similarity than to say that it formulates some similarity antecedently existing."[32] And indeed, it does seem as if the chief clerk's use of "Das war eine Tierstimme" is being used as a simile, as a foreshortening of "That was *like* an animal voice" or "That sounded *as if* it came from an animal." This is because, at this point in the story, the chief clerk has not seen Gregor and has no reason to (reasonably) believe that his voice *is* a *Tierstimme* (even though, actually, it is).[33] So it is reasonable to assess that he is attempting to express the idea that Gregor's voice sounds *like* an animal's. But therein lies the problem: *what* about the way an (unnamed, generic) animal sounds characterizes Gregor's painful squeaking? Do animals, for that matter, even have what humans would reasonably call a "voice" without a severe degree of anthropomorphism? Again, this is not to say that the chief clerk isn't using a metaphor: at this point in the narrative there is every reason to believe that he is. It is, simply, to point out that the metaphor "works" in a far more complicated way than an extended simile does, as the extended simile has to create more meaning than it expresses.

Finally we come to what most closely approximates Black's conception of a "successful" metaphor. The "richer" view of metaphor is what Black calls the "interaction view," whose similarities to (and differences from) the Richards "tenor/vehicle" model will soon become readily apparent. Black's "interaction view" works by summoning up a complex discourse between the literal meaning of the "principal" subject (what Richards will call the "vehicle") and the "subsidiary" one (Richards: "tenor"), the principal being what in a more erroneous view would be called the literal part of the statement and the subsidiary the metaphorical part. In the interaction view, "the effect . . . of (metaphorically) calling a man a 'wolf' is to evoke the wolf-system of related commonplaces."[34]

The "interaction" of metaphor—which I formalize into the template "X is a 'Y,' " with the scare quotes around "Y" implying a constant and dynamic interaction rather than a simple substitution—is particularly important in the Kafkan literal-metaphorical oeuvre. This we can see not only in the examples from *The Metamorphosis* we will examine in more detail in short order, but in telling selections from Kafka's other work as well: in "Ein Hungerkünstler" ("A Hunger Artist") for example, the panther that replaces the hunger artist in the cage calls up the "commonplaces" of a voracious, very alive, ravenous human being (*GW* 1:273); in "A Country Doctor" the narrator's servant being named "Rosa," the rose-colored cheeks of the apparently healthy (but actually quite ill) patient, and, finally, his "rose" of a wound, all "interact" both with each other across the horizontal indices of the story's world, and with both the literal and literary "commonplaces" of the rose itself.[35]

Returning to *The Metamorphosis*, then, and to both the brown liquid and the *Tierstimme*, we can see that both of these metaphors "work" best in the "interaction" view. The brown liquid does work as a metaphor for the replacement of language if we see it as invoking a set of mouth-related "commonplaces," and this, furthermore, concurrently with the set of "commonplaces" that Gregor's transformed body may or may not be evoking simultaneously. The *Tierstimme*, as well, evokes and displaces "commonplaces," both more familiar and more challenging, about the voice, human, animal, and otherwise.

How, then, do some of the other successful metaphors in *The Metamorphosis* interact? Let us first look at the portrait of the lady in fur, as Kafka allows it such terrific primacy. It appears in what we could largely deem the two most important scenes of the story: the first, in the description of Gregor's room that comes during the discovery of his transformation—"Es stellte eine Dame dar, die, mit einem Pelzhut und einer Pelzboa versehen, aufrecht dasaß und einen schweren Pelzmuff, in dem ihr ganzer Unterarm verschwunden war, dem Beschauer entgegenhob" ("It showed a woman dressed in a fur hat and a fur boa, sitting erect and brandishing toward the viewer a fur muff in which nearly the whole of her forearm had disappeared") (1:93)—and later, in which Gregor's drive to protect the portrait causes him to reveal his form to his family and terrify his mother:

> Und so brach er denn hervor—die Frauen stützten sich gerade im Nebenzimmer an den Schreibtisch, um ein wenig zu verschnaufen—wechselte viermal die Richtung des Laufes, er wußte wirklich nicht, was er zuerst retten sollte, da sah er an der im übrigen schon leeren Wand auffallend das Bild der in lauter Pelzwerk gekleideten Dame hängen, Kroch eilends hinauf und preßte sich an das Glas, das ihn festhielt und seinem heißen Bauch wohltat. Dieses Bild wenigstens, das Gregor jetzt ganz verdeckte, würde nun gewiß niemand wegnehmen. (1:131)

> And so he scuttled out—the women were just propping themselves up against the desk, in order to have a little breather—and changed direction several times, not knowing what he should rescue first. Then he noticed, on the otherwise empty wall, the picture of the woman clad only in fur, and he crawled hurriedly onto it and pressed himself against the glass, which held it there and which felt good against his hot belly. At least this picture, which he currently covered up entirely, nobody could take away.

The first metaphorical interaction comes, of course, in the young woman's animal/sexual appointments, for the fur in which she nearly disappears evokes not a single, concrete "meaning" but rather, again, what Black has called a series of fluid commonplaces: about animals (their fur), about unbridled female sexuality (evocative of pubic or other body hair), about some heretofore unconceived amalgam of human and animal physicality. This particular kind of fluid, interactive metaphor appears elsewhere in Kafka as well, most notably in a scene which we have already discussed in great detail in *The Trial*, when K. encounters Titorelli's rendition of the goddess of Justice and Victory as one entity (*GW* 3:153), again evoking not only a logical contradiction as previously discussed, but on a metaphorical level a constantly moving string of associations that bring into question any and all preconceptions about any and all concrete elements depicted (the salesman, the animal, the primal human female; victory and justice).

The second interaction is understandably more difficult, as it has added consequences with Gregor's sister. It is this moment—in which the mother's terrified reaction causes Grete's first instance of direct address to Gregor since his transformation, one of admonishment, "Du, Gregor!"—in which either Grete betrays Gregor or the other way around; in any case, their shaky alliance in which Grete keeps Gregor alive and Gregor stays under Grete's control is over. For Deleuze and Guattari this is a crucial point in Gregor's trajectory of re-Oedipalization, an instance in which Gregor's "deterritorialization through his becoming-animal finds itself blocked for a moment," and whose consequence is death:

> To please him, his sister wanted to empty out the whole room. But Gregor refused to let go of the portrait of the lady in fur. He sticks to the portrait, as if to a lost territorialized image. In fact, that's what the sister cannot tolerate. She accepted Gregor; like him, she wanted the schizo incest, an incest of strong connections, incest with the sister in opposition to Oedipal incest, incest that gives evidence of a nonhuman sexuality as in the becoming-animal. But, jealous of the portrait, she begins to hate Gregor and condemns him. From that point on, Gregor's deterritorialization through the becoming-animal fails; he re-Oedipalizes himself through the apple . . . and has nothing to do but die.[36]

But this only works when an interaction is presupposed: first, a simple reappearance of the previous interaction of the lady in fur, the fluid animal/sexual "meaning" of that portrait, must be present in order for Gregor's protection of it to mean what Deleuze and Guattari seem convinced it means. Gregor can only reject "schizo incest" with Grete if he prefers "schizo" intercourse with something or someone else; that is, she can only be "jealous" of the lady in fur if the lady in fur continues to "mean" in an animal/sexual interactive capacity.

The action that directly succeeds this moment and indirectly causes Gregor's death is what at first appears as the allegory but reveals itself to be another interactive metaphor: the pelting of Gregor's body with apples, thrown by his enraged father:

> Es war ein Apfel; gleich flog ihm ein zweiter nach; Gregor blieb vor Schrecken stehen; ein Weiterlaufen war nutzlos, denn der Vater hatte sich entschlossen, ihn zu bombardieren. Aus der Obstschale auf der Kredenz hatte er sich die Taschen gefüllt und warf nun, ohne vorläufig scharf zu zielen, Apfel für Apfel. Diese kleinen roten Äpfel rollten wie elektrisiert auf dem Boden herum und stießen einander. Ein schwach geworfener Apfel streifte Gregors Rücken, glitt aber unschädlich ab. Ein ihm sofort nachfliegender drang dagegen förmlich in Gregors Rücken ein; Gregor wollte sich weiterschleppen, als könne der überraschende unglaubliche Schmerz mit dem Ortswechsel vergehen; doch fühlte er sich wie festgenagelt und streckte sich in vollständiger Verwirrung aller Sinne. (1:135–36)

> It was an apple, and a second one flew at him after it. Gregor stood still in terror; running was useless, in that his father had decided to bombard him. Out of the fruit bowl on the credenza he'd stuffed his pockets full and now threw apple after apple, without even looking. These small red apples rolled around on the floor as if electrified, bumping against each other. A weakly thrown apple grazed Gregor's back but skidded off harmlessly. But another one, thrown immediately

> thereafter, drove hard into Gregor's back. Gregor wanted to drag himself away, as if he could make this surprising and unbelievable pain disappear with a change of location; alas, he felt instead as if he were nailed to the floor, and lay stretched out in complete confusion of all his senses.

Why is this not an instance of simple allegory, for a father/son relationship all too well documented? It may have allegorical results, to be sure, but in order to *work* as an allegory—to stand in, as an entire gesture, for the physical and psychological domination of a son by a father—the fluid morphing of "commonplaces" must first take place, and that is not an allegorical but rather an interactive metaphorical gesture. That is, the apple must interact twice, with the commonplaces of the concept "weapon" and then "weapon" (and, by extension, "apple") with "phallus"; the first happens in the literal story but the second only by evoking certain prior archetypal narratives. But even that must be exposed as an interaction rather than a "solid" evocation of an archetype (something at least Deleuze and Guattari argue does not exist in Kafka): the Oedipus story involves the son penetrating, not the father, and the sexual congress is with the mother; thus what happens in *The Metamorphosis*, if it is to evoke some sort of Oedipal narrative (that itself evokes a "real" historical one) in some sort of allegorical fashion, can only do so if the interactive perversion of that prior narrative is recognized. Thus the interaction view either takes the place of or is necessary for the full comprehension of gestures that may at first be conceived of as simpler ("substitution" or "comparison") metaphors or pure allegory. This is, then, how several of the "successful" metaphors in *The Metamorphosis* work; though they and their workings are fascinating, we will see that it is the "unsuccessful" metaphors that carry more (and more interesting) implications about what metaphor is and how (or if) it works. Even Black's analysis provokes such an examination, as his rendition of the "interaction view" ends with his acknowledgment that "there is, in general, no simple 'ground' for the necessary shifts of meaning, no blanket reason why some metaphors work and others fail."[37] In other words, there seems to be no explanation for why some ostensibly metaphorical language does constitute a working metaphor and why other ostensibly metaphorical language is just literal language that subjects us to the *illusion* that it is metaphorical—just, so to speak, "metaphorical nonsense."

The *Tractatus* and Nonsense

The relevance of the *Tractatus* to this story, from which it admittedly seems quite distant, comes in the exploration of Wittgenstein's contrast between language that makes sense and language that does not—specifically, in his conception of the logical form of language and how this form has bearing on linguistic sense.[38] As we have already seen with respect to *The Trial*, in the *Tractatus* Wittgenstein determines that the logical form of language is, in effect, what makes language able to express anything at all. And as we have briefly touched upon in Josef K.'s inability to verbalize his true conundrum, this form itself, in its nature as a form, is not expressible in language.

I believe the same can be said about metaphorical language—that, just as literal language has a logical form, metaphorical language has a metaphorical form (X is a "Y"), and that this form is both what makes metaphor metaphorical and, being form, is inexpressible in natural language. For when a metaphor works without incident, we take for granted the mistaken idea that its content has "metaphorical meaning," that there is such a thing as metaphorical meaning at all; I am able to recognize this mistaken way of thinking because Wittgenstein has discovered something remarkably similar about the logical proposition. That is: when it makes sense, we are lulled into assuming that that sense comes from, or is part, of what that proposition actually means. But this, as we are about to see, is most certainly not the case. Instead, although all sentences that make sense have logical form in common, that form is itself inexpressible.

Wittgenstein demonstrates logical form's inexpressibility in language by providing examples that make progressively less sense, but whose logical form remains intact. This demonstration provides the unexpected but vital link to literary study. What we will see now is that Kafka—in a remarkably similar way—demonstrates metaphorical form's inexpressibility in language by providing examples of metaphors that make progressively less sense, but whose metaphorical form remains intact.

Let us first revisit logical form, which we have previously encountered in our exploration of *The Trial*, specifically with the truth table and the "special case" of tautologies and contradictions. Another way to understand logical form is basically to take the opposite tactic as the truth-table method: that is, to force ourselves to begin paying attention to how logical form is present in everyday language, again concentrating on tautologies and contradictions as an excellent example of this. That is, if we hear someone say, "I am going to the store," we do not immediately notice that sentence's logical form; we do not even know what that is. Instead we concentrate on what that sentence is purportedly doing: alerting us to assess the truth or falsity of the speaker's actual state of affairs (*Sachverhalt*), with respect to her motion toward a retail establishment.[39]

The logical form—how "I," "store," and "am going to" disambiguate into formal logic when compared with the actual *Sachverhalt* in the world—should be, in nonlogician households at least, summarily ignored. Thus, the inexpressibility in language of this statement's logical form should not even register with the speaker or the hearer. If, however, we hear a tautological statement, such as "I am either going to the store or not going to the store," we are more likely to concentrate on the fact that a sentence has been uttered when it might as well not have been, because, though uttered, it didn't actually tell us anything (*TLP* 4.442–4.4661).

Now, suddenly, the inexpressible things that make this sentence "language" come to the forefront: how can we tell that something was uttered, if nothing was expressed? Because the logical structure of the sentence signals that something was. It is the logical form of tautologies (as well as contradictions: "I am both going to the store and not going to the store") being apparent, when the tautologies and contradictions themselves say nothing, that causes Wittgenstein to determine the following: first, language can express reality, but it cannot express what it has in common with reality: logical form ("Die Sprache kann die gesamte Wahrheit darstellen, aber er kann nicht das darstellen, was er mit der Wirklichkeit gemein haben muß, um sie darstellen zu können—die logische Form" [*TLP* 4.12]). This is because "um die logische Form darstellen zu können, müßten wir uns mit dem Satze außerhalb der Logik aufstellen können, das heißt außerhalb der Welt" ("In order to represent logical form, we would have to set ourselves, with the proposition, outside of logic; that is, outside the world") (4.12), and of course we cannot go outside the world of things we can express in order to express something. Hence, we have this oft-cited remark: "Was gezeigt werden kann, kann nicht gesagt werden" ("What *can* be shown, *cannot* be said") (4.1212).

Wittgenstein means it literally when he claims that language shows its logical form—for language relates to the world precisely by creating a tangible, easily recognizable logical structure that mirrors (or fails to mirror) the literal situation in the world that the said language is supposed to be describing (the general upshot of the "picture theory" sections of the *Tractatus*, *TLP* 1–3). Thus, in 4.1212, the "was" Wittgenstein is talking about is not merely a singular "was," but rather what all language has in common with whatever reality it purports to express. Logical form, in turn, is what language shows that allows it both to make sense and to alert us to when it does not make sense. The proposition shows but cannot express to us its sense, because it is impossible to explain why a proposition that makes sense makes sense, because logical form exists outside of language, and "explaining" without language is impossible.

The "*was*" in 4.1212 refers to that which language has in common with reality, an assertion that comes out of the picture theory of language, which Wittgenstein develops in the earlier propositions of the *Tractatus*. The picture theory, to recall our earlier brief discussion, is the idea that the language we use with each other shares a logical form with the reality that language is supposed to express. This is why the world must be the totality of facts, and not things (1.1)—what makes it "the world" is *how* these things relate *to each other* in logical space, not the things themselves. And logic, rather than being something *in* a proposition, is the structure that binds and arranges the sentence; the space that allows for that sentence to be arranged and that makes that sentence "match" whatever it is allegedly supposed to depict in reality.

This is the crux of the picture theory, which, as I have mentioned before, biographical legend has it that Wittgenstein developed after being inspired by a famous court case in which an automobile accident was re-created in the courtroom using models, the position of the models corresponding exactly to the position of the "real cars."[40] Propositions, Wittgenstein argued, should—if "the world" actually is "the totality of facts, and not things"—work along similar lines, their *logical form* mirroring the way the actual "things" they refer to in the world are arranged. In the picture theory, then, the argument is that an elementary proposition (*Satz)* is a fact (*Tatsache* [3.14]), "in which the elements, the words," as Black explains, "are united in a definite structure—a definite arrangement or mode of combination."[41] This, as expressed in 2.18, is logical form, the quality about language that makes it "language" (i.e., able to represent reality):

> 2.18 Was jedes Bild, welcher Form immer, mit der Wirklichkeit gemein haben muß, um sie überhaupt—richtig oder falsch—abbilden zu können, ist die logische Form, das ist die Form der Wirklichkeit.
>
> What every picture, of whatever form, must have in common with reality in order to be able to represent it at all—rightly or falsely—is the logical form, that is, the form of reality.

The crucial role the logical form of reality plays in all interpretations of the *Tractatus* (and in my interpretation of Kafka's use of metaphor) does not truly emerge until far later in the *Tractatus*, in the 4s, when it becomes clear that the most important thing about the logical form of reality—that is, what literal language has in common with reality that makes it allegedly able to represent it, that makes it, in the Wittgensteinian conception, make "sense"—is that it cannot be said, but only shown:

> 4.022 Der Satz *zeigt* seinen Sinn.
> Der Satz *zeigt*, wie es sich verhält, wenn er wahr ist. Und er *sagt, das* es sich so verhält.
>
> The proposition *shows* its sense.
> The proposition shows how things stand, if it is true. And it *says*, that they do so stand.

The picture theory of language comes together to work like this: the *Tatsache* that a *Satz* depicts is compared with "reality" (4.05) and then judged on whether it matches or does not match what is "really" there. Thus, although a proposition is the expression of a fact, its sense is independent of what that fact actually is (i.e., whether it matches or does not match with reality).

That is why it is possible to understand why, when pointing to a black dot on white paper and saying "this is black," that such an assertion is "true," but why doing exactly the same thing while pointing to the white part is false (4.063). That is why *propositions always already have a sense*; asserting them doesn't *give* them sense; what a proposition asserts is the sense it already must have to be a proposition in the first place (4.064).

This, then, is why it is impossible to explain *why* a proposition that makes sense makes sense, because it just does, and in order to explain logical form, one would have to go outside of logic to do so, and that is just not possible. It is Wittgenstein's argument as to why certain things about language can only be "shown" that brings this all together in the lead-up to 4.1212, which upon our second viewing (see this book's introduction) should make a substantial amount more sense:

> 4.12 Der Satz kann die gesamte Wirklichkeit darstellen, aber er kann nicht das darstellen, was er mit der Wirklichkeit gemein haben muß, um sie darstellen zu können—die logische Form.
>
> Um die logische Form darstellen zu können, müßten wir uns mit dem Satze außerhalb der Logik aufstellen können, das heißt außerhalb der Welt.
>
> Propositions can represent the whole of reality, but they cannot represent what they must have in common with reality in order to be able to represent it—the logical form.
>
> In order to represent the logical form, we should be able to put ourselves with the propositions outside logic, that is outside the world.

And then, soon thereafter:

> 4.1212 Was gezeigt werden *kann*, *kann* nicht gesagt werden.
>
> What *can* be shown *cannot* be said.

This, then, is what may allow the propositions of the *Tractatus* to retain some sort of worth even though they decidedly fail Wittgenstein's test of what does and does not make sense.[42] For in 6–6.54, Wittgenstein reveals that all propositions dealing with ethics, aesthetics, riddles, or enigmas—in short, what most people consider "philosophy"—cannot possibly make sense, an issue we will take up in far more detail in chapter 3. For now, it is most important to remind ourselves that the ultimate fate of language that doesn't make sense is that it is simply illusion *masquerading* as language.

Now we are pointed once again to the tautology/contradiction example that began this section. For the true moment when one can understand that our language shows its sense and cannot say its sense is the moment language makes no sense at all. For it is not, actually, something like the tautology "I am either going to the store or not going to the store"—which technically falls within the rules of logic by being classifiable as a tautology, but that expresses nothing—that causes logical form's inexpressibility in language to become obvious. Rather, that honor falls to a total violation of logic, in the manner of "I am going to the readily."[43] Why do we recognize this sentence as gibberish? Because, unlike "I am both going and not going to the store," it contains a glaring category error, the substitution of an adverb for a noun. Its linguistic *form* is wrong. Yes, now the speaker has done something noticeably against the rules, and in doing so has made the very existence of those rules—in this case, that a sentence needs a form to make sense—clear. The structure that still makes this recognizable as an English sentence, albeit a nonsensical one, must itself not be expressible within that sentence, since the sentence itself expresses nothing other than nonsense.

Now, finally, we can move on to the way in which Wittgenstein's theory of the inexpressibility of logical form fits in with what I believe to be the illusory "chief question" of *The Metamorphosis* ("What is Gregor Samsa a metaphor *for*?"). I would like to posit that the same form/content separation Wittgenstein insists governs propositional language also applies to literary metaphor, and that the rendering of a failed one, an illusory one, a nonsensical one, is what makes this most evident. For the rules of metaphor are most apparent when a violation occurs, when, for example, the X and "Y" entities of a metaphorical utterance are the same thing. Being the same thing, they cannot "interact" since the prefix "inter" presupposes difference. Thus, the richness of expression we expect (X is a "Y," metaphorically) is displaced by redundancy (X is an "X," nonsensically), and this redundancy, this absence of richness, forces upon us the recognition of the metaphorical form itself.

At last we can begin to see a bit more clearly what connects metaphorical structure in *The Metamorphosis* with Wittgenstein's theory of the logical form of language in the *Tractatus*. It is the idea of something presented in the form of language that cannot be said in language, but nevertheless shows what is important about language. In the end, just as Wittgenstein has shown that what makes language *language* is inexpressible in language, a closer look at nonsensical metaphor in Kafka's *Metamorphosis* will reveal exactly why what makes metaphor metaphorical is also inexpressible in its language.

The Metamorphosis and Metaphorical Nonsense

First let us confront the idea that we "must" recognize Gregor's body as a metaphor in the first place, an act that some critics fear comes as a result of decades of critical conditioning rather than textual necessity. Anderson points out that "few if any readers of *The Metamorphosis* have wished to recognize

Gregor Samsa's metamorphosed body as an aesthetic form," reminding us that "for Kafka's early public the bug was simply too repulsive, and was explained away with allegorical notions like 'alienated labor' or 'unconscious self-loathing.'"[44] The explaining away has, in turn, provoked not only classic interpretations like these, but also others, so many that Anderson is here inspired to the assignation of "negative infinity," a description I have previously invoked. There is, however, a textual reason—over and above the repulsiveness—for this presupposed metaphor, and that is that Gregor's literal body is possible for the reader to picture only in bits and pieces, details Anderson describes as "scant and contradictory"; furthermore, "since the story is narrated largely from Gregor's perspective, his own body tends to disappear from the reader's view."[45] Take, for example, Gregor's first self-appraisal, taken directly after waking up (that is, in the story's second sentence):

> Er lag auf seinem panzerartig harten Rücken und sah, wenn er den Kopf ein wenig hob, seinen gewölbten, braunen, von bogenförmigen Versteifungen geteilten Bauch, auf dessen Höhe sich die Bettdecke, zum gänzlichen Niedergleiten bereit, kaum noch erhalten konnte. Seine vielen, im Vergleich zu seinem sonstigen Umfang kläglich dünnen Beine flimmerten ihm hilflos vor den Augen. (1:93)

> He lay upon his hard, armor-like back and if he raised his head up a bit he saw his concave, brown belly, which was now divided by arches into stiff sections, now so tall that the blanket could not cover it, and indeed seemed ready to slide off it entirely. His many legs, so pitifully thin compared to the rest of his body, waved about helplessly before his eyes.

If Gregor's back is indeed armor-like, then it is a curiously weak armor, as it is pierced fairly easily by an apple; odder still is the absence of number of Gregor's legs—is it six? Is he an insect? Is it more, like a centipede? Is it some fantasy number in the middle? Further, the "noch nie gefühlten, leichten, dumpfen Schmerz" ("light, dull pain he had never felt before") (1:94) Kafka describes Gregor feeling directly after waking up is striking and memorable, and given so much attention that we as readers are sure it must mean something—and not only does it not develop into anything major, it is never mentioned again.

For Anderson, the task is, in spite of or because of these lapses in descriptive coherence, to focus on Gregor's body—in short, to remind ourselves, by removing the necessity for metaphor, of "the audacity of using a human-sized cockroach as a main figure in a literary text."[46] But a problem arises when we only, as Anderson seeks to do, "describe Gregor's form in visual and aesthetic terms, even when the text itself leaves these terms vague or obscures their reference."[47] And that is that in doing this we ignore another bit of audacity—and that is the audacity to create something whose literal and aesthetic being is simultaneously inescapable and vague. Take for example the entire sentence in which the "leichte[r], dumpfe[r] Schmerz" comes into play, in which Gregor is attempting to get out of bed for the first time. Kafka describes Gregor's body in vivid but obscured detail, and here this pain appears that never develops into anything:

> Er versuchte es wohl hundertmal, schloß die Augen, um die zappelnden Beine nicht sehen zu müssen, und ließ erst ab, als er in der Seite einen noch nie gefühlten, leichten, dumpfen Schmerz zu fühlen begann. (1:94)

> He tried it a hundred times, closing his eyes in order not to have to see his floundering legs, and only stopped when he began to feel in his side a light, dull ache he had never felt before.

Gregor's body is being rendered as simultaneously very real, very "experienced" (i.e., not an "absolute metaphor") and yet it is inherently vague—but does this translate directly into the necessity of metaphor? As we will shortly see in detail, the necessity of metaphor comes not just in Kafka's portrayal of Gregor's vague/concrete body, but from the word *Ungeziefer* itself, a term that is literal and metaphorical at the same time, that is, what Corngold will term a "second-order metaphor" for a particular kind of indescribably disgusting insect-esque creature, a "shifting, unsettled constellation of features."[48] So Gregor's body in its original characterization must be a metaphor—and yet he must also be literal.

The idea that Gregor *must* be a metaphor but *can't* be a metaphor has been hinted at (albeit in pieces, and in different phrasing) by Kafka critics, traceable back to Adorno's assertion that everything in Kafka be taken literally ("alles wörtlich nehmen"),[49] but also present in Günter Anders's *Kafka Pro und Contra*, in which he makes the astute observation that the point of departure in *The Metamorphosis* is ordinary language, and in it Kafka's chief accomplishment is that he has forced a metaphor to literalize itself, to take its words "at their word."[50] Corngold reads Anders here as claiming that Gregor is a metaphor come alive, and it is with this assumption that both his 1973 and 2004 examinations of "the metamorphosis of metaphor" begin. Corngold first recognizes the problem with what he sees as the concept of metaphor broadly conceived in *The Metamorphosis* by recalling Kafka's own distaste for metaphor (back again to the idea that they made him "despair" of writing, as wrote in his diary [*GW* 11:196]). Kafka is after all "the writer par excellence who came to detect in metaphorical language a crucial obstacle to his own enterprise."[51]

Corngold's argument hinges on his application of Richards's concept of the metaphor (which resembles Black's "interaction view"), in which some thing (A, a "vehicle") is designated *as* some other thing (B, a "tenor").[52] But if what is supposed to be a "vehicle" that evokes a "tenor" is purposefully forced "out of context," *made into a literal thing*, then it just functions as a name, and directs us not to the qualities of the "tenor" we wanted to ascribe to the "vehicle," but the whole "tenor" itself.[53] Everything that would normally remain in the "metaphorical unconscious" suddenly becomes literal as well, precluding any of what Black would call the "interaction" between commonplaces that do apply in the situation and exclusion of those that don't.[54] Gregor is not "a vermin," a human with *some applicable* vermin-like qualities, he *is a vermin; he has woken up* "in seinem Bett zu einem ungeheuren Ungeziefer verwandelt" ("in his bed transformed into a monstrous *Ungeziefer*") (*GW* 1:93). Not a giant cockroach (*Käfer)*, not a massive spider (*Spinne)*, not even an *Insekt*, or the bug (*Wanze*) Kafka often mentioned to his friends—Gregor is an *Ungeziefer*, a word stemming from the Middle High German word *zebar* (meaning a classification of animals fit for sacrifice) whose modern incarnation the *Duden Bedeutungswörterbuch* defines as "bestimmte [schmarotzende] tierische Schädlinge /bes. Insekten/" ("particular [scrounging] pests, particular insects").[55] This itself is a designation that is both specific and vague; though a particular *sort* (a sort *defined by their observer*) of "pests" is meant, no specific species are designated. With the simple choice of one word—and bolstered by Gregor's inconsistent and perplexing rendering—Kafka has assured that Gregor is both literal (he is not "like a vermin," a man with vermin-like qualities, whatever commonplaces that may or may not evoke; he *is* one) and inherently metaphorical, inhabiting a word, *Ungeziefer*, that has no concrete literal reference. It is this self-collapsing action—a metaphor that acts like a metaphor but cannot be a metaphor—that demonstrates the inability for this metaphor to "be the case" metaphorically, that reveals it as metaphorical nonsense, that shows Kafka to be confronting the meaning limits of metaphorical language in a way remarkably similar to how Wittgenstein uncovered what he saw to be nonsense in philosophical propositions.

But how does this really work? By the structural examination the collapse of Gregor as a metaphor provokes. Corngold argues that Kafka's rendering of Gregor's body is "destructively paradoxical," for if a metaphor becomes literal, "we go to (B) as an object in the world in its totality," while at the same time we know it is a metaphor and read it metaphorically; we "go to (B) only in its quality as a predicate of (A)." That is, we expect, still, Gregor to stand for something even though apparently now all he stands for is himself. And thus we have a problem:

> As literalization proceeds, as we attempt to experience in (B) more and more qualities that can be accommodated by (A), we *metamorphose* (A). But if the metaphor is to be preserved and (A) and (B) are to remain unlike, we must stop before the metamorphosis is

> complete. If, now, the tenor—as in *The Metamorphosis*—is a human consciousness, the increasing literalization of the vehicle transforms the tenor into a monster.[56]

Ergo, "the continual alteration of Gregor's body suggests ongoing metamorphosis, the *process* of literalization . . . and not its end state."[57]

But what does the process of literalization say? It says *nothing* and can only show, and, furthermore, shows *that* it can only show (and cannot say). The idea that governs this argument is that the way Kafka has chosen to use metaphorical language in the creation of Gregor Samsa's body forces us to acknowledge several "ineffable truths" (in the words of Hacker, referring to the *Tractatus*) about the structure of metaphor, foremost among these being that metaphor *is* a structure and not a thing. This is an idea hinted at by Deleuze and Guattari when they argue that Kafka's animals evoke no mythology and no archetypes, but rather

> correspond solely to new levels, zones of liberated intensities where contents free themselves from their forms as well as from their expressions, from the signifier that formalized them. There is no longer anything but movements, vibrations, thresholds in a deserted matter: animals, mice, dogs, apes, cockroaches are distinguished only by this or that threshold, this or that vibration. (*Kafka: Toward a Minor Literature*, 13)

When something is freed from its signifier, so to speak, the movement or threshold of that (empty/misguided) signifying remains. Unlike what Deleuze and Guattari seem to be arguing, however, I see the perseverance of the movement or threshold, the alleged signifying-toward-nothing, to *show* that Kafka's metaphorical rendition of an animal *is* only a structure, a movement, the demonstration of a threshold. The genius of Kafka's story is that he forces us to acknowledge that the metaphorical form is independent of content by way of the recognition of Gregor's body as a failed or metaphorically nonsensical metaphor: one with the proper metaphorical form but only its original literal content.

Metaphor's independence of content is also recognized in the philosophy of language that grew and splintered out of both the early and late Wittgenstein, both in the world of critical theory and that of analytic philosophy. This is the idea that, in the (metaphorical) parlance of Donald Davidson, "to make a metaphor is to murder it," a view (and, more or less, a terminology) shared by Derrida. Before reaching his own death metaphor, Derrida begins "White Mythology" by reminding us:

> If we wanted to conceive and classify all the metaphorical possibilities of philosophy, there would always be at least one metaphor

> which would be excluded and remain outside the system: that one, at least, which was needed to construct the concept of metaphor, or, to cut the argument short, the metaphor of metaphor.[58]

The only way to "get around" this would be to discover, somehow, that metaphors have "another origin" ("White Mythology," 18). For, after all, in an unattributed nod to Blumenberg, "concept is a metaphor, foundation is a metaphor, theory is a metaphor; and there is no meta-metaphor for them" (23). Derrida argues that metaphor is a special linguistic/philosophical moment, "the moment of possible sense as a possibility of non-truth. It is the moment of detour in which truth can still be lost" (42). Metaphor's "real meaning" is in fact the dialectical moment it creates, its existence *as* a "provisional loss of meaning," something that "always has its own death within it" (73–74). That is: metaphor, in having its own death within it (in necessarily "killing" its own content), means *with* its form.

Death metaphors used to describe metaphor are not unique to critical theory; Davidson chooses one as well, when, in his rebuttal to Black, he presents his own more drastic view of "what metaphors mean" in his essay of the same name. Black's interaction view is too permissive for Davidson, whose more dramatic conception of metaphor is that, strictly speaking, there is no such thing. That is, a statement can have a metaphorical *use* but there is no such thing as an inherently metaphorical statement. Davidson demonstrates his theory before he explains it, beginning his essay with the assertion that metaphors are "the dreamwork of language" ("What Metaphors Mean," 31). Rather than explicate what he has done with that metaphor, Davidson leaves it, and argues that metaphors (including presumably the one he just used) "mean what the words, in their most literal interpretation, mean, and nothing more" (32). While he concedes that "metaphors cannot be paraphrased," this is "not because metaphors say something too novel for literal expression but because there is nothing there to paraphrase" (32). This, in turn, is because of the distinction he makes between "what words mean and what they are used to do," a distinction on which the central argument of the essay is based, and one that his use of "metaphor is the dreamwork of language" purportedly demonstrates. For Davidson, "it is no help in explaining how words work in metaphor to posit metaphorical or figurative meanings, or special kinds of poetic or metaphorical truth. These ideas don't explain metaphor, metaphor explains them."[59] Davidson's argument here seems to point back to Derrida's—the uncovering (metaphorically speaking) of a metaphor is an illusion, because all there is underneath is more metaphor. The difference with Davidson is that this death possibility isn't a sort of always-already-contained innate characteristic of metaphor—it is not a possibility at all; it is a constant fact that metaphors are simply literal speech and nothing more. He writes: "If we are to think of words in metaphors as directly going about their business of applying to what they properly do apply to, there is no difference between a metaphor and the introduction of a new term into our vocabulary: to make a metaphor is to murder it."[60] This death metaphor about metaphor Davidson attempts to make stronger with the example that determining *the way in which words are used* is the only way to tell the difference between a metaphor and an outright lie.[61] What could be termed Davidson's "resolute" conception of metaphor (after the "resolute" reading of Wittgenstein we will see developed momentarily) ends in the following directive:

> We must give up the idea that a metaphor carries a message, that it has a content or meaning (except, of course, its literal meaning). The various theories we have been considering mistake our goal. Where they think they provide a method for deciphering an encoded content, they actually tell us (or try to tell us) something about the effects metaphors have on us. The common error is to fasten on the contents of the thoughts a metaphor provokes and to read these contents into the metaphor itself.[62]

Though Black ends up rebutting Davidson's argument, Davidson has managed to strengthen (for better or worse) the final element in Black's own conception of "interactive" metaphor, which is that there is no systematic way to tell why some metaphors work and others don't.[63] If metaphor only exists as a form or a use, and there is no such thing as metaphorical content with meaning (or metaphorical meaning of content), then the "interactive" and skeptical views of metaphor can actually conflate. There *is* such a thing as a "successful" metaphor—one that, though it *might*, as Derrida argues, have its own death within it (after long and protracted-enough use, in the Nietzschean sense), still "interacts" (Black) between some sort of tenor/vehicle combination (Richards), but whose designation *as* metaphor is completely independent of its content and simply rests on the fact *that* it conforms to the form of metaphor. And thus, should the tenor and vehicle happen to be the same thing—the same *Ungeziefer*, for example—it is also possible to have a "failed" or metaphorically nonsensical metaphor whose structure is exactly the same as a "successful" or sensical one (ergo it is also a metaphor) but whose content, once again necessarily independent from the form, may evoke "commonplaces" but also simply evokes itself. This designation takes much the same form as Wittgenstein's examination of the tautologies and contradictions of logic, which he describes as senseless (*sinnlos*) but not nonsensical (*unsinnig*) due to the logical form they take—the same form as sentences that *do* make sense. That is, the sentence "It is raining or not raining" is put together using exactly the same logical and grammatical rules (which Wittgenstein demonstrates using the construction of a truth table) as "It is raining." Thus, though it ends up telling us nothing about the weather (in Wittgensteinian parlance, it makes no "sense" because it does not give us a picture in our head with which we can match or not match reality), it shows us a great deal (everything, in fact), about how logical form is independent of content (*TLP* 4.31).

In Kafka, though the designation of Gregor Samsa as an "ungeheures Ungeziefer" *tells* us only confusing accounts of exactly what kind of animal Gregor is (or what, even, his face looks like), the structure of the metaphor—the way the word *Ungeziefer* is meant, in the German language, to evoke "commonplaces" about unwanted invasive creatures in an otherwise civilized household—*shows* us everything we need to know about metaphor: that it is a structure that must be independent of content. As Gregor's body begins to die after being struck in the exoshell by his father's apple, the very concreteness of his pain, of his serious wound ("schwere Verwundung") of the apple remaining lodged in his shell for a month, is set against the consciously milder behavior of the father, whose act of wounding served somehow to remind him that Gregor was a member of the family (1:136). This scene takes place in the final act of the story, thus reinforcing Kafka's consistent portrayal of Gregor as both inescapably concrete—his pain being the primary evidence of that—and oddly esoteric (his family-member status is still in there somewhere); as embodying the form of a metaphor and the content of himself. A recognition of a parallel trajectory with Wittgenstein in provoking *with form* the importance of form is what both recalls and departs from Corngold's examination, both of the "metamorphosis of the metaphor" and of the "necessity of form" in Kafka's work.

According to Corngold, the real metamorphosis of *The Metamorphosis* is the struggle with the *process* of literalizing a metaphor—the process of concretizing a moving, shifting interaction (Black), solidifying what Derrida called the moment of possible meaninglessness—which is impossible. All that really results (Davidson would argue) is whatever is literally there. The "wahrer Sachverhalt" of the situation (*Sachverhalt* being a term used both by Kafka to describe the Samsa cleaning lady confirming Gregor's demise *and* the centerpiece of Wittgenstein's picture theory) is that Gregor stands only for himself (*GW* 1:153). And here reemerges the original question I sought to avoid: why would Kafka do that? For Corngold the genius seems to be in the demonstration of metaphorical nonsense itself, in the failed literalization of metaphor. Gregor's status as a living "shifting" metaphor either shows us nothing at all about metaphor (in that he is metaphorically nonsensical), or, simultaneously, *everything* there is to say about metaphor, "that metaphor is an enigma, to be grasped, if at all, only by approximations," which would certainly echo Black's sentiment that there is no way to tell why one metaphor succeeds and another fails.[64] But is metaphor really an "enigma" we can grasp only in bits and pieces? Or is it, rather, an easily recognizable structure that, in its status as a structure, makes itself free of its content (and that content's signifying-consistency obligations) and thus is not responsible, in the end, for whether or not this content means, whether or not this content makes metaphorical sense by meaning in a consistent extratextual direction?

Interestingly enough, this is what those who attribute philosophical or metaphysical content to Wittgenstein's *Tractatus* argue he has done with philosophical language (or, in some conceptions, all literal language): he has shown, through the representation of a breakdown of semantic content, the difference between form and content, and the role that form must play in language. And this, then, is what I argue that Kafka has done in confronting the limits of metaphor: he has shown, through the representation of a metaphor that both cannot and must be a metaphor, the role that form must play even in purely literary or heavily metaphorical language. Metaphorical language may just be, as Thorlby conceives it, an "obstacle to be overcome"; but not in the way we might imagine; "overcoming" it results in the acknowledgment of and adaptation to the vital role structure plays in representational language.[65] There is also a moment where Wittgenstein, too, insists that the propositions of the *Tractatus* must be overcome ("Er muß diese Sätze überwinden" [6.54])—the difference, as we will momentarily see, between the metaphysical and resolute readings of the *Tractatus* is that the metaphysical conception argues that the act of conquering, overcoming, or transcending these sentences, of recognizing them as *unsinnig*, is predicated on the discovery that in not saying, they show their form.

Though Gregor Samsa's body is perhaps the largest and most drastic self-collapsing or nonsensical metaphor in *The Metamorphosis*, there are others—some, in fact, we have already examined as "working" metaphors—that bear examination. Anders has said that "Kafkas Welt wird undeutlich, weil seine Metaphern kollidieren" ("Kafka's world becomes unclear because his metaphors collide").[66] And they do—with other metaphors (as in the case of the "negative infinity" of possibilities) but also, and more interestingly, with their literal selves. That is, Gregor Samsa's metaphor body "collides" with his real body; they are the same thing. Or take, for example, the animal voice (*Tierstimme*) about which the chief clerk remarks in the earliest pages (1:105): from the clerk's perspective he is using metaphorical language, but in "reality" he is using literal language; Gregor's voice *is*, in fact, a *Tierstimme*. The dramatic irony of the moment comes in the remarkably simple conflation of literal and metaphorical truth.

Remember, also, Gregor's own recognition of his *Tierstimme* early on, as he has "a shock" to hear his own terrifying warbling juxtaposed with his mother's "gentle voice" (1:96). Here we effectively have Gregor's aphasia standing in for Gregor's aphasia, the inability to communicate with his family that preexisted Gregor's transformed condition. However rich the metaphorical meaning is here—the great joke of Gregor's transformation being that it makes manifest an inability to communicate with his family that was always there—what is truly remarkable is that it is the same as the literal meaning. One subtle kind of aphasia stands in for another, but aphasia it is—the content of the aphasia (i.e., how or "why" Gregor cannot talk) varies, but the form (i.e., that Gregor cannot talk) is consistent. And this continues as he attempts to speak in human language through the door: "'Ich komme gleich,' sagte Gregor langsam und bedächtig und rührte sich nicht, um kein Wort der Gespräche zu verlieren" ("'I'll be right there,' said Gregor slowly and carefully . . . so as not to lose a word") (1:102). Again, we have a language crisis standing in for a language crisis, a fear of losing the efficacy of language standing in for a fear of never having had the efficacy of language in the first place. The metaphorical "truth" may be so prone to overpowering the literal truth in this scene because they are, slight content differences aside, the same truth. In this way they both don't "work" as metaphors and *completely* work as metaphors—they *show* that they are metaphors by the way *that* they both work and don't work. That is, they show that the structure of something purporting to stand in for something else works in exactly the same motion when there is a "something else" as when there is not.

Conclusion

Kafka has not, then, as Deleuze and Guattari claim, "killed" metaphor in some quest for the purification of language which the modernists—including and especially Wittgenstein—apparently sought.[67] Instead, in narrating both a literal metaphor and a failed metaphor, Kafka has just shown us what metaphor is: a form, one that can have a discernible semantic "interaction" between the literal and otherwise, but one that does not have to; one whose content can be said, but whose form can only be shown. For Wittgenstein's *Tractatus*, it seems as if in the end the "saying/showing" distinction is what keeps its nonsensical remarks from being wholly useless. As long as there is *recognition* of the logical form of reality and of language's ability to *show* that form, then the *Tractatus* still has plenty of meaning, both as philosophy and to philosophy. In working with Kafka's *Metamorphosis*, what we can now see after exploring its connections with the *Tractatus* is that, even if the metaphorical "meaning" of Gregor Samsa's body can never be agreed upon and Anderson's "negative infinity" remains, a solid "meaning" the story can have is that with and through this instance of metaphorical nonsense, he shows what metaphor cannot say.

Chapter 3

✦

"The Judgment," Ethics, and the Ineffable

So far, rather than solve two of the problems that have faced Kafka readers for a century—Josef K.'s guilt, what Gregor Samsa's body "means"—we have, in the spirit of Wittgenstein, *dissolved* them by uncovering the illusions that came with the posing of each one. In the case of *The Trial*, the illusion was that of the necessity of a "guilt or innocence" structure. In the case of *The Metamorphosis*, the illusion was the misapprehension that there is such a thing as metaphorical content at all. As Wittgenstein says, the world is all that is the case—all true pictures at once. Because I have only so far presented two cases on behalf of Kafka as exemplar of analytic modernism, it should be apparent that these two major instances of illusory "problems" in Kafka's stories are far from "all that is the case" in his world—and, accordingly, the complex and surprisingly literarily relevant examples of logical form are far from all that is the case in Wittgenstein's *Tractatus*. Indeed, most readers of the *Tractatus* are primarily concerned with how it ends—with the conceit of philosophical language meeting *its* end and would-be philosophers resigned instead to silence (*TLP* 7). Fittingly, the way in which the end of the *Tractatus* exposes logical modernism in Kafka's work comes as we witness another end: that of Georg Bendemann, protagonist of "The Judgment."

When, at the story's climax, Georg's father pronounces his son a "teuflischer Mensch" ("devilish person"), and thereupon "condemns" him to death ("Und darum wisse: ich verurteile dich jetzt zum Tode des Ertrinkens!" ["And now hear this: I sentence you to death by drowning!"] [*GW* 1:52]), we would be right to assume that Herr Bendemann has come to this conclusion based on an ethical judgment. This is especially understandable given the content of the elder Bendemann's preceding rant about Georg's neglect of his family and expatriated friend, not to mention the alleged wantonness of his fiancée Frieda Brandenfeld ("Weil sie die Röcke gehoben hat!" ["Because she lifted up her skirts!"] [1:49]). Georg takes this ethical proclamation to heart, executing what any reasonable person might consider an uncalled-for jump off a bridge, one that Uta Degener has recently summed up nicely, saying that it results in neither Georg nor his father having our sympathy, and thus an ending "less tragic than absurd":[1]

> Er schwang sich über, als der ausgezeichnete Turner, der er in seinen Jugendjahren zum Stolz seiner Eltern gewesen war. Noch hielt er sich mit schwächer werdenden Händen fest, erspähte zwischen den Geländerstangen einen Autoomnibus, der mit Leichtigkeit seinen Fall übertönen würde, rief leise: "Liebe Eltern, ich habe euch doch immer geliebt," und ließ sich hinabfallen.
>
> In diesem Augenblick ging über die Brücke ein geradezu unendlicher Verkehr. (52)

> He swung himself over, as he had in his youth as an outstanding gymnast, the pride of his parents. As he held on with weakening hands, he made out an omnibus between the handrails that would easily obscure the sound of his fall, and called out quietly: "Dear parents, I have always loved you," and let himself fall away.
>
> In this moment an endless stream of traffic went over the bridge.

Indeed, it is because Georg actually does jump to his presumable death that the central act of judgment in "The Judgment" has been, and continues to be, the source of reader consternation: Herr Bendemann is not a professional jurist, and so his son's heeding the "sentence" doesn't really seem to make much sense. To be sure, several decades' worth of Kafka critics describe quite aptly the conundrum of this ending. Stanley Corngold perhaps set the standard by declaring, simply, that "there would seem to be no plausible motivation for Georg's death"; J. P. Stern has phrased similar concern in a different manner, wondering "how acceptable we find the verdict of death at the end; what narrative connection we may discern between the bulk of the tale and its catastrophic conclusion; what Georg Bendemann has done to deserve such a verdict; or more generally, what is the manner of Kafka's motivation."[2] Russell Berman has simply explained: "All seems right in the world of Georg Bendemann, until suddenly, and without a fully compelling explanation, all seems wrong."[3] Ritchie Robertson has asked: "Why is Georg so helpless when faced with his angry father? And why does the father condemn his son to death?"[4] And Walter Sokel, quite recently, writes of Georg's "instantaneous and utterly surprising obedience to his father's verdict."[5]

Further complicating matters, "The Judgment" is in many ways Kafka's most perfect and most flawed piece of work. It is perfect, in that Kafka himself believed it so: it came out of him "like a proper birth" ("wie eine regelrechte Geburt"), in one night of labor, the fully formed literary offspring that solidified the dedication of his "organism" to literature at the expense of everything else (*GW* 9:264): "Nur so kann geschrieben worden," he wrote in his journal in euphoria and exhaustion, "nur in einem solchen Zusammenhang, mit solcher vollständigen Öffnung des Leibes und der Seele" ("One should only write like this, only in such a state of continuity, with such a complete opening of the body and soul") (*GW* 10:101). This is a moment in Kafka's autobiography that seems to entrance the critical world. It is unsurprising, then, how many theoretical—and above that metaphysical—implications we have taken away from the story that "begins the work of [Kafka's] maturity," as Stern has described it, that "usher[ed] in the series of works that has become central to modernist world literature," as Berman has put it.[6] The continuation of Sokel's train of thought from above, for example, is that "The Judgment" is Kafka's "Dionysian text par excellence," one that "was written in a Dionysian vein, in a single uninterrupted stream of words, a flow, the act of writing exactly reflecting its idea, the flow filling the space-time of one night, without break, without interruption, in a single continuous whole."[7] And Peter von Matt describes the single night that changed world literature: "In dieser Nacht hat sich die Gestalt der Weltliteratur verändert und der neuzeitliche Begriff von Literatur überhaupt" ("On this night the entire shape of world literature changed, and the modern concept of literature altogether").[8]

Complicating matters, however, is the nagging realization that "The Judgment" is simultaneously Kafka's least perfect story: its climax is so perplexing and so uniquely commanding of critical attention, but, unlike much of Kafka's canon it has no pretentions of being "unfinished" to excuse this; its climax is intentionally perplexing, perhaps the purest example of what Adorno calls a puzzle with no key.[9] Nearly a century of critical reactions to the story as "problem" are understandably varied in offering a "solution," though some, like James Phelan, strive to "respect and hold onto the story's strangeness rather than trying to master it."[10] This is certainly not the usual case, however: Corngold, already lamenting critical overload in 1977, claims the work nevertheless "invites reflection on its distinctive power to compel interpretation." And this Corngold does, explaining, "a work that invites so much interpretation can have inspired the production of meaning only as a function of its refusal of meaning."[11]

Indeed, the central "problem" of "The Judgment" seems obvious and yet we come back to it again and again: why does Georg obey? That his father can offer an unsubstantiated "charge" and "sentence" (literally "judgment") is one matter; why Georg obeys it is another altogether. With no prior knowledge of Kafka's literary reputation or that of his most famous critics, this moment should strike a reasonable reader as wholly nonsensical in the technical sense; Georg's actions seem, without the solution of psychoanalysis, biographical grafting, or literary intertextuality, wholly inexplicable. But this original assumption—that we should unearth a reason behind the nonsense—is the critic's big mistake.

To see why, Wittgenstein can again be of help to us. It is precisely his characterization of "nonsense" in the *Tractatus*, and his subsequent assertion that nonsensical language cannot be judged, that will hold the key not to the solution, but to the dissolution of the problem of "The Judgment." I certainly agree that the eponymous judgment of this story doesn't make much sense—but not for the reasons previously articulated. Instead, I am reminded of Wittgenstein's elucidation in the final sections of the *Tractatus* about the nonsensicality—and subsequent unjudgeability—of certain alleged "propositions" that actually are not: riddles and enigmas; aesthetics; and, most of all, ethics. For according to the end of the *Tractatus*, the very idea of an "ethical judgment" in language is impossible.

Phelan has purported to investigate this story's "underlying logic." Here I would like to take that impulse further and with more terminological strictness, and in so doing show that there is no "underlying" special logic of "The Judgment," but rather that the story displays, overtly and clearly, in its adherence and its rebellion, formal logic, which as we already know Wittgenstein was instrumental in developing at almost precisely the moment Kafka wrote this story. What this discovery will show us is that the real problem of "The Judgment" deals not with Herr Bendemann's specific *act* of judgment. Rather, the chief problem of "The Judgment" is the act of ethical judgment itself—a contradiction in terms.

Facts, Possible Facts, and the State of Georg's Affairs

As it was with *The Metamorphosis*, the easiest way to see how a Tractarian view of nonsense helps elucidate the otherwise confounding climax of "The Judgment" is first to see how—or if—the story displays any moments that could be defined as having sense in the Tractarian fashion. It turns out that the vast majority of the story does make sense in this way: indeed, the easiest way to look at it would be to say that anything in the story that does not create or attempt to "solve" an enigma, or attempt to make an aesthetic or ethical pronouncement, is the depiction of a true, false, or potentially true "fact," and thus makes sense. The slightly less easy way to solidify this theory is to show exactly how and why most of the prose in "The Judgment" successfully depicts a possible state of affairs. To see why the less-easy way is rewarding nevertheless, let us examine Wittgenstein's remarks about the concept of a possible state of affairs (*möglicher Sachverhalt*) in greater detail. As the second section of the *Tractatus* begins, he explains to us what a fact is: "Was der Fall ist, die Tatsache, ist das Bestehen von Sachverhalten" ("What is the case, the fact, is the existence of states of affairs") (*TLP* 2).

First, the origin of the phrase "state of affairs" in English: the first standard translation of the *Tractatus*, C. K. Ogden and Frank Ramsay's 1922 edition (for which Ogden bears sole credit), translates *Sachverhalt* as "atomic fact," and in doing so places the *Tractatus* within both the linguistic and philosophical context of Russell's atomism.[12] However, as we have seen, the preferred current standard, Stephen Pears and Brian McGuinness's 1961 version, translates *Sachverhalt* as "state of affairs." Unlike the positivist-leaning "atomic fact," "state of affairs" has literary implications, especially when we consider connections with "The Judgment," given Georg's alleged romantic situation—in fact, this exact phrase is used in some of Corngold's most famous criticism of the story. He describes Herr Bendemann's pseudo-juridical sentence and Georg's jump thusly:

> To sentence Georg to death is to set in motion a relentless process which brings about the state of affairs designated in the sentence.
>
> The sentence is in effect a performative. It does not aim in its utterance to designate a state of affairs that is taking place and is extrinsically caused. It aims instead to bring into existence a state of affairs of which it is the sole cause.[13]

This is technically true, and in the second sentence Corngold seems himself to be pointing to a Tractarian conception of language as designating states of affairs, before arguing instead on behalf of a more late-Wittgensteinian or Austinian version ("a performative"). What I would like to show here is that Corngold's early work can be refined even further: the sentence (meant in both senses of the English word) may be a "performative," but that is not why it doesn't designate: it doesn't designate because it can't.

To see why this is, let us return to the concept of *Sachverhalt* as Wittgenstein explains it. The word itself is easily divided into its constituent parts, each of which has a vital place in Wittgenstein's picture theory of logic and language: *Sache*, "things," "objects," and *Verhalten*, or "behavior," itself a compound of *halten*, "to hold," and the multivalent prefix *ver*, which can both strengthen and negate the verb it modifies (in this case, it strengthens). Indeed, Wittgenstein describes a *Sachverhalt* as "eine Verbindung von Gegenständen (Sachen, Dingen)" ("An association of objects [things]") (*TLP* 2.01). For any speaker of German, the synonymy of *Sachverhalt* (the behavior of objects) and *Tatsache* is also apparent: the "behavior" of things is another way of expressing the *deeds* of things.

Thus, according to Wittgenstein, the world is made up of facts, which themselves are the existence of states of affairs, or "das Bestehen von Sachverhalten." And, further, as we have already seen from examples in previous chapters, the way we are able to think, speak, and otherwise communicate about that world is because we think by picturing facts to ourselves: "Wir machen uns Bilder der Tatsachen" ("We make pictures of facts to ourselves") (2.1). Therefore: a picture in our minds is a fact (2.141). But how does such a picture come to *be* in our minds? Again, it depicts a model of the reality around us ("Das Bild ist ein Modell der Wirklichkeit" [2.12]).[14]

But how does language do this? The answer to this returns us again to the important distinction in the *Tractatus* of form from content. That is, a "model of reality" has the ability to depict reality only because they share a common pictorial form ("Form der Abbildung" [2.17]). Again, this pictorial form is "die logische Form, das heißt, die Form der Wirklichkeit" (2.18). Thus, when Wittgenstein repeats in 2.22 how a picture in our minds depicts reality, he adds one crucial word, "logical": "Das Bild hat mit dem Abgebildeten *die logische Form der Abbildung* gemein" (emphasis mine). The pictorial form, which is the form of reality, is logical. This conception (and independence) of form is what allows Wittgenstein to progress from what facts are to how our minds conceive of and express them: in the form of a proposition that makes sense: "Der Gedanke ist der sinnvolle Satz" ("A thought is a sensical proposition") (4).

Here is the crucial element of this theory: in order to make sense, a proposition need not be true—it only needs to be possibly true. The idea of "possibly true" relates back to Kafka's story because both "actual" facts and "possible" facts take important roles in the buildup to the Bendemanns' fatal argument. For example, there are several elements that many of Kafka's best critics have argued we can take as true facts in "The Judgment": Georg lives with his father; his mother has been deceased for two years; since Frau Bendemann's death, Georg has taken an active, and successful, role in the family business.[15] But if we look at the story closely, we will find that none of these "facts" are true facts; they are all merely *possible* facts. Although when it comes to the story's sense this actually doesn't matter, it is worth admitting that it is uniquely difficult to come across pictures in this story we can trust as "true facts": the closest we get is the primary narrative that doesn't come from Georg's or his father's thoughts or memory. But the primary narrative comes courtesy of Kafka's curious omniscient-obtuse narrator, one Berman has aptly described as exhibiting a "subversion of realistic description"; Greenberg adds, "Kafka's narrative mode eliminates every trace of the traditional hauteur of detachment of the narrator from his narration."[16]

And yet we have no choice but to accept that the obtuse-omniscient third-person (sort of) provides a vital service: he presents the closest thing we have to the actual facts of the story, the only facts that are impossible to dispute if we are to understand any of the story as prose narration rather than outright gibberish. First: Georg finishes some sort of document, puts it in an envelope, and looks out the window (1:39–40); then, Georg enters his father's room, presumably to converse about said document (1:42). Thereafter, Georg speaks with his father and adjusts Herr Bendemann's bedclothes, during which time Herr Bendemann becomes agitated (1:45–48); the men argue, and Herr Bendemann performs the "sentence"; Georg runs out of the family apartment and to a nearby bridge, off of which he jumps, almost certainly to his death (1:52); and, finally, an "endless stream of traffic" ("unendlicher Verkehr," with all of its sexual connotations) crosses the bridge postmortem (1:52).

These and only these are the true facts of "The Judgment," or as close as a story like "The Judgment" can get to true facts, because they are given to us directly by the (albeit unstable) narrator, and do not come filtered through Georg's dubious memory, nor do they come skewed through his father's rage.

Everything outside of the primary narration is technically up for dispute—but that does not mean it makes any less sense than the "true facts," for its very ability to be up for dispute denotes what Wittgenstein scholars call truth-functional bipolarity: we may never know if Georg's fiancée Frieda really made such a fuss about not knowing his friend in Petersburg, but the fact that the description is rendered in such a way—a group of declarative sentences—that we can make a true-false judgment about it gives it sense. The same applies to the other instances of possible fact.

These include, for example, the initial description of Georg's friend in Petersburg. We see here what Georg "sees" in either his memory or his imagination, but we do not and cannot see any deeper into Georg's motivations or deeper feelings. What Georg "sees" (and what we, thus, also see) is, due precisely to its correct syntactical German, as well as the truth conditions, the technical ability to match up *with* a real thing in reality, picturable: a sallow, disillusioned man, both alienated from his homeland and uncomfortable in his new environs, said discomfort apparent in the awkward way he wears the facial hair that is in fashion in pre-revolutionary Russia:

> So arbeitete er [der Freund] sich in der Fremde nutzlos ab, der fremdartige Vollbart verdeckte nur schlecht das wohlbekannte Gesicht, dessen gelbe Hautfarbe auf eine sich entwickelnde Krankheit hinzudeuten schien. (1:7)

> So he toiled uselessly abroad, his foreign-style beard doing a poor job of covering up that well-known face, whose yellow hue seemed to betray the onset of a worsening illness.

Here, the picture Georg gives us is remarkably telling: the friend is disguised and estranged, and yet apparently still quite well known; he also appears to be ill. This picture, in fact, is indicative of two vital currents in this story. First is the "unhealthy," with respect to the father's condition and in narrative terms; we can think of this as the unreliability or "off" aspect of the secondary or tertiary narration. Second, we have the disguised; like the friend's face, the instability of said friend's very existence is at this early point in the story disguised, here by the first in a compelling set of vignettes and a descriptive style exactly as intense and blasé as the primary narrative. The importance of the friend in Petersburg has not been understated in the critical tradition: for Greenberg, in fact, it constitutes the "puzzle of the story," the "one failure in a story of vivid, succinct art."[17] And it is precisely in this puzzling nature that the picturability and thus sense of the story begins to drop off—but, since the veracity of the friend, the story's chief enigma, does not come into question until later in the story, let us treat the reader's initial reception of his visage as a proper picture, as a possible fact. We will address the mystery that develops later as it appears.

The astute reader might still be unconvinced that the unsubstantiated "possible facts" of "The Judgment" abide by the same logical rules as the "real facts" do. After all, if Georg (or his father) could be making things up, does that not mean their fabrications abide only by the "limits" of the imagination, which we have been told time and again are none? Here is why the imagination is not exempt: in *TLP* 5.61, Wittgenstein takes the picture theory to its logical conclusion: since a thought is a fact we picture to ourselves, if something is unpicturable it cannot be thought either ("Was wir nicht denken können, können wir nicht denken. Wir können auch nicht *sagen*, was wir nicht denken können" ["We cannot think what we cannot think, and we also cannot *say* what we cannot think"]). This applies to anything we are trying to picture, think, or say, anything at all—true or not.

Let us illustrate this with another example: we reenter Georg's imagination/memory to "witness" the very exchange between Georg and his fiancée whose veracity itself is actually in doubt (even the engagement is introduced as a secondary aside: "daß er selbst vor einem Monat mit einem Fräulein Frieda Brandenfeld, einem Mädchen aus wohlhabender Familie, sich verlobt hatte" ["that he himself had been engaged for a month to a Miss Frieda Brandenfeld, a girl from a good family"]) (1:42). In the exchange, Georg explains to Frieda that it would be in poor taste to invite his friend to their wedding, given the prohibitive expense of travel and, apparently, the unfairness of celebrating one's good fortune in the face of another's growing misfortune. (The same goes for Georg's fortune in the family business: "Georg hatte keine Lust gehabt, dem Freund von seinen geschäftlichen Erfolgen zu schreiben, und jetzt nachträglich hätte es wirklich einen merkwürdigen Anschein gehabt" ["Georg had had no desire to write to his friend about his business successes, and now in hindsight it would have appeared very strange"] [1:41].) To which Georg's depiction of his fiancée replies: "Wenn du solche Freunde hast, Georg, hättest du dich überhaupt nicht verloben sollen" ("If you have such friends, Georg, you shouldn't have gotten engaged"). To which Georg himself allegedly replies, "Ja, das ist unser beider Schuld; aber ich wollte es jetzt nicht anders haben" ("Yes, it's both of our faults, but I wouldn't have it any other way"). At this point the secondary picture takes the story's first (but not last) turn toward the explicit: "Und wenn sie dann, rasch atmend unter seinen Küssen, noch vorbrachte: 'Eigentlich kränkt es mich doch,' hielt er es wirklich für unverfänglich, dem Freund alles zu schreiben" ("And when she then, breathing heavily under his kisses, interrupted once again, 'Actually it still makes me sick,' he thought it really innocuous to write his friend after all") (1:42).

While the imagined/remembered picture of Georg's friend might strike us as hyperbolic but possibly accurate, this interchange appears less so, or even downright implausible. The fiancée's first remark, which seems playful, also seems comparatively realistic. To be sure, Georg's response is tone deaf; however, it still seems somewhat probable. Further, their following moment of passion, itself hinting at exactly the kind of premarital relations to which the father alludes in his obscene rant later, also seems understandable. But her final remark is truly perplexing. And yet, it is still above all the narrative portrayal of a possible fact, of a *Sachverhalt* that is picturable in either Georg's memory or imagination, and this is also equally picturable to us. The moment may seem absurd, but in fact it makes perfect sense. However, as we will now see, the same cannot be said for several other pivotal elements in this story, namely: Herr Bendemann's assessment of Frieda; the surprising debate about the friend in Petersburg's existence; Herr Bendemann's shocking final decision; and the so-called logic of why Georg obeys his father at all.

Enigmas, Ethics, and the Logic of Georg's Death

Although it is interesting to note that even the most dubious "facts" from Georg's memory make perfect sense, it is far more interesting to realize that the most memorable conflicts of the story make no sense at all. These are moments that demand judgment of things that cannot be judged: it's suggested that we ought to "solve" the mystery of the friend in Petersburg, that we side with or against Herr Bendemann in declaring Frieda Brandenfeld wanton, that we agree or disagree that Georg is a "teuflischer Mensch," that we come up with a system in which Georg heeding his father's sentence is a valid conclusion to anything. In looking at these moments, we will discover both exactly why each is nonsensical—and, thus, why most alleged "judgments" in "The Judgment" cannot actually be.

First let us illuminate the enigma of the friend. Herr Bendemann mimics Georg sarcastically when the subject of the friend is first broached between them ("Ja, deinen Freunde" ["Oh yes, your *friend*"] [1:45]). The elder Bendemann chides his son for withholding "the whole truth" ("die volle Wahrheit"), and implies that he, the father, is in possession of this "whole truth," and said truth is being willfully covered up ("gut zugedeckt"), just like the elder Bendemann's aging body (1:45–48). He insists, "du hast keinen Freund in Petersburg" ("You have no friend in Petersburg"); Georg is "immer ein Spaßmacher gewesen" ("You've always been such a joker") (1:47). As Georg protests, Herr Bendemann admits that there is indeed an individual by this description in Petersburg, but he is more the father's friend than Georg's, and that they have been conspiring together this whole time; that, in fact, to facilitate this conspiracy Georg's father hasn't actually been reading the newspaper at all, but in fact just "lying in wait" pretending to:

> "Seit Jahren passe ich schon auf, daß du mit dieser Frage kämest! Glaubst du, mich kümmert etwas anderes? Glaubst du, ich lese Zeitungen? Da!" und er warf Georg ein Zeitungsblatt, das irgendwie mit ins Bett getragen worden war, zu. Eine alte Zeitung, mit einem Georg schon ganz unbekannten Namen. (1:51)

> "For years I have been expecting you to come with this question! Do you think I have been doing something else? Do you think I've been reading the papers? Here!" and he threw at Georg a page that had been with him somewhere in the bed. An old paper, with a name that Georg had never seen.

The relative veracity/friend-ness of the friend in Petersburg seems to be, as Greenberg has said, "the puzzle of the story." Further, accounting for him "in a way that is convincing," in a way that "can be justified," is for Greenberg impossible; the friend, he argues, is "the one failure in a story of vivid, succinct art," and this precisely because of the centrality of his mysterious nature.[18] Greenberg goes on to suggest, after Kate Flores, that the friend represents another, hidden side not of Georg but of Kafka the author; I agree with his first assertion, that the friend's "puzzle" is a failure, but find his second irrelevant to its justification. For it is true that the "puzzle" of the friend fails, but that is not necessarily (or not only) because of some irreconcilable tension in the author's own biography—it is because of the problem inherent in the form of the puzzle.

For the enigma—*das Rätsel*—is for Wittgenstein itself a misnomer. This is because any question that can be asked (properly, with language that makes sense) can also be answered; thus, what we think of as a riddle, enigma, or puzzle does not actually exist as such:

> 6.5 Zu einer Antwort, die man nicht aussprechen kann, kann man auch die Frage nicht aussprechen.
>
> *Das Rätsel* gibt es nicht.
>
> Wenn sich eine Frage überhaupt stellen lässt, so *kann* sie auch beantwortet werden.
>
> For an answer which cannot be expressed the question too cannot be expressed.
>
> *The riddle* does not exist.
>
> If a question can be put at all, then it *can* also be answered.

It's not even that riddles or enigmas can't be solved, it's that *they do not actually exist*—and this because the very idea of a question without an answer is a misnomer. Any question that makes sense has itself either a true/false answer, or as an answer a proposition that itself can be judged true or false. Anything else is simply an illusion. This certainly goes for the apparent enigma in "The Judgment": is the friend in Petersburg a real person, and, if so, is he friendlier with Georg or with Herr Bendemann? I may have just typed that "question" out, but Wittgenstein would say that I cannot actually ask it. Thus, the first problem in "The Judgment" is indeed a failure, but not for the reasons we initially thought it was: the mystery of the friend in

Petersburg is a failure because all mysteries allegedly expressed in language must be. But what is particularly interesting about this is that despite its ineffability, the problem of the friend is not simply the central "puzzle" of the story, but the reason for the central conflict. This is, to my mind, the primary reason this story is so confounding.

From the impossibility of "solving" mysteries Wittgenstein moves on to the impossibility of aesthetic propositions. The most interesting alleged aesthetic judgments in "The Judgment" are two separate proclamations of dirtiness. The first follows the narrated picture of Herr Bendemann's room, squalid and suffocating:

> Georg staunte darüber, wie dunkel das Zimmer des Vaters selbst an diesem sonnigen Vormittag war. Einen solchen Schatten warf also die hohe Mauer, die sich jenseits des schmalen Hofes erhob. Der Vater saß beim Fenster in einer Ecke, die mit verschiedenen Andenken an die selige Mutter ausgeschmückt war, und las die Zeitung, die er seitlich vor die Augen hielt, wodurch er irgend eine Augenschwäche auszugleichen suchte. (1:44)
>
> Georg was astounded at how dark his father's room was, even on this sunny morning. The tall wall that surrounded the small courtyard cast such a shadow. His father sat at the window in a corner, which was decorated with various remembrances of his late mother, and read the paper, which he held before his eyes and to one side, in the hopes of compensating for his weakening eyesight.

When confronted with this scene, Georg proclaims the room "unerträglich dunkel" ("unbearably dark"), an obvious aesthetic judgment (1:44). And the second, and in some way parallel, aesthetic judgment I'd like to revisit is the moment wherein Herr Bendemann attributes his son's negligent behavior to the sexually impure Frieda Brandenfeld, who "lifted her skirts" for Georg, who is a "widerliche Gans" ("strumpet"):

> "Weil sie die Röcke so und so und so gehoben hat, hast du dich an sie herangemacht, und damit du an ihr ohne Störung dich befriedigen kannst, hast du unserer Mutter Andenken geschändet, den Freund verraten und deinen Vater ins Bett gesteckt, damit er sich nicht rühren kann. Aber kann er sich rühren oder nicht?" (1:49)
>
> "Because she lifted up her skirts like this, you had to have a go at her, and that's how you could have your way with her without serious disturbance—and you have disgraced Mother's memory, betrayed your friend, and stuck your father in bed so that he can't move. Or can he after all?"

Here it is easy to see why Wittgenstein insists that ethics and aesthetics are the same thing (6.421: "Ethik und Ästhetik sind eins"); in deriding Frieda's sartorial actions Herr Bendemann is of course really deriding her virtue. Further, it will be unsurprising to discover that Wittgenstein believes that aesthetic "judgments," like ethical ones, do not actually exist. To see why this is, we must then discuss what is by far the most interesting moment of unjudgeability (that is still stubbornly treated like a working "judgment") in this story: the father's alleged ethical proclamation and ensuing titular judgment.

Directly out of the "skirts" screed comes Herr Bendemann's primary ethical judgment: "Ein unschuldiges Kind warst du eigentlich, aber noch eigentlicher warst du ein teuflischer Mensch!" ("You were actually an innocent child, but more actually you were a devilish person!") (1:52). The strange designator of "noch eigentlicher" is the first indication that something in this declaration is seriously off, although it is not as odd if we think back to the beginning of the argument, wherein Herr Bendemann insists that Georg is not telling him "the whole truth":

> "Georg," sagte der Vater und zog den zahnlosen Mund in die Breite, "hör' einmal! Du bist wegen dieser Sache zu mir gekommen, um dich mit mir zu beraten. Das ehrt dich ohne Zweifel. Aber es ist nichts, es ist ärger als nichts, wenn du mir jetzt nicht die volle Wahrheit sagst." (1:45)
>
> "Georg," said his father and pulled his toothless mouth open, "listen! You came to me about all of this for my advice. That is without a doubt to your credit. But it is nothing, it is worse than nothing, if now you don't tell me the whole truth."

And it is indeed this self-proclaimed expertise in "the whole truth," the one that allows Herr Bendemann even to possess differing grades of actuality, that also seems to allow him to "sentence" Georg to death:

> "Jetzt weißt du also, was es noch außer dir gab, bisher wußtest du nur von dir! Ein unschuldiges Kind warst du ja eigentlich, aber noch eigentlicher warst du ein teuflischer Mensch! – Und darum wisse: Ich verurteile dich jetzt zum Tode des Ertrinkens!" (1:52)
>
> "Now you know what exists outside yourself; until now you knew only of yourself! You were an innocent child actually, but even more actually you were a devilish person! And now hear this: I sentence you to death by drowning!"

If we are to buy into Herr Bendemann's system, "die volle Wahrheit" would then correspond to the "more actual," "noch eigentlicher"; regular-actual, "eigentlich," then becomes secondary (and corresponds, then, to Georg's lesser and not-as-correct perspective), and the two grades of actuality seem contradictory. I would like to posit again the idea that while the impulse to take a side in the "reality" debate between the Bendemanns is compelling, and the many differing theories equally so, that we are once again looking at the problem all wrong—it is indeed impossible to determine whose version is "more actually" the "whole truth," but not for the reasons we think.

Again, our impulse is to side with either Herr Bendemann or Georg, to judge for ourselves the story's titular judgment. Berman's account of why this act may both draw us in but inevitably fail us is particularly compelling, as he reminds us, "proper judgment is presumed not to be arbitrary, but must instead be based on adequate evidence and its proper evaluation, according to established rules of judgment." The problem in "The Judgment" is, however, that "most evidence is indicated . . . to be corrupt and inconclusive, open to such a range of interpretation that it turns out to be useless for the cases at hand."[19] This is quite true; and what's more, Georg's facility for interpretation seems crucially lacking. For Berman later argues that (juridical) judgment is impossible because Georg lacks control over his own language: "Language gets the better of him, remains beyond his grasp, sometimes erratic, sometimes recalcitrant, but never fully under his control. Without an effective command of language, he is hardly in a position to argue his own case."[20] I agree to a certain extent with Berman here: specifically, that language remains beyond Georg's grasp—but this is not the case through any fault or shortcoming of Georg's grasp. The real reason that neither side of the Bendemann argument regarding the relative good or evil of Georg's conduct is ultimately justifiable or convincing is that there is no such thing as ethical language at all.

The first reason Wittgenstein gives for the impossibility of "ethical propositions" takes us back again to why and how propositions make sense. We have already learned that a proposition cannot say its sense, that the sense of a proposition thus cannot be in it. It must instead show that it has sense by way of its form and its truth functionality. Therefore, because a proposition cannot say its sense, and because the limits of language are the limits of the world (*TLP* 5.6: "Die Grenzen meiner Sprache bedeuten die Grenzen meiner Welt"), said world, being "alles, was der Fall ist" (i.e., all true propositions at once), contains only what the true propositions say. What these propositions show, their sense, cannot be within them, and it is with this idea that the *Tractatus* veers into a "hybrid document" of semi-mysticism and truly confounding pseudo-propositions Monk has discussed so compellingly. As the *Tractatus*'s penultimate section—by far its most interesting and its most severely "hybrid"—draws to a close, Wittgenstein reveals that because the sense of the world cannot be in the world, there is only one other place for it to be: outside it. And because of this, what lies in all sentences is equal—it is the possibility to depict a state of affairs, nothing beyond that:

6.41 Der Sinn der Welt muss außerhalb ihrer liegen. In der Welt ist alles, wie es ist, und geschieht alles, wie es geschieht; es gibt in ihr keinen Wert - und wenn es ihn gäbe, so hätte er keinen Wert.

Wenn es einen Wert gibt, der Wert hat, so muss er außerhalb alles Geschehens und So-Seins liegen. Denn alles Geschehen und So-Sein ist zufällig.

Was es nichtzufällig macht, kann nicht in der Welt liegen, denn sonst wäre dies wieder zufällig.

Es muss außerhalb der Welt liegen.

The sense of the world must lie outside the world. In the world everything is as it is and happens as it does happen. *In* it there is no value, and if there were, it would be of no value.

If there is any value which is of value, it must lie outside all happening and being-so. For all happening and being-so is accidental.

What makes it nonaccidental cannot lie *in* the world, for otherwise again this would be accidental.

It must lie outside the world.

Precisely because of this—because all propositions that make sense are of equal value (of truth value, specifically)—no proposition can express something "higher": how one ought to live; what is the best way to be; the meaning of life. Because a true proposition can express only a state of affairs and higher things cannot be contained within that state of affairs, there can simply be no such thing as an ethical proposition: "Darum kann es auch keine Sätze der Ethik geben. Sätze können nichts Höheres ausdrücken" ("Hence there can be no ethical propositions. Propositions cannot express anything higher") (6.42). There being no such thing as ethical propositions, however, does not mean that there are no such things as ethics themselves—indeed, Wittgenstein insisted that the entire point of the *Tractatus* was "an ethical one," and that its inability to express ethics, its "unsaid" and ineffable section was its most important purpose. Wittgenstein had, he insisted, an entire ethical corpus—and anyone who understood the *Tractatus* would understand immediately and clearly that said corpus simply could not be put into words. And this was because ethics are not of this world—by not being of this world, they are thus transcendental: "Es ist klar, dass sich die Ethik nicht aussprechen lässt. Ethik ist *transzendental*" ("It is clear that ethics cannot be expressed. Ethics are *transcendental*") (6.421). If we find Wittgenstein convincing, then the "solution" to an ethical "problem"—say, for example, "Is my son actually a terrible person who deserves to die?" is actually to recognize that said problem cannot be put into words correctly or clearly, and thus of course cannot be solved; it can only be dissolved: "Die Lösung des Problems des Lebens merkt man am Verschwinden dieses Problems" ("One notices the solution to a problem upon the dissolution of this problem") (6.521). If we then render all "ethical problems" only dissolvable and thus all "ethical questions" unaskable, what is left? Is it, simply, an austere silence as apparently commanded by the *Tractatus*'s final proposition? Not necessarily, if one is to adhere to the "standard" readings of the text—also, called the "metaphysical" readings, because of exactly what appears in these sections, and largely because of 6.421 and this remark: "Es gibt allerdings Unaussprechliches. Dies *zeigt* sich, es ist das Mystische" ("There is indeed the inexpressible. This *shows* itself; it is the mystical") (6.522).

"The mystical," the transcendental, what does not lie in the world, what can be shown but not said—all of this, according to this particular reading of Wittgenstein, still exists, but it is simply nowhere our language can reach. With all of this in mind, it should now be clearer that what Herr Bendemann actually says when proclaiming Georg "devilish" and "sentencing" him to death (the weight of ethical judgment contained clearly in the word "beurteilen") is nothing; he may be trying to express the ethical, but that is impossible. This still, however, fails to address what I see as the central problem of "The Judgment." We may have dissolved the problem of why Herr Bendemann's proclamation makes no sense, but since we never really thought it did, what does that help? After all, most critics agree that the truly confounding moment in the story is Georg's obedience.

As with *The Trial*, however, there is "logic" and then there is logic—and before Wittgenstein determines ethics and enigmas to be mystical or transcendental (because they are outside the world), he does this with logic when he proclaims that the sense of the world lies outside it. The logical form of reality is the "was" in 4.1212's "Was gezeigt werden *kann*, *kann* nicht gesagt werden"; logic is not only ineffable, but its ineffability is what makes possible the ineffability of ethics and the rest of the "Unaussprechliches," or "das Mystische." So again, it is not that Phelan's or any other critic's breakdown of the "logical" progression of Herr Bendemann's excoriation and Georg's obedience is errant; it is that said "logic" first of all cannot actually be logic because it contains too much pure nonsense (as opposed to contradiction or tautology, which is still allowed to participate), and second of all the actual logic of it, like the ethics of it, cannot be put into words. Thus, try as we might with theories about Georg's family troubles (which is usually code for Kafka's family troubles), we cannot map out a logic to Georg's jump; we cannot justify it, we cannot give a good reason for it—or any reason at all. And again, this is not because Herr Bendemann has not provided adequate evidence for his "judgment" (though obviously he has not), but because even if there were some logic to Georg's jump, we still would not be able to explain it using language.

The Unjudgeable and the Ineffable; the Metaphysical and the Resolute

All of this still leaves a major problem untouched, however: does it really matter that Herr Bendemann's proclamation is unproclaimable, and no reason for Georg's jump can ever be given, when Georg appears to both understand and heed this proclamation? This is where another parallel surfaces between the Kafka and Wittgenstein texts, as perhaps the hallmark gesture, the most memorable moment at any rate, of both works is that they both do things that have been specifically precluded by previous events. In Wittgenstein's case, the remarkable trick he accomplishes at the end of the *Tractatus* is to reveal its own nonsensicality through this meticulous progression: he shows us how the world is arranged (into facts; *TLP* 1–2); then how we are able to think about the world (3); then, how we are able to speak about possible facts in the world (4–5); and then, finally, how we are not able to picture, think about, or speak about anything else, including and especially the philosophy of the *Tractatus* itself. As we have seen before, at the end of the *Tractatus*, Wittgenstein determines that what philosophers have heretofore been calling "philosophical propositions" are contradictions in terms; that the alleged propositions of philosophy are nonsensical (6.54).

I would like to reexamine this revelation in the context of the act of judgment. The act itself is not obscured in the least in the *Tractatus*, but forms of the word *Urteil* (which translates as both "judgment" and "sentence") appear only four (albeit important) times in total. The first is in Wittgenstein's introduction, when he explains that it is of no concern to him how this work fits in with his philosophical peers: "Wieweit meine Bestrebungen mit denen anderer Philosophen zusammenfallen, will ich nicht *beurteilen*" ("I do not wish to *judge* the extent to which my aims coalesce with those of other philosophers") (introduction 2, emphasis mine). What appears, however, to be Wittgenstein's trademark glibness is simply yet another instance in which he follows his own rules: he does not want (*wollen*) to judge the disciplinary verisimilitude of his *Tractatus* because he cannot. Such a thing cannot be judged, because this exact work is about to determine that the language of both his philosophical peers and the *Tractatus* itself is only pseudo-propositional nonsense, and therefore unjudgeable. This in turn is exactly the point of both times a form of the word *Urteil* appears in the body of the *Tractatus* itself, first at 4.063, as Wittgenstein explains the importance of truth conditions (which he modifies from Frege's *Wahrheitswert*, truth value) to the logical form of the proposition (i.e., the logical form of reality, the form of a picture):

> Ein Bild zur Erklärung des Wahrheitsbegriffes: Schwarzer Fleck auf weißem Papier; die Form des Fleckes kann man beschreiben, indem man für jeden Punkt der Fläche angibt, ob er weiß oder Schwarz ist.

> Der Tatsache, dass ein Punkt schwarz ist, entspricht eine positive—der, dass ein Punkt weiß (nicht schwarz) ist, eine negative Tatsache. Bezeichne ich einen Punkt der Fläche (einen Fregischen Wahrheitswert), so entspricht dies der Annahme, die zur Beurteilung aufgestellt wird, etc. etc.
>
> An illustration to explain the concept of truth. A black spot on white paper; the form of the spot can be described by saying of each point of the plane whether it is white or black. To the fact that a point is black corresponds a positive fact; to the fact that a point is white (not black), a negative fact. If I indicate a point of the plane (a truth value in Frege's terminology), this corresponds to the assumption proposed for judgment, etc. etc.

Wittgenstein goes on that in order to be able to say (to judge) whether a point on a beflecked paper is white or black, one must first know under what conditions a spot can be black or white; that is, one must have a common understanding of "white," "black," and probably "surface" or "paper," and probably "spot" as well. We must be given these conditions before the pointing begins, else the gesture makes no sense:

> Der Punkt, an dem das Gleichnis hinkt ist nun der: Wir können auf einen Punkt des Papiers zeigen, auch ohne zu wissen, was weiß und schwarz ist; einem Satz ohne Sinn aber entspricht gar nichts, denn er bezeichnet kein Ding (Wahrheitswert) dessen Eigenschaften etwa "falsch" oder "wahr" hießen; das Verbum eines Satzes ist nicht "ist wahr" oder "ist falsch"—wie Frege glaubte—, sondern das, was "wahr ist," muss das Verbum schon enthalten.
>
> The point at which the simile breaks down is this: we can indicate a point on the paper, without knowing what white and black are; but to a proposition without a sense corresponds nothing at all, for it signifies no thing (truth value) whose properties are called "false" or "true"; the verb of the proposition is not "is true" or "is false"—as Frege thought—but that which "is true" must already contain the verb.

Another way of looking at this is that the fact of "being true" or "being false" does not give a proposition sense in the Fregean definition (or, for that matter, *Bedeutung*, "reference" in the same)—rather, sense, which is the quality of being able to be true, must be present in the propositional structure to begin with. This again emphasizes the divorcing of logical form from linguistic content, for if the fact of truth or falsehood gave the proposition sense, that would mean its logic was somehow contained within it, instead of it being contained within logic. Instead, because the proposition inhabits the form, and indeed must inhabit it in order to be a proposition, any proposition that makes sense must make sense regardless of its truth; the fact that it can be either true or false is what gives it sense in the first place: "Jeder Satz muss *schon* einen Sinn haben; die Bejahung kann ihn im nicht geben, denn sie bejaht ja gerade den Sinn. Und dasselbe gilt von der Verneinung, etc." ("Every proposition must *already* have a sense; it cannot be given a sense by affirmation; indeed its sense is just what is affirmed. And the same applies to negation, etc.") (4.064).

The inevitable conclusion of this line of thinking is that since any proposition that makes sense must have the capacity to be judged true or false, anything that looks like a proposition but does not have said capacity for judgment is not a proposition at all, but rather nonsense. Any legitimate analysis of the form of any proposition that claims that one thing judges another must, then, also show definitively that only sensical propositions can be judged, and nonsense cannot. This is the full implication of remark 5.5422, the second and last time a form of the word *Urteil* appears in the body of the *Tractatus*: "Die richtige Erklärung der Form des Satzes 'A urteilt p' muss zeigen, dass es unmöglich ist, einen Unsinn zu urteilen" ("The proper explanation of the form of the proposition 'A makes the judgment *p*' must show that is impossible to judge a piece of nonsense").

Since Wittgenstein's conception of sense as providing the space for, rather than being contained by, the proposition is in conflict with Frege's earlier *Begriffsschrift*, his insistence that only a sensical proposition can be judged has its roots in breaking from Frege as well; it is in a footnote quoting Frege's earlier formal logic that the word *Urteil* appears in the *Tractatus* for the final time. For in the *Begriffsschrift* Frege employed a curious mechanism that was one of the first symbols dropped from what we now know as first-order logic: the *Urteilsstrich*, or "judgment stroke." This was to appear above all propositions written in the *Begriffsschrift* and to signal that a judgment was being made in that proposition; Wittgenstein points out that such a stroke is redundant, as anything that can be judged can be judged obviously and clearly, and anything else is unjudgeable and no symbol can help it (4.442).

This then ties in perfectly to the *Tractatus*'s remarkable ending, in which Wittgenstein determines that since all philosophical "propositions" are nonsensical and thus also unjudgeable, so is the *Tractatus* itself. And yet, we just read it, it contained all sorts of developments in logic that logicians still use today, and the vast majority of the philosophical community believes that the text still contains unsayable truths (that we have thus judged true and thus can judge true) about the logical form of reality, and about language's ability and inability to portray said reality. Let us compare this to what I believe to be a remarkably similar gesture at the end of "The Judgment": we have discovered the major "judgments" in this story to be unjudgeable—and yet they have tangible, mortal results. Thus, both texts stubbornly do exactly that which they are not supposed to be "able" to. Wittgenstein, for his part, has given us little choice but to apply, retroactively, to his own "nonsensical" propositions the scrutiny of their own allegedly nonsensical rules. We are to throw the ladder away, but the only reason we know this is because we have climbed it, and as we were doing so the rules enunciated on those "rungs" were (allegedly) easy to understand and obey—so are they really nonsensical? Indeed, the soundness of Wittgenstein's own proclamations on the logical structure of language, many of which are still taught in logic classrooms around the world, seem to make this possible.

And Kafka, in a similar gesture, has all but dared us to find motivation and sense in a series of events whose structure explicitly prevents these things from ever being found. It is actually most helpful to examine these gestures—defiantly self-negating (or in Kafka's case, self-preventing), yet stubbornly proceeding in spite of or even because of that self-hampering—against the backdrop of a debate surrounding the very status of the act of self-negation at the end of the *Tractatus*, of what that gesture actually means (or, more accurately, does not mean).

As we have discussed previously, interpretation of the end of the *Tractatus* often finds its way into two main camps: the standard or metaphysical readings and the "resolute" readings. This is immensely important because of each reading's vastly divergent opinion on what exactly Wittgenstein means when he relegates something to the unsayable. In one case, we can take "das Mystische" or the transcendental at face value, and in the other we cannot, as we must recognize the sentences that contain those words as utterly meaningless.

In the more standard conceptions, what remains after the seventh remark's call to "silence" are, as we have seen before, pseudo-propositions. These have been revealed to be nonsensical, but they are still supposed to show what they cannot say: indescribable truths about the logical form of language and reality. In this more commonly accepted canon of *Tractatus* interpretation, the reader who "understands" Wittgenstein "correctly" no longer suffers from the illusion that philosophy says anything, but recognizes that it shows us why that actually is the case.[21] This leaves ample room for "the mystical" really to be mystical, and for the *Tractatus* to be the truly "hybrid" document Monk, for example, argues that it is.

The faction of "new" or "resolute" readers, most prominently Cora Diamond and James Conant, argue on the other hand that the *Tractatus* cannot actually show anything about language, and thus the nonsense that Wittgenstein insists the book is in 6.54 is just that, "plain nonsense." While the metaphysical reading argues that the act of conquering, overcoming, or transcending these sentences, of recognizing them as *unsinnig*, is predicated on the discovery that in not saying, they show their form, Diamond dismisses this action as "chickening out."[22] If, she asks, in 6.54 Wittgenstein says that all of the *Tractatus* should be read as *unsinnig* and that the ladder must be thrown away, does that not also apply to 4.1212, which claims that what can be shown cannot be said, and 2.18, which explains the logical form of reality? What is supposed to be keeping the phrases "Die Logische Form . . . der Wirklichkeit" and "Was gezeigt werden *kann*, *kann* nicht gesagt werden" from being read as nonsensical and thrown away? And, were that to be the case, what is left of the idea that something can be shown but not said with logical form?

The most crucial recognition we undergo as the result of a "resolute" reading of the *Tractatus* is that of what Diamond refers to as Wittgenstein's "transitional vocabulary." This is what enables the resolute reading of the *Tractatus* (or any other text) to differ from never reading it at all. Diamond envisions a transitional vocabulary as a specific proposition or set of propositions that can, even if they prove themselves invalid as a result of their own rigid application, be necessary and useful as part of a transition. And, further, it is this transition that constitutes the most vital part of the discovery about these statements' processes of proving themselves invalid. The "transitional vocabulary" discussion validates the new readers' designation of the *Tractatus* as "plain nonsense." In Diamond's conception, it is the reader's responsibility to take 6.54 as seriously as possible. This means we are not to "chicken out" and hold onto concepts allegedly "elucidated" in the body of the work, such as, for example, the argument in 4.1212.[23] For Diamond, the very "notion of something true of reality but not sayably true is to be used only with the awareness that it itself belongs to what has to be thrown away."[24] The more traditional view that the "wo" and "da" in "Wovon man nicht sprechen kann, darüber muß man schweigen" actually refer to something is, in Diamond's conception, an illusion, and a reader who truly understands Wittgenstein will come to see this illusion for what it really is. The real reward of reading the *Tractatus* carefully is to understand how confused we have been to believe that there is such a thing as a philosophical vocabulary in the first place.[25]

In this view, then, we succeed in reading the *Tractatus* when we come to distinguish the difference between perspective "and the illusion that there has to be perspective" at all.[26] What Diamond is trying to make us see is that with the resolute reading, once the transitional language has been made unnecessary and we can look back on it as pure nonsense, we have been liberated. Liberated, that is, from the pressure of trying to communicate something philosophical—and all the way liberated, more liberated than we would be were we simply to acknowledge that we can't communicate anything philosophical because our language precludes this kind of expression. Diamond's view is at once more extreme and more optimistic: for if, according to her, we read the *Tractatus* correctly, we "see the world correctly" as Wittgenstein says in 6.54, we are freed not just from the pressure of communicating philosophy when we can't, but also from the illusion that there was any philosophy to communicate in the first place. Through analysis of the transitional vocabulary concept, we can now see that the supposed breakthrough of the resolute reading of the *Tractatus* is the realization that if "Was gezeigt werden *kann*, *kann* nicht gesagt werden" is plain, austere, non-elucidatory nonsense, then nothing it says about showing can be taken seriously, and thus all insights gleaned from the say/show distinction disappear.

The resolute approach to the *Tractatus* is a compelling choice for literary critics, especially those interested in Kafka—as we have seen, recent scholarship by Karen Zumhagen-Yekplé uses the idea of "the resolute" in Kafka to quite successful effect.[27] For the question of judgeability in "The Judgment," however, I see undeniable potential in both approaches. Each would address the problem of Herr Bendemann's death sentence making no sense, and then reconcile that with the seemingly irreconcilable action Georg takes in response. In the metaphysical view we are left with a nonsensical proclamation followed by a suicide whose logic is impossible to articulate (and, again, not actually because of the nonsensical proclamation)—but with this we are also left with room for the transcendental, "das Mystische," a vastly important ethical presence that simply does not reside in our world.

Conclusion

As Kafka seemed to spend his entire career striving to cheat this dichotomy by writing the impossible (chargeless arrests, senseless metaphor-vermin, etc.), it is only fitting that he continue to do so by creating a story where the characters seem to be able to understand and access "ineffable" truths about each other in spite of their complete failures in the linguistic realm. Indeed, in a different context remark 6.44 of the *Tractatus* feels like it could have been written by Kafka himself: "Nicht wie die Welt ist, ist das Mystische, sondern dass sie ist" ("The mystical is not *how* the world is, rather *that* it is"). With this in mind, it would at first seem that the metaphysical approach to the dissolution of the problem of "The Judgment" is the obvious choice.

And yet: what is more senseless, more defiant of a justification, more profane—really, more anti-transcendent—than a filial suicide? And what's more, one whose profanity is exacerbated by a sexual entendre in the story's final two words: "unendlicher Verkehr" ("endless intercourse [of traffic]")? Does this moment, jarring and obscene (itself preceded by Herr Bendemann's "skirt lift," also jarring and obscene), portend, deserve, or even act like it wants a metaphysical or transcendent significance? In the resolute view, Georg is simply dead, and it does not matter why—it is in fact our discovery of why it does not matter why that matters. This view would both fit well with and slightly reconceive the original conclusion I have just put forth about *The Metamorphosis*, where I have taken great pains to argue that Kafka takes something we all take for granted—metaphor—and twists it into impossibility so that we can see its limits and how it works. In a "resolute" view of "The Judgment"—or even in a partially resolute view—we can see that here

Kafka has described and undermined the very act of (ethical) judgment in the same way.

Wittgenstein, in his initially failed search for a publisher for the *Tractatus*, insisted that the "point of the book was an ethical one"—that the most important part of the treatise, the ethical "section," was the part that was necessarily left unsaid (presumably coming after remark 7's command of silence). Similarly, what we could call the point—the narrative climax—of "The Judgment" is also an ethical one, but, not unlike the *Tractatus*, the most important thing this climax should reveal is that the very ethical proclamations that constitute its core conflict are actually impossible to proclaim.

Part Two

✦

Analytic Skepticism

Kafka and the *Philosophical Investigations*

Preface to Part Two

✦

Wittgenstein's Transition and a More Analytic Kafka

The philosophical component of the following chapters marks an important transition from the "early" Wittgenstein to the "later," and thus a further development of what I call analytic modernism. As I have discussed in this book's introduction, after the *Tractatus*'s publication, a disgruntled Wittgenstein, fed up with what he saw as a grievous misunderstanding of his slim volume's main point (despite said slim volume being accepted, quite unconventionally, as his doctoral dissertation and granting him the Ph.D. from Cambridge), left philosophy for school teaching and architecture. What returned him to the discipline he attempted to dismantle was, in the end, a desire to attempt to dismantle it again in a different and possibly better way. The result was the *Philosophische Untersuchungen* (*Philosophical Investigations*), the volume upon which Wittgenstein worked for the rest of his life, and which at the time of his untimely death of prostate cancer in 1951 was still incomplete.

While the *Tractatus*'s unconventional numbered structure, resolute interconnectedness, and small stature necessitated a pre-exegesis before the first half of this book could even truly begin, the structure and (if we are to take Wittgenstein at his word) purpose of the *Investigations* are different. Ostensibly, the *Investigations* are a set of landscape sketches upon which we are to gaze, not a whole whose trajectory we must understand before we begin—indeed, as we are about to see, the entire conceit of "trajectory" is contrary to the spirit of the project. While the *Tractatus* was just seven numbered propositions long, with all the subsequent text simply (or not so simply) modifying sub-propositions, as I mentioned briefly in my introduction, the first half of the *Investigations* consist of *hundreds* of propositions, again numbered, but not always progressing in a linear fashion (for remember the "problem with progress"?). What really distinguishes the *Investigations* from their predecessor, however, is not just the little-cited second half, which transitions into full prose essays, but the confounding detail that the first half's numbered propositions take the form of an argument between at least two disagreeing voices, one of whom is meant to be a sort of metaphysicist's straw-everyman, and the rest of whom (there is debate about whether there is but one "interlocutor" or several) are meant to disabuse this everyman of his illusions.[1] Here, however, is where the differences between the texts begin to converge once more: although Wittgenstein goes about his task in a markedly different way, in the *Investigations* he tackles the same issues he did in the *Tractatus*: the mystery of how our language works, and what it can and cannot do.

Though the *Investigations* are in many ways far more complex than the *Tractatus*, their format makes them far easier to integrate into literary study without much of a preface; thus, my concurrent exploration of the *Investigations* and the Kafka works that bring them to life—*The Castle*, "In the Penal Colony," and "Josefine the Singer, or the Mouse Folk"—sets directly off on the proverbial hike, rather than preparing for many pages at base camp as was necessary with the *Tractatus*. However, just because the structure of the *Investigations* hints literary does not mean that the structure of my arguments surrounding them must (or even can). Indeed, it may be surprising to realize that despite its total lack of formulae and truth tables, the second half of this book takes a structure that is oftentimes even more analytic than the first.

What I mean by an analytic structure is this: while the *Tractatus* offered us a logicist's take on "dissolving" the central problems of several of Kafka's best-known works, the *Investigations* offer us something wholly different, and, some might say, markedly less analytic. For there are no truth tables to be found in the *Investigations*, no sub-propositions, no clear and triumphant demarcation of what language can and cannot do, no rules. On the contrary: one of the text's most interesting sections, which I visit in great detail in chapter 5, dismantles the conceit of "rules" entirely. But if the *Investigations* do not subject language to analysis, then why, we may ask, do they still belong to the analytic canon, and why does a concurrent exploration with Kafka still merit the term analytic modernism? As we are about to see, the *Investigations*' status as ordinary language philosophy (a term that will be explored in the detail it deserves momentarily), as well as the volume's relationship to the *Tractatus*, makes Wittgenstein's second book one of the analytic canon's most discussed.

Its relationship to literature is, however, not the same as that of the *Tractatus*, and thus I have termed the result of its pairing with Kafka not "logical modernism," but rather "analytic skepticism," putting an analytic twist on the radical language skepticism whose multifaceted relationship to Kafka's canon I have already discussed at some length in earlier chapters. All this is to say that while their primary philosophical source is not as analytic on its surface, the following chapters' exploration of the *Investigations* as a literary companion, structurally and in my argumentation, take a highly analytic approach, perhaps even more so even than previous chapters.

In writing the following chapter, for example, I found that a more philosophical structure was the most successful in bringing the most clarity possible—to me, and thus also hopefully to readers—to Wittgenstein's paradox of ostensive definition, which is quite complex and far-reaching in its implications. What I do in this half of the book, in particular with the chapter that follows, on *The Castle*, is very much in the philosophical (or perhaps social-scientific) vein: I offer bold hypotheses about the appearance of particular and important paradoxes from the *Investigations*, and then a systematic analysis of the appearances of said paradoxes throughout Kafka's texts. In doing so, my hope is twofold: I want to offer a multidisciplinary approach to literary analysis that is welcoming to and inclusive of readers from other disciplines such as philosophy or cognitive science, and I also want to offer a thesis that is both dramatically clear and clearly presented, with as little jargon as humanly possible. Therefore, it is my hope that in both content and method, the following exploration continues to make the case for an analytic modernism.

Chapter 4

The Castle and the Paradox of Ostensive Definition

Just as most criticism of *The Trial* addresses Josef K.'s guilt, and the majority of examinations of *The Metamorphosis* and "The Judgment" concentrate on Gregor's metaphorical meaning and the reasons for Georg's jump respectively, the scholarly canon of *Das Schloß* (*The Castle*) often returns to variations on two basic themes: Why is the community of the Castle so closed off, and why is the character of K. so obtuse? Why, as John Zilcosky asks, "does Kafka choose to make the faceless hero of his most mysterious novel a land surveyor," given that "K. never actually does any surveying in the novel (he doesn't even possess surveying equipment)"?[1] Why, asks Mark Harman, did Kafka write K. as flatly and opaquely as possible—deliberately, through a series of relentless deletions of K.'s inner monologue, effectively "stripping" K. of "'interesting' traits that a more conventional novelist would choose to emphasize"?[2] Indeed, as Elizabeth Boa has aptly pointed out, the variations on these themes are multitudinous, and equally plausible, for "just as the castle buildings present different aspects depending on who is looking at them, so the reader . . . will find different meanings depending on choices of interpretive strategy."[3]

As I have discussed previously in light of the *Tractatus*, I believe that these questions about *The Castle*, while they have inspired some truly spectacular insights into the text and Kafka's "late" oeuvre, also obscure another question that has been largely ignored. Instead of asking why the Castle village is so closed to outsiders and why K. is a land surveyor who surveys no land, why not ask how? To some extent, Sussman has done this already in his exegesis of Kafka's "aesthetics of fragmentation," arguing that a fragmentary aesthetic is present "when The Castle surveys the gaps and misprisions in the bureaucratic approaches linking the power-nexus to the village below it."[4] I would like to take Sussman's idea a step further, and the following exploration uses the earliest passages of Wittgenstein's *Philosophical Investigations* to do just that. In the *Investigations*' introduction, Wittgenstein insists once again that anyone who reads his volume as a philosophical text is misguided. While the *Tractatus* is allegedly for entertainment purposes only, the *Investigations* are to be leafed through as "an album," a collection of "landscape sketches" (*Landschaftsskizze*).[5] The following chapter serves as both an introduction to the form and early content of Wittgenstein's major late work, and a demonstration that Wittgenstein's challenging collection of landscape sketches will help us to chart the plight of Kafka's strangely embroiled land surveyor (*Landvermesser*; due to this chapter's focus on the ability of this single word to mean, I will refer to K.'s job title primarily in German).

Reconceiving the Central "Problem" of *The Castle*: Is He or Isn't He?

A strange man arrives in a remote village late one night and goes to sleep on a straw mattress in the bar of a dingy inn; upon being roused and asked to leave because he lacks the proper permissions, he insists he is there for a reason, and does so by naming himself official land surveyor (*Landvermesser*) hired by the Count: "Sonst aber lassen Sie es sich gesagt sein, daß ich der Landvermesser bin, den der Graf hat kommen lassen" ("Otherwise let it be said that I am the land surveyor for whom the Count has sent") (*GW* 4:11). This claim is first disputed: "Ich habe es ja gesagt," says one of his interrogators, "keine Spur von Landvermesser, ein gemeiner lügnerischer Landstreicher, wahrscheinlich aber ärgeres" ("I told you . . . no trace of 'land surveyor,' a common lying vagrant, probably worse") (4:12). But immediately thereafter, the telephone rings and K.'s self-identification is confirmed: "Ein Irrtum also? Das ist mir recht unangenehm. Der Bureauchef selbst hat telefoniert? Sonderbar, sonderbar. Wie soll ich aber jetzt dem Herrn Landvermesser erklären?" ("A mistake? But this is quite awkward for me. The Chief telephoned himself? Remarkable, remarkable. How should I explain this to Herr Land-Surveyor?") (4:13). And yet, when Kafka's final novel cuts off mid-sentence after nearly 400 pages, its protagonist has failed to survey a single square meter of land. Thus, it should be unsurprising that one of the most enduring and oft-cited interpretations of *The Castle* is that of Walter Sokel nearly half a century ago, who suggests that K. is an impostor:

> K.s Reaktion erlaubt zwei Deutungen. Er wurde überhaupt nicht berufen, und seine Behauptung, berufen zu sein, ist ein kecker Versuch, die Anstellung zu erzwingen. Sein Anspruch wäre also ein Erpressungsversuch. Oder aber die Berufung ist an ihn ergangen, doch unter so zweifelhaften Umständen und mit so vielen Widersprüchlichkeiten verknüpft, daß sich K. auf einen schweren Kampf gefaßt machen mußte. In beiden Fällen ist eines klar. Er ist kein ahnungsloses Opfer einer Justizverweigerung, einer plötzlichen Sinnesänderung des Schlosses.[6]

> K's reaction allowed two possible interpretations. The first was that he was not called at all, and his claim to have been called would

> simply be seen as a bold attempt to force himself into the job, as attempted blackmail. Or he was indeed called for the job, but under such dubious circumstances and so tied up in contradictions that he [had unwittingly just put himself up for a tremendous struggle going forward]. In both cases, one thing was clear. He was a clueless victim of a miscarriage of justice, of the Castle's sudden change of mind.

Sokel effectively turns the entire basis of interpretation of this novel on its head—for if K. is not an innocent victim of an untenable bureaucracy, what is he? In collecting and processing the vast array of critical turns encompassing even Kafka's least-studied works, Stephen Dowden pays particular attention to Sokel's argument, positing that in this view "K. is not so much a rebel as a fraud," and thus "the novel's basic theme is K.'s attempt to make everyone, including the reader, believe that justice is the problem and that the injustice inflicted upon him is his motive in his struggle with the castle." And yet:

> One of the few things we can know for certain is that K. is a liar. He claims to have left behind a wife and child. He also says he is going to marry Frieda. He has to be lying about one or the other, unless he is a remorseless bigamist. Sokel somewhat arbitrarily decides that K. is lying about the wife and child, arguing that it is a part of K.'s need to invent a past for himself.[7]

There are indeed many ways for K. to be an impostor—he may be, as Sokel suggests, an opportunistic stranger with no land-surveying experience, one who merely claims (*behauptet*) to be the *Landvermesser*, as K. himself seems to acknowledge in attempting to see his rude initial treatment through the eyes of the villagers: "Das Geweckt-werden, das Verhör, die pflichtgemäße Androhung der Verweisung aus dem Grafschaft habe K. sehr ungnädig aufgenommen, übrigens wie sich schließlich gezeigt hat vielleicht mit Reicht, denn er behaupte ein vom Herrn Grafen bestellter Landvermesser zu sein" ("Being awoken, the interrogation, the compulsory threat of double-checking his credentials from the Count's people—all this had put K. in a very ungracious mood, possibly justifiably so, as he claimed to be the land surveyor ordered by the count") (4:12).

K. may also indeed be some sort of *Landvermesser*, but not the "real" *Landvermesser*, *actually* sent for by the actual Count Westwest, to survey this particular castle. Sokel's suggestion remains so compelling because, as Dowden has shown us, K. certainly does act like an impostor: he does not recognize his "assistants" Artur and Jeremias, he neither possesses any surveying equipment nor seems to know what to do with it, and agrees somewhat incomprehensibly to take a position as unpaid school janitor after taking up with Frieda.[8] And thus, for Dowden "Sokel is certainly right that K.'s claim to be a surveyor summoned by the castle is untrustworthy." However, as much as I reluctantly admit the "impostor thesis" is quite likely the strongest one, Dowden makes the excellent point that "it undermines the novel's fundamental hovering between possibilities," instead positing the impostor thesis as fact, and thus discounting "Kafka's cunning ambiguity."[9]

To resist this "cunning ambiguity" is to resist what may be the most important element of Kafka's last novel. What I mean is that K. is *probably* an impostor, but this is actually the wrong focus to be granting *The Castle*. To show why, I would like to introduce in earnest Wittgenstein's later work, which, not unlike *The Castle*, is quite a bit longer than its author's previous work, as well as more sweeping, more intricate, and quite a bit more unreliable, all also qualities we might correctly attribute to *The Castle*. I do of course see the clever companionship between the *Investigations* and *The Castle* because of the similarity between Kafka's *Landvermesser* and Wittgenstein's *Landschaftsskizze*, both of which appear in off-kilter contexts: the former surveys no land, the latter contains no land. But beyond this clever connection, the *Investigations* also highlight another aspect of Kafka's place in the modernist canon, one that is decidedly more radical than the skepticism we have seen so far. For the *Investigations*' first major issue, the paradox of ostensive definition (§§1–28), is played out clearly and with remarkable repercussions in the fictional world of Kafka's *Castle*.

Ostensive definition (*hinweisende Definition*) is the action of pointing to something and/or using a particular sort of word—"this" or "that," for example—in order to name it, and in order for others to understand its name in a consistent manner. Wittgenstein insists this entire concept is an illusion. The initial conflict of *The Castle* is also, when we think about it, one of purported ostensive definition. That is: is K. or isn't he the "real" *Landvermesser*? But with the help of the *Investigations* we can dissolve this apparent problem and reveal the real problem it obscures. That is: it is not whether or not K. is the "real" *Landvermesser* that is truly at issue *even if he is probably not*.

The New Problem: (What) Does *Landvermesser* Mean?

Our first step is to discuss the progression of the paradox of ostensive definition itself, which begins with the *Investigations*' opening remark, which Wittgenstein takes from Augustine's *Confessions*. Allegedly, when humans invented language, they gave every word a meaning:

> Die Wörter der Sprache benennen Gegenstände—Sätze sind Verbindungen von solchen Benennungen.—In diesem Bild von der Sprache finden wir die Wurzeln der Idee: Jedes Wort hat eine Bedeutung. Diese Bedeutung ist dem Wort zugeordnet. Sie ist der Gegenstand, für welchen das Wort steht. (§1)

> The words of language signify objects—propositions are relationships between such significations.—In this picture of language we find the roots of the idea that every word has a meaning. This meaning is allocated to the word. It is the object for which the word stands.

In this view, the primitive human language is one of pure ostension: "This . . ." (*person points to something*) "is called a [name]" (*says something*). Thus the "given" view of language development is one of successful semiotic acts—semiotic acts such as, to use a random example, the verbal indication of oneself, *ich*, the conjugated verb that designates self-identification, *bin*, and the predicate noun *Landvermesser*.

Speaking of which, let us now finally begin to see how problematic this ostensive act comes across in Kafka's text. Of the 117 times this word appears in the 1994 Pasley edition of *Das Schloß*, five appear in acts of direct naming of K., the first being the aforementioned endeavors not to be ejected from the inn ("daß ich der Landvermesser bin, den der Graf hat kommen lassen"). Another important instance also occurs early on, as Schwarzer asks, "Wie soll ich das dem Herrn Landvermesser erklären?" This is a question that causes K.'s attention to pique: "K. horchte auf. Das Schloß hatte ihn also zum Landvermesser ernannt" ("K.'s ears pricked up. So the Castle had referred to him as the land surveyor") (4:13). With some help from a mysterious voice on the telephone K. appears to have named himself, and then been named, with success. This pattern repeats moments later, when K. walks himself to exhaustion in the snow and seeks shelter in one of the overcrowded village houses: "'Ich bin der gräfliche Landvermesser,' sagte K., und suchte sich so vor den noch immer Unsichtbaren zu verantworten. 'Ach, es ist der Landvermesser,' sagte eine weibliche Stimme und noch folgte eine vollkommene Stille'" ("'I am the official land surveyor,' said K., and searched for the person to whom he was answering, though that person remained invisible. 'Ah, it's the land surveyor,' said a female voice, which was followed by total silence") (4:20). So what can be the problem with the ostensive gesture here? It seems to have worked fine.[10]

But according to Wittgenstein, that is exactly the problem—just because everyone seems to understand that K. is the *Landvermesser* now doesn't mean that they actually know what he is supposed to be doing. In fact, soon it becomes obvious that this act didn't work *at all* the way K. hoped. Interestingly, the onslaught of changes in parameters that occur as K. gets to know the village better contain the same structure as what in his text Wittgenstein calls a *Sprachspiel*, or language-game, a method repeated throughout the *Investigations*.

It is certainly important to examine the *Sprachspiel* phenomenon in greater detail before we progress, although I also return to it in the following chapter when discussing "In the Penal Colony." For now, it is necessary to know that Wittgenstein dismantles (his version of) the Augustinian theory piece by piece, until we are left with a paradox, and calls this a "game." He also calls the "game" the "method of §2," so named after the second remark, which sets forth a "primitive language" between a builder and his assistant that contains only the words for cube, pillar, slab, and beam: "Würfel," "Säule," "Platte," and "Balken." The builder, named A, calls out each word when he needs the correspondingly shaped block; the assistant, B, "bringt den Stein, den er gelernt hat, auf diesen Ruf zu bringen" ("brings the stone that he has learned to bring at this particular call") (§2). In the remarks that follow, Wittgenstein reveals that the assistant is not learning the four-word "language" of the builder, but rather simply being trained—and, he continues, the way a child learns a first language is indeed through this kind of training ("Abrichten," §5).

As Wittgenstein demonstrates here, a "language-game" ("Sprachspiel," §7) presents a scenario with clearly defined parameters and context; the game's creator uses it to offer a "thesis" about how language works, and bases this apparent thesis on the evidence in this particular scenario. The "game" takes off when the creator then alters either the parameters or context little by little until the thesis is no longer valid—in §§2–5, Wittgenstein does this by reminding us that we are mistaken in conceiving of the four-word "language" as a complete model for a system of how language is acquired, as this "model" is rather simply a description of a single case ("Ja, brauchbar, aber nur für diese eng beschriebene Gebiet, nicht für das Ganze, daß du darzustellen vorgabst" ["Yes, it is appropriate, but only for this narrowly circumscribed region, not for the whole of what you were claiming to describe"] [§3]).

Now we can address the question of how this echoes the form of Kafka's text. In *The Castle*, after that first fateful night in the inn, by the time K. engages again in pure self-identification it is over 300 pages later, when he is deeply embroiled in local drama—and thus his parameters have changed dramatically. K. has been hired (and fired) as school janitor; his engagement with Frieda has stagnated; he has become a player in the drama of the shunned Barnabas family. It seems like an afterthought at this point that he has not surveyed a single hectare of land as he narrates his own Castle history to the marginally sympathetic Olga: "Ich war hier zwar als Landvermesser aufgenommen, aber das war nur scheinbar, man spielte mit mir, man trieb mich aus jedem Haus, man spielt auch heute mit mir, aber wie viel umständlicher ist das" ("I was taken on here as land surveyor, but that was only appearance. They toyed with me, they drove me out of every house, they're playing with me still, but how much more intricate it's become") (4:289). K. seems here to be under the misguided impression that the word *Landvermesser* as he was originally named when he was "taken on" has a meaning with consistent and wide applicability, rather than the narrowly circumscribed case of his first night in the village. Further, in addition to K.'s initial instance of self-naming and the morphing it undergoes, there are numerous other instances in which K. refers to himself as a *Landvermesser* casually, and others do so, and the meaning of the word seems wildly inconsistent at best and utterly opaque at worst. For example, early on, in response to the landlady (*Wirtin*, also sometimes translated as "innkeeper's wife"), who makes the first of many claims that the Castle folk do not have use for outsiders, K. insists self-referentially that sometimes they do: "zum Beispiel mich, den Landvermesser" ("for example, me, the Land Surveyor") (4:15).

From Wittgenstein's point of view, something like this should come as no surprise. To see why this is, let us return to the original *Sprachspiel* of §2, which takes the parameters "language with four words" and thesis "we define things in a first language by pointing to things and assigning meaning to them." Wittgenstein then widens the scope of the idea of "ostensive language learning" just enough to demonstrate its inherent weakness: in order to define something ostensively, we have to have ostensive words, words such as "this" and "that one"—and how do we ostensively define those (or, for that matter, "those")?

> Wird auch "dorthin" und "dieses" hinweisend gelernt?—Stell dir vor, wie man ihren Gebrauch etwa lehren könnte! Es wird dabei auf Örter und Dinge gezeigt werden,—aber hier geschieht ja dieses Zeigen auch im Gebrauch der Wörter und nicht nur beim Lernen des Gebrauchs.— (§9b)

> Are "there" and "this" also learned ostensively?—Imagine how one might perhaps teach their use! It would be by pointing to things and places—but here the pointing occurs in the use of the words and not only in learning the use.—

In the case of the *Landvermesser* problem, the ostensive phrase is *ich bin*—but how do we know that the villagers and K. both conceive of that phrase in the same way? One of Wittgenstein's interlocutory voices argues that we could just narrow the parameters of the game again and argue that ostensive language only works for nouns or certain other parts of speech that are not themselves ostensive in purpose—but, counters the voice most critics attribute to Wittgenstein's straw man, how does that explain a child understanding the meaning of "these"? Wittgenstein ends up with the idea that there is no such thing as pure ostension, and that all of what we misleadingly call ostensive definition is actually, in its own way, explanation:[11]

> Was bezeichnen nun die Wörter dieser Sprache?—Was sie bezeichnen, wie soll sich das zeigen, es sei denn in der Art ihres Gebrauchs? Und den haben wir ja beschrieben. Der Ausdruck „dieses Wort bezeichnet das" müßte also ein Teil dieser Beschreibung werden. (§10a)

> What do the words of this language *mean*?—What they mean. What is that supposed to show, if not the kind of use they have? And that we've already described. The expression "this word means that" would also have to become part of this description.

When we are pointing to something or otherwise signaling that "*this* is called a [that]," or "I am called a land surveyor," the target of our explanation has *to know already* the logical form of an ostensive gesture and that, further, the use of this logical form is itself an act of description, explanation, and not pure ostension.

And indeed, the chief problem in K.'s case is that while "Herr Landvermesser" effectively becomes his name, at no point does anyone in the novel do what must be done to clarify what a *Landvermesser* actually is: explain it. Instead, we have one instance of so-called pure ostension after another, bare naming with no context. Unsurprisingly, these instances do not help clarify K.'s place in the village in the least—even when, as at the beginning, they are supposed to vindicate K. This original instance would seem to offer sufficient proof that (1) a land surveyor was ordered to this village, and (2) K. is that land surveyor, by honest or dishonest means—and yet, it fails to. Yet another way K. is "legitimized" (and yet not explained) as *Landvermesser* comes through Frieda, who names him upon first meeting him ("so weiß ich doch alles, Sie sind der Landvermesser" ["everybody knows, you're the land surveyor"] [4:51]), and whose fall from grace stems directly from her involvement with K.—her public utterance—twice, for emphasis— of "Ich bin beim Landvermesser! Ich bin beim Landvermesser!" ("I'm with the land surveyor!") (4:56). It is almost like that sex act is the final seal of his name—but this name refers only to "the man who committed this act with Frieda"—because that is all reference can do; contrary to Frege, but in the later Wittgenstein, reference no longer works.

Here instead is how reference "works," according to the *Investigations*' §28, which contains a three-stage language game that culminates in the sentence to which most philosophers point as the paradox of ostensive definition in its pithiest form. The first stage in the game brings us a voice attesting the thesis that will eventually be dismantled:

> Man kann nur einen Personennamen, ein Farbwort, einen Stoffnamen, ein Zahlwort, den Namen einer Himmelsrichtung etc. hinweisend definieren. Die Definition der Zahl Zwei "das heißt 'zwei' "—wobei man auf zwei Nüsse zeigt—ist Vollkommen exakt.
>
> One can ostensively define a proper name, the name of a color, the name of a material, a number, the name of a geographic direction, etc. The definition of the number two, "that is called 'two' "—at which point one points to two nuts—is entirely exact.

But is that really so? A second voice begs to differ by expanding the parameters set out by the first voice. How, the second voice begs to differ, is the person receiving the assertion "this is two nuts" supposed to know that the quantifier "two" applies to all groups of two things, and not just nuts?

> —Aber wie kann man denn die Zwei so definieren? Der, dem man die Definition gibt, weiß ja dann nicht, was man mit "zwei" benennen will; er wird annehmen, daß du *diese* Gruppe von Nüssen "zwei" nennst!
>
> —But how, then, can "two" be so defined? The person to whom one gives the definition doesn't know what one wants to call "two;" he will suppose that "two" names *this* group of nuts!

There is no reason the word "two" can't be misunderstood to apply only to nuts—to understand that it should *quantify* everything, one must first understand what quantification is. Thus ends the game, with the paradox of ostensive definition: "Die hinweisende Definition kann in jedem Fall so und anders gedeutet werden" ("Ostensive definition can be variously interpreted in every case"). This leaves us back where we started, wondering how—or if—ostension works.

Also back where he started, interestingly enough, is K. in his own bizarre journey of ostension. Let us rejoin him in his final instance of self-identification as *Landvermesser*, which takes place just before the novel cuts off in mid-sentence: the landlady, at once K.'s biggest detractor and greatest purveyor of information, asks him, equally existentially as factually: "Was bist du denn eigentlich?" ("What are you really?"). To which K. answers: "Landvermesser." The landlady's rebuttal to this is one many of us have been leveling silently since the novel's opening: "Was ist denn das?" ("What is that?") (4:455). And it is Kafka's narration hereafter that marks one of the finest examples of the "cunning ambiguity" Dowden attributes to him. The landlady, it seems, finds K. to be the same sort of impostor Sokel does—but the choice as to whether or not to accept K.'s version of events is cleverly left out on Kafka's part, forcing us to put all of our still-feeble understanding into the word *Landvermesser*, which, in all these instances, K. has done a spectacularly poor job of defining. As Wittgenstein has said, what we mistake for ostension is really explanation; *explanation*, not the repeated acts of naming, is what could allow us to know what exactly K. conceives of as a *Landvermesser*. And this explanation fails to satisfy the landlady regardless, for reasons we can and will never know. It is as if the word *Landvermesser* meant something different in every case.

Wittgenstein clarifies the paradox of ostensive definition in §30, when he explains that its problem is that it only "works" when its target already knows what role the word or expression being "shown" takes in a language:

> Man könnte also sagen: Die hinweisende Definition erklärt den Gebrauch—die Bedeutung—des Wortes, wenn es schon klar ist, welche Rolle das Wort in der Sprache überhaupt spielen soll.
>
> . . .
>
> Man muß schon etwas wissen (oder können), um nach der Benennung fragen zu können. (§30a, b)

> One could also say: ostensive definition explains the use—the meaning—of the word, when it is already clear what role in the language overall the word should play.
>
> . . .
>
> One must already know something (or know how to do it), in order to be able to ask about what it's called.

Now that this game has been played in full, we can see that (Wittgenstein's version of) Augustine's "Lernen der menschlichen Sprache" presents not a disputable philosophical thesis about how first-language learning proceeds, but rather an illusion about what first-language learning is:

> Und nun können wir, glaube ich, sagen: Augustinus beschreibe das Lernen der menschlichen Sprache so, als käme das Kind in ein fremdes Land und verstehe die Sprache des Landes nicht, das heißt: so als habe es bereits eine Sprache, nur nicht diese. Oder auch: als könne das Kind schon denken, nur noch nicht sprechen. Und "denken" hieße hier etwas, wie: zu sich selber reden. (§32b)

> And now I believe we can say: Augustine describes learning human language as if a child were to come to a foreign land and not understand its language, as if it had a language already, just not this one. Or we could also say: as if the child could already think, just not speak. And "to think" means here to talk to oneself.[12]

Therefore, the problem with ostensive language learning is that in order to "learn" a language you already have to know enough about how it works that you can correctly figure out its constituent grammatical parts. It seems, then, as if Wittgenstein's first paradox has actually offered a solution to the problem of why K.'s self-naming has not worked in the way we (or he) have hoped or expected: K., who already ostensibly speaks his own language and thus understands how language works, simply needed to have treated communication in the village like second-language learning. He should have understood, after the tenth misunderstanding, that his interpretation of the ostensive phrase "Ich bin der gräfliche Landvermesser" did not mean in the same way their understanding of the same phrase meant. He should have made an effort to learn *their* language, which, though it sounded and seemed to be the same as his, was actually foreign.

And this is where the exploration of Kafka and the *Investigations* becomes truly remarkable, and far more than an unconventional explicative tool for literature: we have thus far seen how Wittgenstein's paradox helps us to see why K. has so many problems understanding his new community—but what we might not expect is that we can also use *The Castle* to illuminate *Wittgenstein's* issues with ostensive definition. That is: in creating the exclusive, preclusive, deliberately misunderstanding-provoking world of the Castle village, Kafka has unwittingly added a remarkable dimension to Wittgenstein's *Sprachspiel*: if one can learn a foreign language ostensively, that would mean that the foreign language *itself* contained the concept of ostension. Remarkably, the system of communication in the Castle village does not—or at least not in any conventional way. What we will now see, then, is that not only does the Wittgenstein text offer a novel interpretation of the Kafka text, but also that the Kafka text actually illuminates the Wittgenstein text.

The Reverse-Ostensive Systems of the Castle

The obtuseness of the Castle's communicative system is a common and rich focus of Kafka criticism, including some interesting work from outside German studies, such as that of historian Mark E. Blum, who frames K.'s troubles with the villagers in terms of Max Weber's distinction between *Gemeinschaft*, "community," and *Gesellschaft*, "society," with a *Gemeinschaft* being an organic collective made up of people who have substantive commonalities, and a *Gesellschaft* an artificial construct. For Blum, the onus is at least partially on K., who fails to "commit himself fully to be a member of this community."[13] But there is a direct relationship between the presence of a community, or in this case the alleged commitment to that community, and how that community is also what Wittgenstein would call a "language community," or *Sprachgesellschaft*.

As an outsider, K. has no possible way to understand how anything in the Castle village means, because the Castle's system of meaning does not itself mean in anything resembling the way K.'s own language does. In fact, he has no potential to understand what anything there means without somehow learning the village's own backward system of ostension. And this proves near impossible, both because K. understandably does not seem to be aware of the paradox of ostensive definition on his own, and because, more simply, the Castle "system" is deliberately obtuse. A closer examination of why and how the Castle "system" rejects established assumptions about how communication works will adequately round out our survey of the paradox of ostensive definition as it appears in *The Castle*.

Kafka has already brought to life Wittgenstein's revelation that we cannot understand what a word means through pure ostension. If K.'s self-identification as *Landvermesser* is one thing, it is pure ostension devoid of context, and it fails spectacularly. What remains to be seen is Kafka's depiction of a culture in which the *very concept* of ostension itself is undermined—a depiction that in many ways serves to make Wittgenstein's point better than he himself did. For the village effectively demonstrates the most extreme case of this paradox of ostensive definition—that is, when ostension has been demystified and use made purposefully inscrutable, language is all but meaningless and communication with outsiders who depend upon the illusion of ostension thus impossible.

This is most certainly the case in K.'s dealings with every single person in the village—he simply cannot communicate with anyone, even when he believes he can. Furthermore, this delusion is his real problem, not the perceived bureaucratic injustice (for to claim injustice one would have to understand what was just). Wittgenstein addresses this issue in §31 with the example of an attempt to explain the pieces of chess—if a person simply points to the king and says, "That is the king," this will make sense only to a person who understands all the rules of chess except what the king looks like or what he does. Or take the case of someone who doesn't understand chess at all—the only way she would be able to understand an explanation of the king ("Das ist der König. Er kann so und so ziehen, etc. Etc." ["That is the king; he can move like such and such, etc."]) would be if she already knew what a board game of this sort was, and had observed previous games with rules with understanding ("mit Verständnis"). Now it is easy to see that, as Wittgenstein has put it, "Nach der Benennung fragt nur der sinnvoll, der schon etwas mit ihr anzufangen weiß" ("Only someone who already knows what to do with it can significantly ask a name") (§31). Now imagine attempting to explain a king to someone who comes from a culture where the entire concept of representative board games has never existed: where would one even begin? And now imagine *refusing* to explain a king to that same person, whose understanding of a king, it turns out, is necessary for her survival. This takes Wittgenstein's game to a fascinating new extent, and it would be the closest possible scenario to the one in which K. finds himself. Thus it is impossible for K. to parse any of the regulatory minutiae in the village because that would be like giving a king to the person above and forcing him to play.

And while K. never manages to survey a single piece of land, readers have much to gain from a survey of the anti-communicative landscape of the village. Through a systematic failure to parse the unparsable signals K. encounters—from a Castle that isn't one, to helpers that hinder, to scrambled telephone lines and roads that refuse to lead anywhere—we can see the full might of the ostension-challenging language community of the village.

Case Study 1: Schloß, Dorf, Gehilfe

No study of *The Castle* and ostensive definition can exclude the odd way in which both the word *Schloss* (in Kafka's spelling, *Schloß*) first appears in the text—leaving aside even the fact that in German it means both castle and lock, a double denotation of barricading exclusivity. What I would like to concentrate on here is the triumphant lack of pictorial fulfillment our first "picture" of the Castle brings: there is, in fact, no discernible castle in this castle: "es war weder eine alte Ritterburg, noch ein neuer Prunkbau, sondern eine ausgedehnte Anlage, die aus wenigen zweistöckigen, aber aus vielen eng aneinander stehenden niedrigen Bauten bestand" ("it was neither an old knight's castle nor a newer opulent building, but rather an expansive compound composed of two-story buildings all built very close to one another") (4:16).[14] Initially, K. thinks, mistakenly, that a traditional castle is present, only impossible to make out because it is obscured by fog: "Vom Schloßberg war nichts zu sehn, Nebel und Finsternis umgaben ihn, auch nicht der schwächste Lichtschein deutete das große Schloß an" ("Of the castle hill one couldn't make anything out; it was surrounded in fog and darkness, and indeed the large castle failed to be illuminated by even the weakest flare of light") (4:9). Instead, this fog and darkness merely obscure an alleged castle that is itself impossible to see as a castle; instead it is only the peculiar little buildings, so that to a stranger no castle appears whatsoever: "hätte man nicht gewußt das es ein Schloß ist, hätte man es für ein Städtchen halten können" ("were one not to know it was a castle, one could easily have taken it for a small city") (4:6). In fact, the only way to know what the word *Schloß* means in this context is to be part of the Castle apparatus itself, to "come from the Castle," as so many villagers seem to do. What's more, as we and K. both learn—in the novel's most important sentence—and as the schoolteacher explains: "zwischen den Bauern und dem Schloß ist kein Unterschied" ("there is no difference between the peasants and the Castle") (4:19).

How can the castle *equal* the village? This is an unexpected referential equation indeed, one that seems to defy the act of reference itself; this is an act echoed formally in K.'s fruitless attempt to find the castle using the village roads that never actually lead to it:

> Die Straße nämlich, diese Hauptstraße des Dorfes führte nicht zum Schloßberg, die führte nur nahe heran, dann aber wie absichtlich bog sie ab und wenn sie sich auch vom Schoß nicht entfernte, so kam sie ihm doch auch nicht näher. Immer erwartete K., daß nun endlich die Straße zum Schloß nicht entfernte, so kam sie ihm doch auch nicht näher. (19)
>
> This street in fact, this main street of the village, did not lead to the Castle hill; it led only in its general direction, but then as if on purpose turned away, and if this did not necessarily lead away from the Castle, it didn't lead any nearer to it either. K. always expected that the street, in the end, wouldn't separate him from the Castle entirely, and yet on it he did not draw any closer.

Instead of leading to the castle, these roads lead elsewhere and nowhere—this is not unlike K.'s (and our) expectation that the word *Schloß* point to something approximating a traditional picture of a castle. But a traditional system of reference is nowhere to be found. It seems instead to have been deliberately and categorically rejected, leaving both K. and the reader bereft and at the mercy of the actions of a system that nobody from outside it is allowed to understand.

And yet, that does not stop us from trying. This system, as best we can tell, seems to encompass a three-part structure of anti-ostension, meaning that the triad works in place of the ostensive gesture in the way that the villagers communicate, and further that none of its three parts functions in a correctly ostensive fashion. First: as we have seen, neither the physical castle nor the word *Schloß* points to any traditional castle structure in K.'s expected sense of the word; just as the physical castle is indiscernible from the physical village, the word points only to the word *Dorf*, which itself points rather tautologically back to the word *Schloß*, and thus expresses only the collection of ramshackle buildings and the insistent insularity of the inhabitants. This defiance of the act of picturing returns at a pivotal moment in the narrative, as the landlady reveals to K. her previous affair with Klamm and shows him a photograph that does not depict what it appears to depict:

> "Einen jungen Mann," sagte K. "Richtig," sagte die Wirtin, "und was macht er?" "Er liegt glaube ich auf einem Brett, streckt sich und gähnt." Die Wirtin lachte. "Das ist ganz falsch," sagte sie. "Aber hier ist doch das Brett und hier liegt er," beharrte K. auf seinem Standpunkt. "Sehen sie doch genauer hin," sagte die Wirtin ärgerlich, "liegt er denn wirklich?" "Nein," sagte nun K., "er liegt nicht, er schwebt und nun sehe ich es, es ist gar kein Brett, sondern wahrscheinlich eine Schnur und der junge Mann macht einen Hochsprung." (4:98)

> "A young man," said K. "Correct," said the landlady, "and what is he doing?" "I believe he is lying on a plank, stretching himself out and yawning." The innkeeper's wife laughed. "That is quite incorrect," she said. "But here is the plank and here he lies," K. insisted. "Look closer," said the innkeeper's wife, annoyed, "is he really lying down?" "No," said K. now, "he's not lying, he's floating and now I see that it's not a plank at all, bur rather probably a cord, and the young man is doing the high jump."

The landlady is kind enough here to force K. through an interpretive act that could greatly help him understand the systems of the community he seeks to join, if only he would pay more attention. For in the looping discovery of what the picture "really" shows—a high jumper rather than a man reclining, effectively the opposite of its original impression—perhaps the landlady is showing K. how to understand not just the castle's photographs, but its people. Perhaps the act of referential ostension works here after all—just in an opposite sort of way.

Opposite ostension is a theory that seems to be fully supported, in fact, by the peculiar way the Castle inhabitants demonstrate the use of the word

Gehilfe. In German, as in English, the word for "assistant" contains the word for "help" inside it; any German speaker would assume that an assistant assists, *ein Gehilfe hilft*. In *The Castle* this will turn out very much not to be the case. This leaving aside the phrase "meine alten Gehilfen," which signifies only the lie that it is (again lending credence to the K.-as-impostor theory), as K. has quite obviously never seen either Artur or Jeremias before:

> "Wer seid Ihr" fragte er und sah von einem zum andern. "Eure Gehilfen," antworteten sie. "Es sind die Gehilfen," bestätigte leise der Wirt. "Wie?" fragte K. "Ihr seid meine alten Gehilfen, die ich nachkommen ließ, die ich erwarte?" Sie bejahten es. (4:27)

> "Who are you," he asked and looked from one to the other. "Your assistants," they answered. "These are the assistants," the innkeeper confirmed quietly. "How?" asked K. "You are my old assistants, whom I sent for and whom I expect?" They nodded.

K.'s reaction to this is, again, this sort of pure-ostension-by-the-seat-of-its-pants that we have seen in Kafka before: specifically, we have seen it in a *Dienstmädchen* with no name who becomes "Rosa" after the narrator defines her, Goethe-style, as a rose about to be plucked ("A Country Doctor"). In a slightly different way—K. seeks, unsuccessfully, to exploit Artur and Jeremias, whereas the country doctor was at least passively concerned with Rosa's virtue—the Kafkan protagonist is very much making things up as he goes along, allowing his prior use (which he mistakes for a universal rule) of the gesture of ostension to create, ever so briefly, a reality where there is none: with "real" assistants, K. must then be the "real" *Landvermesser*, and his designation of Artur and Jeremias as "my old assistants" gestures weakly and shakily in that direction.[15] This impulse makes sense in a way—as nothing in the castle village has made sense to K. up until this point, he seems to see no reason why he can't just fudge his way into some assistants—but, in the end, his act of what J. L. Austin might call "illocutionary" ostension fails—Artur and Jeremias come from the Castle, and accomplish precisely the opposite of their name: "aber die Gehilfen . . . hinderten ihn daran durch ihre bloße aufdringliche Gegenwart" ("but the assistants . . . hindered him in this, simply by way of their meddlesome presence") (4:58).

Interestingly enough, it is not simply because the assistants are impish man-children that they fail to assist K. in the way he believes he needs to be legitimized in the village—it is, again, because K. himself fails to understand the upside-down way in which the word *Hilfe* in the village actually works. Like *Schloß*, it points not to the definition with which the average German speaker is familiar, but instead to another, haphazard and undermining form of "assistance," one that appears in K.'s meaning system to be hindrance, but that may very well according to Castle doctrine be helping.

But, despite the clues K. receives, it is necessarily impossible for him to understand this particular Castle doctrine—because, in effect, the cardinal rule of this doctrine is that it distrusts outsiders to the point of subverting their assumptions about how language works. We might now say that K. must simply connect the opposite signification of the Klamm figure to the opposite signification of the word *Gehilfe* and conclude that things in the village simply mean the opposite of his original referential expectation. But Wittgenstein would caution us severely, and remind us that what we have here is not a blueprint for a general form of Castle reverse ostension, but two particular cases that bear a "family resemblance" ("Familienähnlichkeit") to each other (§§65–81). To assume that a causal connection between them could solve the puzzle of the Castle's system would be to make a grievous error, as for every instance of opposite ostension he encounters, there is at least one competing instance in which the Castle culture undermines the act of reference in a completely new way.

Case Study 2: Telephones, Letters, Explanations

Several of exactly these instances occur when K. encounters three separate modes of communication in the village—the telephone, the written dispatch, and the act of explanation (which Wittgenstein has said all purported acts of "ostension" actually are). Unsurprisingly, each of these acts of purported communication actually undermines it rather than enabling it. As we have seen, a telephone conversation is the basis of K.'s first interaction—and altercation—with the officials of the Castle: Schwarzer makes a call to check out K.'s story; that story is at first roundly dismissed (hearing the laughter over the line, etc.), and then, in a separate call, unexpectedly confirmed (4:12). An unsuspecting outsider would assume, first, that the phone call was directed at the Castle itself; and, thereafter, that the second phone call came from the recipient of the first phone call. But these would be substantial misapprehensions based on a false understanding of how communication in the village works—just like roads that do not lead to the expected destination, and words that do not point to the expected definition, telephone lines again do not lead in a direct or expected fashion, providing another fascinating structural echo of the village's inscrutable system.

Instead of a "direct line" to the Castle, telephone "communication" there goes into a confusing void that seems designed specifically not to reach anyone directly. This Sussman attributes to Kafka's "aesthetics of confusion,"[16] an apt designation when attempting to parse the scene in which the mayor "clarifies" how the telephone works:

> "Und was das Telefon betrifft . . . Es gibt keine bestimmte telefonische Verbindung mit dem Schloß, keine Zentralstelle, welche unsere Anrufe weiterleitet; wenn man von hier aus jemanden im Schloß

> anruft, läutet es dort bei allen Apparaten der untersten Abteilungen oder vielmehr es würde bei allen läuten, wenn nicht, wie ich bestimmt weiß, bei fast allen dieses Läutwerk abgestellt wäre. Hie und da aber hat ein übermüdeter Beamter das Bedürfnis sich ein wenig zu zerstreuen—besonders am Abend oder bei Nacht—und schaltet das Läutwerk ein, dann bekommen wir Antwort, allerdings eine Antwort, die nichts ist als Scherz." (4:91)

> "And as to the telephone . . . there is no direct telephone connection with the Castle, no central location where our calls go. If we want to call someone in the Castle, all of the telephones in the lowest departments ring, or rather they should ring, but the ringer has been disabled on most of them. But now and then an overtired official will let his work go a bit—especially in the evening or late at night—and the ringer goes off, and we get an answer. However, this answer is usually nothing more than a joke."

Effectively, the initial call "proving" K.'s job was little more than a prank—which, because of its structural signals and the assumptions created by the existence of a telephone altogether, K. (and we) assumed instead was a sincere acknowledgment of credentials. Once again, K. is precluded from knowing this; whether the purpose of this preclusion is deserved punishment for his impostorish derring-do or undeserved punishment for a mild-mannered "actual" *Landvermesser* does not matter. What matters instead is: there is no way for K. to understand what it means to telephone somebody if, to echo the words of Wittgenstein, he does not understand what the gesture of telephoning actually entails.

Further, explains the mayor, not unlike the photo where Klamm originally appears to lie prone on a bench, "Alle diese Berührung sind nur scheinbar" ("All these contacts are only apparent") and, further, "Alle diese Äußerungen haben keine amtliche Bedeutung" ("All these appearances have no official meaning") (4:90, 92). And, further still, in what is tantamount to the mayor outright admitting that the village rejects the act of ostension: "Sie haben darin recht, daß man die Äußerungen des Schlosses nicht wortwörtlich hinnehmen darf" ("You are correct that one should not take the appearances regarding the Castle literally") (4:92).

The telephone was a rather newfangled device at the time Kafka wrote *The Castle*, and thus the idea that its lines reach arbitrary destinations is not terribly far-fetched even to a reader who still expects shades of realism in Kafka's work. The same cannot be said for the paper letter, at this time by far still the most popular and relied-upon means of distance communication, one that any Kafka enthusiast knows played a role in his life whose importance cannot be exaggerated (he sometimes sent two letters to Milena Jesenská in one day).[17] And yet, we see once again that letters—especially official letters, the currency of the Austro-Hungarian bureaucracy—do not seem to serve their expected purpose, instead working once again to muddle communication rather than enhance it.

One major example of this in *The Castle* is K.'s peculiar "communication" with Klamm, the highest-ranking Castle official that anyone in the village knows.[18] One might wonder why K. simply doesn't just give up, given how many words and gestures do refuse to mean what he expects them to—but remember, the reason he is so tempted to view these modes the way he wants to is that they use so many words and conventions he believes to be universally referential within his language (presumably German). Thus, because K. speaks German and the innkeepers also speak German, there is no discernible reason for him not to expect to be able to speak directly to Klamm.

Instead, Klamm is and remains unavailable, even with K.'s various entreaties to him, and the "responses" they provoke. And further, from the content of these "responses," it is actually impossible to determine whether they are indeed responses or simply prewritten letters to anyone who happens by claiming to be a *Landvermesser*, as they begin "Herr!" and contain neither K.'s name (initial) nor any identifying details of his predicament as cuckolder and school janitor. Take for example, K.'s first letter from Klamm, which he takes to be official confirmation of his position. Klamm writes:

> "Sie sind, wie Sie wissen, in die herrschaftlichen Dienste aufgenommen. Ihr nächster Vorgesetzter ist der Gemeindevorsteher des Dorfes, der Ihnen auch alles Nähere über Ihre Arbeit und die Lohnbedingungen mitteilen wird und dem Sie auch Rechenschaft schuldig sein werden. Trotzdem werde aber auch ich Sie nicht aus den Augen verlieren. Barnabas, der Überbringer dieses Briefes, wird von Zeit zu Zeit bei Ihnen nachfragen, um Ihre Wünsche zu erfahren und mir mitzuteilen. Sie werden mich immer bereit finden, Ihnen soweit es möglich ist, gefällig zu sein. Es liegt mir daran zufriedene Arbeiter zu haben." (4:33)

> "You have, as you know, been hired into the Count's service. Your nearest superior is the superintendent of the village, who will explain to you the conditions and particulars of your position, and to whom you will also be responsible for reporting. Nevertheless, I will also not lose sight of you. Barnabas, the bearer of this letter, will report to you now and then learn of your wishes and communicate them back to me. You will find that I am always ready to be of assistance to you, as much as this is possible. I endeavor to have satisfied workers."

Despite the letter's confusing lack of specificity ("in die herrschaftlichen Dienste"), K. takes it for official Castle correspondence—another mistake, as according to the mayor that letter is more of a personal letter, which carries both more and less significance than would an official one. Explains the mayor:

> "Dieser Brief ist überhaupt keine amtliche Zuschrift, sondern ein Privatbrief. Das ist schon an der Überschrift 'Sehr geehrter Herr!' deutlich erkennbar. Außerdem ist darin mit keinem Worte gesagt, daß Sie als Landvermesser aufgenommen sind, es ist vielmehr nur im allgemeinen von herrschaftlichen Diensten die Rede und auch das ist nicht bindend ausgesprochen, sondern Sie sind nur aufgenommen 'wie Sie wissen,' d.h. die Beweis lasst dafür daß Sie aufgenommen sind, ist Ihnen auferlegt. . . . daß Sie, ein Fremder, das nicht erkennen wundert mich nicht. Im ganzen bedeutet der Brief nichts anderes als daß Klamm persönlich sich um Sie zu kümmern beabsichtigt für den Fall, daß Sie in herrschaftliche Dienste aufgenommen werden." (4:89–90)

> "But this letter is not at all official correspondence, but rather a private letter. That is apparent in the salutation 'My dear Sir!' Besides this, it doesn't say anywhere that you have been taken on as land surveyor, the language in it is much more general about 'the Count's service.' And even this isn't binding language; rather, it says you've been taken on 'as you know'; that is, the proof that you've been taken on at all lies with you. . . . That you, a stranger, don't recognize this is no wonder. On the whole this whole letter means nothing other than that Klamm has the intention of looking out for you, should you be taken into official service."

Here the mayor outright says that K. as an outsider has no way of seeing how, and thus also what, the letter means—it turns out that the letter actually "means" quite a bit as a personal letter, but there is no way K. would have known that: "Ein Privatbrief Klamms hat natürlich viel mehr Bedeutung als eine amtliche Zuschrift, nur gerade die Bedeutung die Sie ihm beilegen hat er nicht" ("A private letter from Klamm has, of course, far more meaning than an official correspondence, just not the meaning that you think it has") (4:90). Thus the phrases for "official letter" and "personal letter" join the growing cohort of words and gestures that defy K.'s expected meaning—that, again, seem to be, as Wittgenstein would put it, variously interpretable in every case (and most definitely differently interpreted in this specific one).

Speaking of the mayor, let us not forget the curious set of letters that seem to have brought about K.'s predicament in the first place: there was the letter claiming the village did have need of a land surveyor, even though the village professes no need for one: "Vor langer Zeit, ich war damals erst einige Monate Vorsteher, kam ein Erlaß . . . daß ein Landvermesser berufen werden solle. . . . Dieser Erlaß kann natürlich nicht Sie betroffen haben" ("Long ago, I had only been mayor for a month, a notice came . . . that we should hire a land surveyor. . . . This notice could obviously not have been the one you got") (4:76). Then there was the subsequent letter claiming they were mistaken—which apparently reached the wrong department ("B," rather than the originating department, which the mayor calls "A" [4:79]).

As neither letter seemed to have reached its destination, this results in the final and most intimate instance of anti-communication in *The Castle*: the act of face-to-face direct explanation, which instead actually works to obscure the act of explanation. Not unlike the painter Titorelli's "explanation" of the modes of acquittal in *The Trial*, the mayor most certainly fails to explain to K.'s satisfaction the predicament in which he finds himself (if, indeed, he is an actual land surveyor who was actually summoned to the Castle; this scene provides the most convincing evidence of Kafka's masterful ambiguity). The mayor professes to tell K. the "unangenehme Wahrheit" ("uncomfortable truth") of his situation, which is this:

> "Sie sind als Landvermesser aufgenommen, wie Sie sagen, aber, leider, wir brauchen keinen Landvermesser. Es wäre nicht die geringste Arbeit für ihn da. Die Grenzen unserer kleinen Wirtschaften sind abgesteckt, alles ist ordentlich eingetragen, Besitzwechsel kommt kaum vor und kleine Grenzstreitigkeiten regeln wir selbst. Was soll uns also ein Landvermesser?" (75)

> "You are hired as land surveyor, as you say, but unfortunately we don't need one. There wouldn't be the least bit of work for one here. The borders of our little businesses are well defined, everything has been recorded in an orderly manner, changes in possession happen almost never, and we regulate all small border disputes ourselves. What good would a land surveyor be for us?"

K. replies that he can only hope there has been some sort of misunderstanding; "Leider nicht," replies the mayor, "es ist so, wie ich sage" ("it's exactly how I say it is") (4:75). This situation, now so convoluted as to have made a full circle back to the first page of the novel while affecting no substantial change to the situation, brings us back through the closed-off system of "communication" in the village and once again to the designator *Landvermesser*, whose fate is now more clearly sealed. That is, not only does the designation *Landvermesser* not at all mean in the way K. thinks it should or wants it to, but it turns out it does not point to anything or anybody, since the Castle never wanted someone to actually survey their land in the first place.

And yet, the problem here isn't how all these things point or fail to point, as Wittgenstein has shown that to be necessarily impossible to determine, as that would involve charting out a system of ostension that would be universally applicable in this community. However, the only certainty available to an outsider of the community's system seems instead to be the acknowledgment of a rejection of that very applicability, and nothing beyond that. Thus the real problem is that as an outsider who cannot parse what the later

Wittgenstein would call the "family resemblances" or join the "forms of life" in the village (see chapter 6 for further discussion of these two terms), K. lacks the ability even to understand why it is that he doesn't understand anything there. He chooses instead, mistakenly, to blame a vast and untenable bureaucracy that he believes he could navigate if only he were allowed. But it is not a question of being allowed, it is a question of understanding *how*. And this, K. never manages to figure out.

Conclusion

One of the most important later developments in Wittgenstein's career was the rejection of the notion of "progress" altogether. In the particular case of *The Castle*, this also very much seems to include the "progression" through the act of figuring out how an unfamiliar system works—at every step of K.'s navigation of the system, his progress certainly appeared greater than it actually was. The act of progress itself was perhaps the greatest illusion of all, one brought to life in K.'s initial failed and exhausting walk through the snowy village. For Wittgenstein, all that is left to do, all that can be done, is—ironically enough—to survey the landscape. For K., even that is too much to ask.

Let us return for a moment to the scene wherein K. is discussing the mysterious photograph of a young Klamm with the landlady. During their conversation, she scolds K. in a way that actually reveals more about the structure and modes of communication in the village than it does scold—if only K. would listen correctly. What she tells him is this: "Sie mißdeuten alles, auch das Schweigen" ("You misunderstand everything, even silence") (4:101). The landlady's use of *deuten* (to interpret) here, taken together with Wittgenstein's assertion that "hinweisende Definition kann in jedem Fall so und anders *gedeutet* werden" (emphasis mine), sums up perfectly the hopelessness of K. as an outsider ever understanding the trick signifiers of the village: even (and especially) silence, the lack of language, can be—and is—interpreted variously in every case. And the landlady is not wrong: K. has in fact already misunderstood (and then misused) silence at least once prior to this event: early on in his time in the village, he sets off with Barnabas under the mistaken impression that Barnabas is about to deliver K.'s message directly to the Castle, and instead ends up at Barnabas's home, thereby also putting him in cahoots with one of the village's most shunned families. Frustrated, K. chides Barnabas: "'So,' sagte K., 'Du wolltest nicht ins Schloß gehen, nur hierher . . . warum hast Du mir das nicht gesagt?'" To which Barnabas replies simply, "'Du hast mich nicht gefragt'" ("'So,' said K., 'you didn't want to go to the Castle, only to here. Why didn't you tell me?' . . . 'You didn't ask'") (4:42).

Yes, K. misinterprets everything, silence and words; this happens too many times in the novel to count, but arguably the most glaring instance comes in

K.'s revelations during the mayor's convoluted "explanation:" "Ein Mißverständnis war es also gewesen, ein gemeines, niedriges Mißverständnis und K. hatte sich ihm gar hingegeben" ("So it had all been a misunderstanding, a common, vulgar misunderstanding, and K. had bought it completely") (4:42). Again, there was no way for K. to have known that the village had previously both requested and canceled a request for a land surveyor with no prior experience with the Castle culture. For, of course, to know what anything means there, one must first know how meaning there works; effectively, to know how anything works there one must first already know how everything works there. *The Castle* is, in short, among other things (a curious depiction of female sexuality, a frustrating sketch of the act of exclusivity itself), a tremendously successful dramatization of the paradox of ostensive definition: a word or phrase can be variously interpreted in every case if one does not already understand the system to which that gesture belongs, and K.'s plight shows just how dire our deluded belief in successful ostension can be.

Thus, the "moral" to *The Castle*, if there is one, is more than simply to beware untenable bureaucracies if one is an outsider, or to beware the wishes to assimilate oneself in a foreign society as an impostor, lest one get one's wish. Above all these, I believe, is a different moral: there is no way to learn the ways of a place like the Castle village—or, if we extend our understanding of exclusivity to other Kafka works as a trope, of a place like the Court. Instead, either one knows them innately or inherently, or one is forever destined to be on the outside even when one is so fully enmeshed there seems no hope for extrication. In the end, Kafka has provided a more compelling language game to illustrate Wittgenstein's paradox of ostensive definition than Wittgenstein himself did.

So what remains? If language doesn't "work" ostensively, then (how) does it work? In a word: *use*. That is, language "works" through use in a particular case that its users *feel* they understand or don't:

> Man kann für eine große Klasse von Fällen der Benützung des Wortes "Bedeutung"—Wenn auch nicht für alle Fälle seiner Benützung—dieses Wort so erklären: Die Bedeutung eines Wortes ist sein Gebrauch in der Sprache. (§43)
>
> For a large class of cases—though not for all—in which we employ the word "meaning" it can be defined thus: the meaning of a word is its use in the language.

In the particular case of *The Castle*, Kafka's triumphantly vacuous use of the word *Landvermesser*, as well as his intricate structure of a language community whose language is on the surface identical to that of the outsider K., but which in reality demands a priori understanding of its (completely different) systems as a prerequisite for ever understanding any of its systems, demonstrate the paradox of ostensive definition with astonishing might—for what better way to grasp the full uselessness of an ostensive gesture than with a vast network of miscommunication between people who ostensibly speak the same language? The only feasible solution to this paradox, according to Wittgenstein, is the above discovery, the hallmark of what is now called "ordinary language philosophy," the idea that language takes meaning not from an a priori or universal system of logic, but from repeated and agreed-upon use. We may be unsurprised to discover that Wittgenstein ultimately rejects the meaning-in-use "solution" as well—what may be surprising is that this very rejection also appears in one of Kafka's best-known works.

Chapter 5

✦

Rule-Following and Failed Execution: "In the Penal Colony"

If the *Philosophical Investigations* ended after §43, Wittgenstein's brevity would usher in both good news and bad. The good news: Wittgenstein would finally have presented us with a theory of language with no caveats. With the meaning of language now definitively determined through its use, the picture theory of the *Tractatus* would have been discarded and replaced with this viable new theory. The bad news would be that Wittgenstein would be proven a hypocrite, as his insistence that this work does not advance philosophical theses would have been soundly disproven by a philosophical thesis. Fortunately for Wittgenstein's cohesion, but unfortunately for our desire for a theory of language that works, the paradox of ostensive definition is but the first of the *Investigations*' many such revelations of the delusions under which language users continually labor. In fact, its unmasking leads directly into a new and more complex unmasking: one that effectively dismantles §43 soon after introducing it. This comes in §201, the culminating remark in what philosophers commonly call the paradox of rule-following. The following chapter will bring this second major paradox together with one of Kafka's most paradoxical stories, "In der Strafkolonie" ("In the Penal Colony"). In the course of the chapter, I hope to show that this story is not paradoxical in the way we assume it is—that is, because its torture machine fails to do the only thing it is supposed to do—but in an entirely new way that we can only understand in light of Wittgenstein's rule-following remarks.

This chapter is also an exploration of Kafka's powerful and resonant failure as a prose narrator—at least when it comes to one major work. The point of departure for a meditation on Kafka as a failure is, undoubtedly, Benjamin's statement that the "beauty" and "purity" of his work is "die von einem Gescheiterten" ("that of a failure").[1] Here we will not concern ourselves as much with *why* his work exemplifies the beauty and purity of failure, but rather *how* it accomplishes such a task, and how once again Wittgenstein's philosophy fits in with this dubious accomplishment.

Narration, Description, and "Murder, Pure and Simple"

Until its penultimate scene, what we have assumed to be the previous narrative progression of "In the Penal Colony" leads us to believe that its "eigentümlicher Apparat" ("remarkable apparatus"), whose adulatory officer opens the story by observing it with a "gewissermaßen bewundernden Blick" ("certain look of wonder") despite how "doch wohlbekannt" ("nevertheless well known") it is, works in a certain way. Instead, it apparently malfunctions and impales its greatest adherent in what the visiting explorer terms "unmittelbarer Mord," murder pure and simple (*GW* 1:161, 192). Critical interpretation of "In the Penal Colony," and especially this act, has purported it to mean many things: the terminal existential guilt of man and the struggles with creation of the "true self" (Sokel); Kafka's own desire to purge himself and his writing of late-Hapsburg decadence and degeneracy (Anderson); cultural hybridity and the violence of the colonized body (Goebel); the writing or artistic-creation process in general (Danielle Allen, Andreas Gailus, Richard Jayne); Kafka's specific writing process with respect to a single work (Corngold); violent metaphors for the onset of modern technology (Kittler); the act of reading (Koelb); and, in Heinz Politzer's classic *Parable and Paradox*, no less than "the inevitability of fate" itself.[2] Or, as Anderson describes the situation using a reference to the visiting explorer (*Forschungsreisende*) and one of his earliest gestures in the face of the colony's punishing sun, the story has understandably

> provoked a series of allegorical readings which, like a shielding hand over the eyes or an averted gaze, shifted attention away from the first and literal level of the story, away from its troubling surfaces, in an attempt to get behind or beyond this level and understand its "deeper" significance.[3]

The investigation that follows is a journey filled with denial and disappointment, foremost but not solely for those seeking to understand the story's "deeper" significance. For just as Gregor's metaphorical collapse upon himself in *The Metamorphosis* transformed our conceptions of static metaphorical meaning and solid metaphorical structure, so will the theory of meaning in use, also portrayed in the world of Kafka's prose narration, ultimately fail. This will take place in Kafka's penal colony, in the form of a fascinating conflation of Kafka's exquisitely failed narrative execution of the officer's failed literal execution:

> Die Egge schrieb nicht, sie stach nur, und das Bett wälzte den Körper nicht, sondern hob ihn nur zitternd in die Nadeln hinein. Der Reisende wollte eingreifen, möglicherweise das Ganze zum Stehen bringen, das war ja keine Folter, wie sie der Offizier erreichen wollte, das war unmittelbarer Mord. (1:192)

> The Harrow didn't write at all, but rather just stabbed, and the Bed did not turn his body over, but rather just lifted it, shaking, up closer to the needles. The explorer wanted to reach in, possibly to bring the whole thing to a stop—this was not the torture the officer so wanted to bring about; it was murder, pure and simple.

As many astute voices in literary theory have pointed out, among them Klaus Scherpe in a highly convincing reexamination of Georg Lukács's theories of modernism and critical realism, in writing the story's climax the way he has, Kafka has triumphantly destabilized the very notion of prose narration itself, and any meaning we may have mistakenly attempted to derive from it (or more specifically, as Scherpe writes, any "sense": "Eine Erzählung, so sagt man, macht Sinn und dessen sind wir bedürftig" ["A narration, so we say, makes sense and this is something we need"]).[4] In his "Penal Colony," however, Kafka sabotages any chance of an objective progression of a narration—the presence of which, Lukács has famously argued, makes Thomas Mann's work a triumphant work of critical realism, in comparison to Kafka's decadent modernism, which contains its own highly unreliable subjectivity.[5] Scherpe points out that Kafka's alleged work of prose narration actually fails to unfold a traditional narrative progression, this being due to the primacy of description, which Scherpe contrasts with the progress of narration as such:

> [Die Beschreibung] macht in besonderer Weise aufmerksam auf die Dinge, die Natur, die Landschaften, die Menschen, auch das Nicht-Menschliche, das Anorganische. Auch auf Geschichte? Nicht auf Geschichte im Fortschritt der Zeit, sondern im Räumlichen von Flachen und Figuren.[6]
>
> [Description] makes us aware, in a particular way, of things—nature, landscape, humans, also the non-human, the inorganic. Also aware of (hi)story? Not of history in the sense of the progress of time, but rather in the sense of space, of planes and forms.

Whereas a successful (or, at any rate, realistic) narrative places events in a sequence with the express purpose of allowing the reader to make sense of them, description creates a story (*Geschichte*) that is not necessarily a history (also *Geschichte*), in that it does not make an authoritative claim to objective time or reality, nor to any sort of explanation. Whereas narration concerns itself with such preoccupations as "chronology and causality," description "studies the things." The reader of a description, as opposed to a blatant narration, "erwartet nicht das Ende, sondern die nächsten Worte, im Prinzip ad infinitum" ("does not expect the end, but rather the next words, in principle ad infinitum").[7] As we will soon see in more detail, the officer's description of how the machine should work hijacks almost the entire story, and thus also does away with any reasonable expectations of narrative causality. This has the confounding effect of making the climactic event more nonsensical rather than more explicable; and further, Scherpe argues that the officer's failed execution is an apt demonstration of this overly descriptive character describing his way to his own death.[8] Scherpe as well has little concern over "what" this gesture means, and is instead interested in how it means. While description is a process (*Beschreibungsverfahren*), narration is a progress; further, Kafka's officer's descriptive process in the penal colony seems to work in dramatic rejection of narrative progress: the "substance" of description ("Ihre Sache") is "die Zuständlichkeit und nicht der Progress, das Fortschreiten einer Handlung. Die Beschreibung operiert in der 'Auszeit,' der Erzählung; sie sistiert die Handlung" ("the cognizance and not the progress, the progression of a plot. Description operates in the 'time-out' of the narration; it suspends the plot").[9] While this does not necessarily take place in the authorial voice in Kafka's story, a similar movement does occur as the result of the dominance of one character's description, and the responsibility given to that description to "narrate" important past events. The ability of description to eclipse narration in Kafka's colony is, then, the embrace of *situation*—the painful and protracted awareness of the condition one is presently in—rather than progress, which as Wittgenstein (via Nestroy) has reminded us, always looks greater than it really is. The conundrum upon which I would like to focus here in the Kafka text deals with exactly this: progress, or the delusionary nature thereof. And while Wittgenstein works through the *Investigations* with the coy goal of undermining the conceit of philosophical progress (a trajectory I explore in great detail in chapter 6), the progress that Kafka begins to dismantle in "In the Penal Colony" is narrative progress.

As we will see, Kafka's mastery in crafting "In the Penal Colony" lies in appearing to tell a story but really doing something else, much like in crafting Gregor Samsa's transformation, he appeared to create a metaphor but really did something else. This time, he has created something that takes the shape of a narration and creates the expectation of one. But the narration of "In the Penal Colony" does not actually make sense of anything, but rather makes things more obscure, offers static and arresting descriptions of things and actions that seem to be floating in space. We know Wittgenstein's problem with philosophical progress; now I venture that for Kafka, or at the very least for "In the Penal Colony," the problem with narrative progress is that it also, contrary to Lukács, seems greater than it really is. All of this comes to light when we view Kafka's story alongside the paradox of rule-following.

Revisiting the Paradox of Ostension: The Case of the *Zeichner*

In order to see why the paradox of rule-following even arises as in Kafka's penal colony, we must first revisit the paradox that precedes it—that of ostensive language, which itself leads to the "meaning in use" argument of §43. As in *The Castle*, "In the Penal Colony" offers a remarkably astute take-down of ostension, with which I believe Wittgenstein would be impressed despite his professed dislike of Kafka's fiction. In addition to being prescient, "In the Penal Colony's" dismantling of ostension could not be more apt, for it comes in the breakdown of the apparatus's component known in English as the "Designer," and in German, *Zeichner*.

I will continue to use the German here, as the English fails to betray the orthographic relationship between the verb *zeichnen* (to sketch, to draw) and *Zeichen* (a sign or symbol). Indeed, the alleged literal purpose of the *Zeichner is* to be a "sign maker," to create the shape of the text that is to be written upon the body of the condemned—to de-sign (*zeichnen*), to create the *Zeichen* that is meant somehow to signify (*be-zeichnen*) the law the condemned has transgressed. As, following Wittgenstein's interpretation of Augustine (see chapter 4), the first users of human language gave primacy to ostension, so does the officer give primacy to the ostensive purpose of the machine—the *Zeichner* must work *first* in order for the rest of the execution to be carried out. Further, the officer's description *of* the *Zeichner* must succeed in order for the narrative to proceed.

The problem that arises here is that either the *Zeichner* does not seem to work the way the explorer expects it to, or the officer has not described its working satisfactorily; either way, progress has been hampered (either narrative, cognitive on the part of the explorer, or both). This is because the condemned's sentence remains (at least in the explorer's understanding) incomprehensible to him. For it is de-signed/*gezeichnet* in the "special" language of the deceased old commandant; the explorer cannot even make out the characters that the machine is actually supposed to carve into the condemned's body, which he recognizes only as "labyrinthartige, einander vielfach kreuzende Linien, die so dicht das Papier bedeckten, daß man nur mit Mühe die weißen Zwischenräume erkannte" ("lines that crisscrossed each other labyrinth-like, and covered the paper so thickly that one could only see the white space between them if one looked very closely") (*GW* 1:172).

It is therefore not difficult to understand why the officer's description of the *Zeichner* might not sit right with the explorer (who, throughout the acts of description, remains "nicht befriedigt" or "unsatisfied" [1:169]). As with the word *Landvermesser* (or *Schloß*, or *Dorf*) in *The Castle*, some sort of alternative understanding would predicate a definition (or at least use) of the concepts of *Zeichen*, *zeichnen*, and *bezeichnen* with which the explorer seems unfamiliar. Again, in a result Wittgenstein would deem inevitable, it is impossible for the explorer to discern what the primary act of the machine does because he is not already familiar with its system, with *how* it does what it does. And yet, in Kafka's officer's lengthy and passionate description of the machine, at no time does he truly succeed in showing *how* the machine works.

For the machine's actions to make sense, they cannot simply be described: they must be removed from the officer's descriptive control and instead be the fictional equivalent of "shown in action." This has, at this point in the story, necessarily not occurred, and thus the true purpose and workings of the machine remain mysterious to both the explorer and the reader. In other words: the real "meaning" the machine offers—despite the efforts of the officer to describe it or the *Zeichner* to write or communicate a sentence, both grammatical and penal—comes *only* in its use. And this the officer admits when he explains that the condemned "experiences" the sentence "on his body"—but again, even this "experience" is related in an act of description rather than a narrative experience, and thus still remains obscure:

> "Kennt er sein Urteil?" "Nein," sagte der Offizier und wollte gleich in seinen Erklärungen fortfahren, aber der Reisende unterbrach ihn: "Er kennt sein eigenes Urteil nicht?" "Nein," sagte der Offizier wieder, stockte dann einen Augenblick, als verlange er vom Reisenden eine nähere Begründung seiner Frage, und sagte dann: "es wäre nutzlos, es ihm zu verkündigen. Er erfährt es ja auf seinem Leib." Der Reisende wollte schon verstummen. (1:167)

> "Does he know his sentence?" "No," said the officer, wanting to continue right along with his explanation, but the explorer interrupted him: "He doesn't know his own sentence?" "No," said the officer again, and paused a moment, as if he were requesting from the explorer a more detailed reason for his question, before saying: "it would be useless to avail him of that information. He will experience it on his body." The explorer thought it best to stay quiet.

"Er erfährt es ja auf seinem Leib"—how exactly? Many in the theoretical community posit that the old commandant's language and its method of "communication" are simply a new and different kind of writing. Kittler argues this "neue Art zu schreiben erzeugt ein anderes System der Macht" ("new way of writing creates a different system of power"), which to him is a system of technology-based recording of language, a technology-driven power that makes the new kind of writing possible.[10] Gailus, on the other hand, places primacy on the prisoner's sentence being communicated not onto the body but rather "*through* the body," and that justice or the law can then be "deciphered through the pain of a body subjected to mechanical torture."[11] For Allen's silence thesis, however, the machine's writing causes *non-language*, a silence by way of succumbing to the machine's might through both the gagging of the prisoner and the content of the old commandant's "opaque script," which Allen sees as being "as good as silence" because the explorer claims he cannot read it.[12]

Yet all of these theories must remain purely in the esoteric realm, for as the notion of experiencing a sentence on the prisoner's body is never actually experienced and only described, we never see a prisoner experience the law in any of the ways he "should." There is no actual narrated intersection of the "symbolic and somatic," nor a sacralization of silent acquiescence, nor an epiphany of the "master signifier" of justice, because we never see a prisoner executed. All we see of the prisoner are the pre-execution and post-release versions of him, and in his pre-execution stage he appears ignorant of both the content and form of his execution—evident by his eerie mimicry of the officer's movements: "Er beugte sich hierhin und dorthin. Immer wieder lief er mit den Augen das Glas ab" ("He bent himself this way and that way, the whole time following the movements of the glass with his eyes") (1:171).

What the prisoner seems to be doing here is a continuation of his daily life (the saluting of the captain's door on the hour), which consists of *training*. Training is, of course, the method, rather than ostension, whereby Wittgenstein claims human beings learn a first language (*PI* §5). But the trouble is that there is an obvious potential disjunction between simply being *trained* to do something and understanding what that gesture means.

So how, then, does the prisoner "understand" something on his body? By "Er erfährt es ja auf seinem Leib" the officer seems to be claiming that a penal sentence receives meaning *in its use*, not unlike Wittgenstein argues of a grammatical sentence in §43. In the case of Kafka's colony, the (penal and also allegedly grammatical) sentence the officer so painstakingly and yet obscurely describes only receives meaning in *its* use in its context: that is, not its use in language ("sein Gebrauch in der Sprache") but rather, so to speak, its *Gebrauch in der Strafe*, or use in the punishment. And this is dependent upon the bringing about of a specifically prescribed dose of pain, which the victim is supposed to feel in a specific way and, in this specific use of the old commandant's language, "understand" and "decipher" its meaning:

> Verstand geht dem blödesten auf. Um die Augen beginnt es. Von hier aus verbreitet es sich. Ein Anblick, der einen verführen könnte, sich mit unter die Egge zu legen. Es geschieht ja nichts weiter, der Mann fängt bloß an, die Schrift zu entziffern. Er spitzt den Mund, als horchte er. Sie haben gesehen, es ist nicht leicht, die Schrift mit den Augen zu entziffern; unser Mann entziffert sie aber mit seinen Wunden. Es ist allerdings viel Arbeit; er braucht sechs Stunden zu ihrer Vollendung. (1:173)

> Understanding dawns on even the dumbest ones. It begins around the eyes. From here it spreads. A look that could tempt one to lie down on the Harrow beside him. Nothing else happens—it's just that the man begins to decipher the script. He purses his lips as if he were

> listening. You have seen that it's not easy to decipher the script with your eyes: our man deciphers it with his wounds. It's obviously a lot of work; it requires six hours to complete.

It is as if the officer expects that his description will itself cause an understanding of the machine's working, a "deciphering" of *its* seemingly altered semiotic function, to dawn upon the explorer, who surely must be brighter than the dumbest of prisoners. And yet the secondhand experience of the machine, as relayed by its most passionate and possibly unreliable adherent, is not sufficient to grant the explorer "understanding," nor does he seem to be pressured into feigning it under implied threat of being considered dull-witted by the same dubious source. It seems instead that any sort of meaning—traditional, altered, as an object of description—offered by either the *Zeichner* or the officer's description of it and its surrounding components is useless without the prior experience of the machine in use, which is nominally impossible (after all, the officer insists on describing the machine first [1:164]). Allegedly there has been prior experience of the machine in *correct* use. However, a major problem in accepting this prior use as evidence of correct use is that said correct use takes place entirely outside the narrative space, and evidence of its existence comes from a remarkably dubious source: the officer. The experience of the machine in use during a "successful" execution (that is, one that takes place in the manner the officer describes them) would itself constitute an act of what Scherpe has called successful narration (events that take place over a period of narrated time and that allow the reader to make sense of what is happening).

But in Kafka's story no such execution takes place. Neither, then, does the execution of a narrative, in the sense of "precise completion." The only execution that takes place is the metaphorical execution of the act of narration; in carrying out this execution instead of the others, Kafka has brought about several potential conflicts while simultaneously avoiding the successful bestowing of meaning or sense upon the machine destined instead to remain opaque, disjunctive, seemingly nonsensical, and thus potentially meaningless. In *The Metamorphosis* we discovered a metaphor that had the shape, trajectory, and necessity of a metaphor but no actual metaphorical content. So, too, does the execution (penal, narrative) in Kafka's colony reveal itself to be starkly different from the form it appears to take. In replacing the narration of an actual execution with the description of an alleged execution (and thus the "execution" of narration), Kafka has brought the following seemingly stable elements of his story into contention: first, despite the officer's painstaking description of the machine, we still have no idea whether or not an execution means in the way the officer claims it means, whether or not a prisoner can truly experience the understanding on his body. This is, further, a problem neither solved (on a nonmetaphorical level) by literary criticism, nor *dis*solved in a Wittgensteinian manner. But the Wittgenstein text is far from irrelevant, because as we are about to see, the lack of narrated evidence of the machine in prior successful use—seen through the lens of the paradox of rule-following—allows us to question as forcefully as possible whether such an execution has ever even taken place at all.

Rule-Following and the Execution of Sense

In connecting the officer's explanation that the condemned experiences his sentence on his body with Wittgenstein's assertion in §43 that for a large class of words the meaning of a word *is its use* in language, an incompatibility or contradiction appeared when it became apparent that any "use" of the penal colony's machine that has the potential to grant it meaning takes place outside the narrative space and is thus useless for our purposes. Or rather, this "use" takes place outside the narrative space *if it takes place at all.* Here we will bring in another of Wittgenstein's paradoxes to shed light on the fascinating implications of this very real uncertainty.

Let us return to the previously discussed moment in which the officer describes a penal colony execution to the explorer (1:167–69). He begins by claiming that the method of execution does not sound particularly harsh, and then elaborates:

> "Dem Verurteilten wird das Gebot, das er übertreten hat, mit der Egge auf den Leib geschrieben. Diesem Verurteilten zum Beispiel"—der Offizier zeigte auf den Mann—"wird auf den Leib geschrieben werden: Ehre deinen Vorgesetzten!" (1:167).

> "The command that the condemned has transgressed will be written by the Harrow upon his body. On this one, for example"—the officer pointed to the man, "will be written: Honor thy Superiors!"

Much of what appears in this interaction consists of the explorer voicing his expectations to the officer, and then reacting with dissatisfaction, a dynamic that becomes apparent when the officer answers the explorer's follow-up question ("Aber daß er überhaupt verurteilt wurde, das weiß er doch?" ["But he knows that he's been sentenced in the first place, doesn't he?"]):

> "Auch nicht," sagte der Offizier und lächelte den Reisenden an, als erwarte er nun von ihm noch einige sonderbare Eröffnungen. "Nein," sagte der Reisende und strich sich über die Stirn hin, "dann weiß also der Mann auch jetzt noch nicht, wie seine Verteidigung aufgenommen wurde?" "Er hat keine Gelegenheit gehabt, sich zu verteidigen," sagte der Offizier. (1:167)

> "No, he doesn't know that either," said the officer and smiled at the explorer, as if he expected from him yet more special revelations. "No?" said the explorer, rubbing his forehead, "so the man also doesn't know how his defense was received?" "He has had no opportunity to defend himself," said the officer.

This results in the moment I have already referenced: the explorer is unsatisfied, and he continues not to be satisfied when the officer shows him the transparent Harrow with its long needles that "write" and shorter ones that squirt liquid to clean away the blood, so that the sentence always remains "klar zu erhalten" ("clear to make out") (1:170). The trouble here is that the old commandant's "scripture" is not—given what the explorer seems to expect from the word "klar" and the word "erhalten"—"klar zu erhalten."

Scherpe's notwithstanding, much analysis of this moment tends to bypass the fairly obvious presence here of a description that makes for quite a dissatisfactory explanation. Instead, many critics understandably concentrate on the perceived juridical impropriety described, best exemplified in the officer's proclamation that "Die Schuld ist immer zweifellos" ("Guilt is never to be doubted") (1:168). Koelb, for example, sees the disconnect or lack of clarity in both the old commandant's writing and its assumed manifestation on a prisoner's body as itself the point of the story, which is the "act of reading" rather than writing.[13] He sees the central act of the story as the "scene of reading" (after Derrida); the "successful" application of the penal sentence is actually "the embodiment of the intellectual reproduction that we ordinarily call 'reading.' "[14] And by "reading" Koelb actually means a struggle between what Derrida has characterized as two types of reading, the first being "deciphering," which "escapes play" and "the order of the sign," and the other kind, which is "no longer turned toward the origin, affirms play and tries to pass beyond man and humanism" by way of Nietzsche and the "joyous affirmation of the world and of the innocence of becoming."[15] Koelb argues, then, that while the explorer seems dissatisfied because he cannot "decipher" the old commandant's writing nor can he figure out how the prisoner is supposed to experience an epiphany "with his wounds," his problem is not that he lacks the experience that would make such deciphering possible, but instead that the kind of "reading" a user or beholder of the machine must undertake is actually this second, Derridean type of reading.

All this seems to be criticism applied to the machine in its state of working *correctly*—but again, this is a state that is only described to us secondhand; it is a moment of action the explorer does not witness and an act of narration we do not witness. Where, then, is the proof that this state of working correctly exists at all? The sole instance during which we *and* the explorer actually see the machine in action is its alleged malfunction. As we now explore the officer's suicide—one of the story's few moments that resembles traditional narration—uncertainty about whether the machine ever has worked in the manner in which the officer describes should emerge.

One of the first indications that the execution may not go according to plan comes when the officer complains that he overheard the new commandant's words of invitation to the explorer and that he understood "sofort, was er mit der Einladung bezweckte" ("immediately what was meant by that invitation") (1:179–80). In this moment the officer takes great care to emphasize that his act of reaching out is not an institutional or "community" act. Rather, it complicates the community dynamic more than anything else:

> "Wenn ich eine Meinung aussprechen würde, so wäre es die Meinung eines Privatmannes, um nichts bedeutender als die Meinung eines beliebigen anderen, und jedenfalls viel bedeutungsloser als die Meinung des Kommandanten." (1:181)

> "If I share an opinion here, it's the opinion of a private citizen, no more significant than anyone else's, and in any case far less significant than that of the Commandant."

Although the officer insists that there are indeed adherents to the old commandant throughout the colony (they are simply silent), there is really only a "private citizen" self-described to legitimize the antiquated method of execution. This moment in the narrative will become crucial after the officer has died and the explorer stumbles upon the sole piece of evidence that there had potentially been a community with a shared "understanding" of the old method of execution, a particular "form of life" (*Lebensform*), as Wittgenstein will call it (§§19, 23, 241).

But for now, let us take the officer at his word as a "Privatmann." The officer's status as a lone "private citizen" is what some critics, Sokel and autobiographical adherents foremost among them, argue makes him "special" and thus also have a strong affinity to his creator, "creator" being used in a loose sense to describe the old commandant whom, it goes almost without saying, we also never truly encounter in the textual space.[16] And when this "specialness" is challenged? First, the officer suggests to the explorer that, should anyone in the outside world ask, he shouldn't lie about his opinions, if indeed he does believe what he has witnessed is barbaric, but could he not simply omit his judgment (1:183)? Since the explorer seems not to "understand" the machine, would it really be too much trouble for him to grant the officer what Allen terms the silence of assent, a sort of perverted version of *TLP* 7, "Wovon man nicht sprechen kann, darüber muss man schweigen"? This the explorer will not do, and thus the officer apparently decides to sacrifice himself to the machine. Here we have what is arguably the most easily understandable gesture in the story—a gesture which also happens to be one of the most strongly narrated rather than described, as the sense of objective time, of moving forward, of action suddenly becomes utterly sharp, if not also utterly devoid of context: the officer, who has until now shown himself to be a barbaric and irrational person searching for approval, makes a desperate overture and reacts to rejection of that overture in a proportionately barbaric manner. In fact, this seems to be a sole provoked payoff in an otherwise causality-bereft narrative universe. To be sure, this payoff is bitter and bloody: the punisher becomes the punished—but it is easily understood, given this context, where the officer's love affair with torture was bound to lead to some sort of violent consummation.

Thus it is only surprising in the way alleged twist endings in all *narrative* (i.e., sense-making) fiction are surprising when the explorer tells the officer he cannot comply with the odd request to further the old commandant's agenda through silence, and then the officer says that "now it's time" ("Dann ist es also Zeit"), and proceeds to free the prisoner and prepare to execute himself (1:186). The officer rearranges the designer to "spell" out a new sentence, which the officer must "translate" for the explorer's benefit: "'Sei Gerecht!' heißst es," sagte er, 'jetzt können Sie es doch lesen'" ("'Be just!' it says," he said, "'surely now you can read it'") (1:187). But, unfortunately, the officer's twelve hours of epiphany do not occur. Instead, as we have seen before, the Harrow fails to write, the officer is simply impaled in a gruesome act the explorer terms "murder, pure and simple" (1:192).

What is at first apparent is that the twist in the plot has twisted again, this time not quite so understandably. The officer's execution fails—according to all prescriptions by the officer himself of what would in this context constitute "success"—to result in him "deciphering" "sei gerecht" on his body. So, then, what has happened must be dramatic irony: the officer has failed in the very gesture of sacrificing himself to his own machine, because the machine didn't work in the way he claimed it would. However, dramatic irony only itself works if the machine did indeed malfunction—but did it? In fact, to reiterate the earlier problem of "The Judgment," most possible interpretations of "In the Penal Colony" only seem to "work" when the act of the officer's suicide is judgeable, and thus judged—nonsensical, ironic, symbolic, fateful, anything. Here I would like to offer a counter-argument: that the story "works," thanks in part to its clever subversion of the narrative medium, largely allowing narration to be eclipsed with the officer's lengthy descriptions up until the moment he decides to end his own life, by *disallowing* that gesture any sort of interpretive judgment, any sort of sense-making privilege the successfully executed narrative might normally bring. Any judgment of the action as ironic, symbolic, fateful, or otherwise is predicated on the recognition of the final "twist" in the plot: that the machine failed or malfunctioned, that it did not work in the way it was supposed to work. The problem with this is that there is actually no irrefutable textual evidence that the machine has ever worked the way it was "supposed" to work. Instead, it is possible to argue that the machine simply did what it was "supposed" to do when its most passionate adherent turned it on himself.

This discovery—that it is impossible to prove the validity of a prescription for how something is "supposed" to go, most commonly referred to as a "rule"—is at the heart of Wittgenstein's paradox of rule-following, which comprises the approximately one hundred remarks up to and including §201, and further complicates development on the previously discussed paradox of ostension (and that of "explanation" or logic, which we have not discussed here). As such the paradox unfolds in a similar way: through demonstration in a complex language game, it is shown that this particular construct of language (the concept that one might "follow a rule" set forth *in* language) does not actually work—because in order to understand how it works, *one must already know how it works*:

> Unser Paradox war dies: eine Regel könnte keine Handlungsweise bestimmen, da jede Handlungsweise mit der Regel in Übereinstimmung zu bringen sei. Die Antwort war: Ist jede mit der Regel in Übereinstimmung zu bringen, dann auch zum Widerspruch. Daher gäbe es hier weder Übereinstimmung noch Widerspruch. (§201a)
>
> Our paradox was this: no behavior could be determined by a rule, because all behavior can be made to agree with the rule. The answer was: if everything can be made to agree with the rule, so can it also to contradict it. Thus there would be here neither agreement nor contradiction.

This is a remarkably complex and prolifically debated passage, itself following a remarkably complex and interwoven series of remarks, several of which we must examine in more detail before we can begin to see what §201 actually might mean. As the entire methodology of the *Investigations* necessarily eschews platitudes and propositions in favor of examples, "samples" (*Muster*), and "games," Wittgenstein must *enact* the fallibility of the superconcept; in order to do this, he comes up with examples that need their own examples, which also need their own examples. The examples that can make the rule-following paradox clearest are, inspired by David Stern's reading, those of "fit," of learning the meaning of a word "in a flash" (which is borne out of "fit"), of learning to count by twos (which will come into play again when we work with Kripke's Wittgenstein), and, finally, of "reading," paying particular attention to Wittgenstein's example of a human who is a "reading machine" ("Lesemaschine"), a term that harkens back to Koelb's Derridean interpretation. In each of these cases, the superconcepts of "fit" ("Passen"), "understanding" ("Verstehen"), and "ability" ("Können") will turn out to need governing superconcepts of their own in order to "work," thus highlighting the fallibility of rule following.

Wittgenstein begins his discussion of "fit" by dismantling the assumptions the "author of the *Tractatus*" had to have been acting under in order to come up with the general form of all propositions. The form ("die Allgemeine Form des Satzes") claims that what all propositions have in common is that they all, in one form or another, say "such and such is the case," and they do this by connecting a group of simples or atomic propositions by some combination of the "neither-nor" operator, and as such they are truth-functional (*TLP* 6). In *Investigations* §§134–37 Wittgenstein seems to undermine this bipolarity thesis, which is essentially the culminating systematic idea of the *Tractatus*. In §136, he takes his former self to task by pointing out that in order to judge a proposition, one must already have an extra-propositional conception of "truth" that exists apart from the proposition but "fits" together with it:

> Im Grunde ist die Angabe von "Es verhält sich so und so" als allgemeine Form des Satzes das gleiche, wie die Erklärung: ein Satz sei alles, was wahr oder falsch sein könne. Denn, statt "Es verhält sich . . ." hätte ich auch sagen können: "Das und das ist wahr." (Aber auch: "Das und das ist falsch.") Nun ist aber
> 'p' ist wahr = p
> 'p' ist falsch = nicht-p.
> Und zu sagen, ein Satz sei alles, was wahr oder falsch sein könne, kommt darauf hinaus: Einen Satz nennen wir das, worauf wir in unsere Sprache den Kalkül der Wahrheitsfunktionen anwenden. . . .
> Was in den Begriff der Wahrheit eingreift (wie in ein Zahnrad), das ist ein Satz.
> Aber das ist ein schlechtes Bild. (§136b–d)

> Ultimately, the designation of "Such and such is the case" as General Form of Proposition is the same as the declaration: a proposition is something that can be true or false. Because instead of "such and such . . ." I could also have said "such and such is true." (But also: "Such and such is false." Now let us say:
> 'p' is true = p
> 'p' is false =~p.
> And to say a proposition were everything that could be true or false comes down to this: what we call a proposition is that to which we apply the calculus of truth-functions in our language. . . .
> What engages with the concept of truth (like in a cogwheel) is the proposition. But this is a poor picture.

So here the problem of "fit" is introduced: "true" and "proposition" must fit together, and to do this "true" must exist independently of "proposition" and, somehow, also "fit" with it like the teeth of a gear wheel with the gaps of another gear wheel. The "true" has to exist independently *and* simultaneously be dependent on context—which leads us, understandably, to ask: which is it? (or at any rate to think that the gear wheels are a "schlechtes Bild"). This leads Wittgenstein into one of many instances wherein he links the idea of understanding something "in a flash" with the idea of "fit" (that is, to understand whether a proposition is true or false, you also have to have understood the concept "true" on its own and yet in this context, all at once, which would require some sort of in-a-flash development). Wittgenstein's main example of the problems of this phenomenon come in §139, when he talks about hearing or reading the word "cube"—and concludes that if we do happen to get a picture of a cube in our minds as a result, this is merely because the word has *suggested a certain use to us*, not that the word is inextricably linked to the picture by a governing force of referentiality. This finding, however, far from being conclusive, merely opens the proverbial Russian doll to three new examples, one of which is the aforementioned "fit" and the others of which are *Verstehen*, *Passen*, and *Können*:

> Die Kriterien, die wir für das "Passen," "Können," "Verstehen" gelten lassen, sind viel kompliziertere, als es auf den ersten Blick scheinen möchte. D.h., das Spiel mit diesen Worten, ihre Verwendung im sprachlichen Verkehr, dessen Mittel sie sind, ist verwickelter—die Rolle dieser Wörter in unserer Sprache eine andere, als wir versucht sind, zu glauben. (§182b)
>
> The criteria we allow for "fitting," "being able to," and "understanding" are much more complicated than they might appear at first glance. That is, the game with these words, their use in linguistic circulation that is carried on by their means, is more involved—the role of these words in our language other than what we are tempted to think.

Thus "to fit" creates the problem of "to understand," which itself creates the problem of "to be able to" do something, such as reading. Is it possible that in order to understand the general form of proposition, we have to somehow "understand" the idea of "truth" instantly, or "in a flash"? This is how the problem of "fit," instead of being at all resolved, reveals the problem of *Verstehen*, that is, instant understanding, the idea of grasping a word "in a flash," the *Investigations*' major argument on behalf of a superconcept.

In order to demonstrate the problem with "being able to do something" (and thus also, implicitly, with "understanding" and then, were something to be able to be understood, the idea of "fit") Wittgenstein turns in §§156–58 to the problem of "reading," which he characterizes as the act of reproducing language to oneself as a result of having the eyes register marks on paper. The problem as Wittgenstein sees it is that the human being has the potential to be simply a "reading machine" who does not actually "understand" anything he reads, just as much as he has the potential to be a human being reading in the manner we expect. To help us understand this point, the "reading machine" example digresses into yet another example of reading without really reading, this one of a schoolchild who is ostensibly "learning to read," and in his first attempt, happens to reproduce a word correctly by chance, though he does not actually know how to read yet, and this is followed by many incorrect guesses, and so his teacher says, "No, that's not reading," it was just luck. Now we see that several months later, when his reading has become consistent, the teacher says, "Well, *now* he can read." Was the first word he read actually a correct act of reading? Or was it really an accident? When did the child "really" start reading? (§157). It is, Wittgenstein argues, a matter of the student's behavior ("Verhalten") in context, and not at all the superconcept of "to read correctly."[17] This brings Wittgenstein back to the example of the reading machine:

> Im Falle aber der lebenden Lesemaschine hieß "lesen": so und so auf Schriftzeichen reagieren. Dieser Begriff war also ganz unabhängig von dem eines seelischen, oder andern Mechanismus.—Der Lehrer kann hier auch vom Abgerichteten nicht sagen: "Vielleicht hat er dieses Wort schon gelesen." Denn es ist ja kein Zweifel über das, was er getan hat.—Die Veränderung, als der Schüler zu lesen anfing, war eine Veränderung seines Verhaltens; und von einem "ersten Wort im neuen Zustand" zu reden, hat hier keinen Sinn. (§157d)

> In the case of a living reading machine "reading" meant: reacting to written signs in this way and that. This concept was thus quite independent from that of a mental or other mechanism.—Nor can the teacher here say of the pupil: "Perhaps he has already read this word." For there is no doubt as to what he did.—The change, when the pupil began to read, was a change of his behavior; and to speak of a "first word in his new state" makes no sense.

This, as Stern argues, leads us to the realization that "fit" (such as the "fit" of "reading correctly" with "knowing how to" or "proposition" with "truth") describes a situation, or, in less Tractarian terms, a behavior and not a rule,[18] and thus the full scope of the contentiousness of the idea of a superconcept has come full circle by the time we get to the paradox of §201, which Stern paraphrases as follows:

> No occurent act of meaning or intending can give a rule the power to determine our future actions because there is always the question of how that act is to be interpreted. As a result, the idea that a rule, taken in isolation, can determine all its future applications turns out to be misguided . . .

> Nothing taken in isolation from its context can determine how we go on, as all determination is dependent on our proceeding in the usual way.[19]

As we said before: in order for a rule to "work," there would have to be a rule governing how that rule worked; in order for *that* rule to work . . . and so on. The only thing that could stop that infinite chain would be a superconcept, which Wittgenstein begins dismantling with the "in a flash" discussion, weakens further as each example further chips away at "fit," and to which he seems to deliver a death blow not long after §201:

> "Ein Ding ist mit sich selbst identisch."—Es gibt kein schöneres Beispiel eines nutzlosen Satzes, der aber doch mit einem Spiel der Vorstellung verbunden ist. Es ist, als legten wir das Ding, in der Vorstellung, in seine eigene Form hinein, und sahen, daß es paßt.
>
> Wir könnten auch sagen: "Jedes Ding paßt in sich selbst."—Oder anders: Jedes Ding paßt in seine eigene Form hinein." Man schaut dabei ein Ding an und stellt sich vor, daß der Raum dafür ausgespart war und es nun genau hineinpaßt.
>
> "Paßt" dieser Fleck [*shows ink stain*] in seine weiße Umgebung?—Aber genau so würde es aussehn, wenn statt seiner erst ein Loch gewesen wäre, und er nun hineinpaßte. Mit dem Ausdruck "er paßt" wird eben nicht einfach dies Bild beschrieben. Nicht einfach diese Situation.
>
> "Jeder Farbfleck paßt genau in seine Umgebung" ist ein etwas spezialisierter Satz der Identität. (§216)

> "A thing is identical with itself."—There is no finer example of a useless sentence, which is somehow still connected with a play of the imagination. It is as if in imagination we put a thing into its own shape, and saw that it fit.
>
> We could also say: "Every thing fits into itself."—Or otherwise: "Every thing fits into its own shape." At this we look at a thing, and imagine that there was a spot made for it, into which it now exactly fits.
>
> Does this spot [*shows ink stain*] "fit" into its white surrounding?—But that is exactly how it would look, if there had at first been a hole in its place, and it then fit into that hole. But when we say "it fits," we are not just describing this appearance, not simply this situation.
>
> "Every colored spot fits exactly into its surroundings" is a somewhat specialized form of the law of identity.

Again, now we see here that by recognizing the absurdity of saying that a black ink stain "fits" perfectly in its background, we are recognizing the absurdity of the idea that "fit" can be a superconcept, and are instead coming to recognize that "fit" instead describes *a specific use or situation*, as do all instances that attempt to claim they are following rules.

So, to place the paradox of rule-following in similar terms as we have placed that of ostensive definition, we can say that the problem with "learning" to follow a rule is that when we follow a rule, we already have to know what it means to follow a rule, and thus must be following a rule (Wittgenstein mulls on this very dilemma even as far back as §84, when his interlocutory voice asks: "—Können wir uns nicht eine Regel denken, die die Anwendungen der Regel regelt? Und einen Zweifel, den *jene* Regel behebt,—und so fort?" ("—can we not think of a rule that regulates the application of this rule? And a doubt that eliminates *that* rule—and so on?") (§84a).

In appropriate fashion, we can illustrate the relevance of the rule-following paradox to the officer's suicide in Kafka's penal colony using an example not of its "Gebrauch in der Sprache," but of its use in the failed execution. Looking once again at the moment in which the officer expresses disbelief that the explorer cannot "read" the old commandant's writing, we must also look again at Wittgenstein's problem with "reading," which was actually an example of his problem with "rule-following" altogether. And again back to Wittgenstein's example of the reading machine and the schoolchild who "accidentally" reads correctly in an isolated incident. Through these language games, Wittgenstein has demonstrated that there is no way to know what it means "to know how to read," that there is thus no such thing as following an actual "rule" for "learning to read"—that would require a super-rule for knowing how to follow a rule, and Wittgenstein has rejected the superconcept solution.

The question then arises: (how) is the paradox of rule-following relevant to Kafka's penal colony? In the alleged malfunction of the machine, in the moment of the officer's suicide, when the Harrow does not write and instead simply impales the officer in an act of what the explorer dismisses as "murder, pure and simple" (1:192)? What, exactly, has happened in this moment? Is it, as Goebel has argued, a symbolic suicide of colonial power?[20] Has the machine, as Politzer argues, taken on human characteristics or "acquire[d] human life"?[21] Or is the malfunction simply the completion of the story's "pornological fantasy," as Margot Norris argues, and a necessary plot twist, given that, in her reading, Kafka saw to it that the officer was "robbed of a transcendence that was always fraudulent, and [his] carcass . . . therefore disposed of with the unceremonious dispatch of animal burial"?[22] Is the machine's malfunction necessary for the story itself to function, specifically as a "blow at reason," at "the 'rationalization' of suffering," the transcendence of pain?[23] If Norris is correct, then the point of the machine has always been to malfunction, its function being simply as a narrative (or, rather, descriptive) construct created to show the futility (and incorrectness) of the sacralization of pain. Koelb also seems to argue that the machine's malfunction is, if not the only important aspect of its function, at least immanent, for after all, "[a] machine that *did* run by itself—what would that be? No longer a pure representation, it would deconstruct the very notion of a 'machine.' A machine running by itself, especially a reading/writing machine, would deconstruct itself. Perhaps it would also self-destruct."[24] This is because, according to Derrida, a "pure representation, a machine, never runs by itself."[25] And thus further:

> The machine, liberated by the traveler's disbelief, destroys itself by rebelling against the condition of its existence, which stipulates that such a machine may not run by itself. The apparatus transcends its own nature by its act of self-destruction, for in doing so it ceases simply to represent the system of reading and writing the law.
>
> The purpose of a machine that ostensibly runs by itself *must* be to self-destruct, because inherent in the concept "machine" is "cannot run by itself."[26]

Like Norris or Koelb, we can also argue that the "purpose" of the machine may indeed be to malfunction—but that this purpose may also carry this property without a "higher" (that is: metanarrative or structural) purpose (i.e., something more intrinsic to the story than "it had to happen for the story to 'work' "). Indeed, constructions of pornological fantasy aside, what appears to have happened here is that the machine has malfunctioned. But I would like to argue that the error is not the machine's; it is everyone else's, for laboring under the illusion that there was a set way in which the machine was to "function" at all. In §143, Wittgenstein argues that it is never really possible to tell the difference between a "random" and a "systematic" mistake, and this argument should resonate when we ask, regarding the "mistake" of Kafka's machine: *has the machine "malfunctioned" for the first time?* There is, in the context of the narration, no way to tell. Further, the only evidence that the machine had any prior human contact at all, the saliva-soaked wool gag that causes the prisoner to lose his meager lunch after he bites down on it, could easily have gotten into its condition in countless other ways ("Wie kann man ohne Ekel diesen Filz in den Mund nehmen, an dem mehr als hundert Männer im Sterben gesaugt und gebissen habe?" ["How can one not take this felt into his mouth without revulsion, knowing that more than a hundred men before him have sucked and bitten on it?"] [1:176]). To understand on a purely literal level the officer's suicide in this story—much less to afford oneself the luxury of interpreting said act as "meaning" any number of its metaphorical equivalents—we must accept the moment of surprise and fulfilled dramatic irony that occurs when the machine, instead of allowing its greatest admirer to "sacrifice" himself to it in "Folter," *mal*functions. But because there is no textual evidence of the prior "correct" functioning that would determine a malfunction other than that provided by a remarkably unreliable source.

This unreliable source—the officer—is self-proclaimed engineer, judge, jury, and executioner of the colony (1:168): the architect of all of its present rules (or at any rate the mouthpiece of the architect of its past rules). We can see using simple common sense that these "rules" are arbitrary at best and unintelligible at worst, and that there is no objectively narrated evidence to support them. But what is truly fascinating about this story's connection with the Wittgenstein text is that—just as Kafka's characterization of failed metaphor helped elucidate the problem with *all* metaphor, which echoed structurally Wittgenstein's problem with *all* philosophical language—Kafka's own characterization of *this* particular example of untrustworthy narrated rule-making and sabotaged narrative execution demonstrates rather incredibly Wittgenstein's contention with *all* rule-making.

We will extrapolate on this idea in the forthcoming discussion of Saul Kripke, a philosopher whose interpretation of §201 is both extraordinarily elucidatory for our purposes and highly problematic, but at the moment it remains crucial to understand the rule-following paradox as it relates to Kafka's story: a "rule" is a misnomer because the one thing it is supposed to do—determine *what one is supposed to do*—it *cannot* do without some sort of super-rule to control "how it is to be interpreted," which Wittgenstein has dismissed. Furthermore, Wittgenstein argues that the only way to tell whether a rule really works or not is to examine its behavior in "normal" cases, the "control experiments," as it were—with an abnormal case, which Wittgenstein argues every case can be made out to be (a remark which the only "actual" execution in Kafka's story handily demonstrates), there is no way to tell whether the rule works or not (and further, "je anormaler der Fall, desto Zweifelhafter wird es, was wir nun hier sagen sollen" ["the more abnormal the case, the more doubtful it becomes what we should say here"] [§142]). Wittgenstein argues again and with more force on behalf of this notion later in the rule-following section, shortly before the paradox of §201, when he comes to the conclusion that it is not possible for *one* person to follow *one* rule *once*:

> Es kann nicht ein einziges Mal nur ein Mensch einer Regel gefolgt sein. Es kann nicht ein einziges Mal nur eine Mitteilung gemacht, ein Befehl gegeben, oder verstanden worden sein, etc.—Einer Regel folgen, eine Mitteilung machen, einen Befehl geben, eine Schachpartie spielen sind Gepflogenheiten (Gebräuche, Institutionen). Einen Satz verstehen, heißt, eine Sprache verstehen. Eine Sprache verstehen, heißt eine Technik beherrschen. (§199b–c)

> It is not possible for there to have been only one occasion on which someone obeyed a rule. It is not possible that there could have been but one occasion on which a report was made, an order given or understood, and so on.—To obey a rule, to make a report, to give

> an order, to play a game of chess, are habits (uses, institutions). To understand a sentence means to understand a language. To understand a language is to master a technique.

And this has been, in effect, what the officer has done in Kafka's story as well: he has described the rule for how the machine works and then attempted to follow it, but because he is but one man attempting to follow one rule once, we have no idea whether the machine's malfunction was random, systematic, a normal case, a special case, or, in fact, a "malfunction" at all, because all of the officer's actions have existed in his own personal juridical and punitive microcosm, with parameters of his choosing and his choosing only (or, at any rate, with help only from the deceased old commandant). Thus we realize that it is indeed impossible to tell whether the machine has malfunctioned, because no super-rule governing all of the officer's other rules was possible, and thus none of his rules are provable as rules.

As Robert Fogelin puts it, the "notion of following a rule" is "a natural source of philosophical illusion. Pressures seem to come from every side to turn this notion into a super-concept," and, further, "it is a central task of Wittgenstein's later philosophy to fight this tendency by showing that rules are neither sublime nor are they mysterious."[27] That is: rules are not "sublime" because there is no super-rule governing the rules for following all rules; they are not "mysterious" because they are taken to be a rejection of the Platonism Norman Finkelstein analyzes, which he claims "makes communication look miraculous." That is, the Platonist would argue that though there is no super-rule for governing all rules, the idea of "rule" has an abstract, mysterious, but nevertheless existing Platonic truth concept somewhere, so that we can, when, for example, following a recipe for meringue, "come to grasp which of [our] activities would accord, or fail to accord, with a sequence of noises that [we've] heard."[28] A Platonist, Finkelstein suggests, "might say":

> My words and gestures can be interpreted any which way, but the thing behind them—the meaning—needs no interpretation. Now, I can't convey this item directly to my interlocutor. All that I can do is talk to him, or gesture to him, and all my words and gestures can be interpreted in various ways. But if he's lucky, he'll guess what I have in mind and understand me.[29]

Wittgenstein, Fogelin argues, wholly rejects this kind of Platonism (and this should be no surprise), and instead seems to enjoy that

> interpretation [of a rule] is an obvious candidate to play the role of bridge, but—under the pressure of an insistence that there's a gulf between *any* string of words and what it calls for—every interpretation seems inert as well. The paradox of . . . §201 has its roots in the

> thought that there is always a gulf between the statement of a rule—a string of words—and the rule's execution or application.[30]

Wittgenstein relishes the struggle to resist, always, not only the existence of a sublime superconcept, but also that of a prelinguistic abstract truth. Rather, he simply presents us with the "gulf," the paradox of §201. And it is with an acceptance of this "gulf," rather than the reliance upon an extratextual truth easily assumed (that an execution has taken place as planned before), that we can best appreciate the depth and nuance of the uninterpretability of the officer's suicide in Kafka's story.

It is also through an exploration of the rule-following paradox that we can discover why at least two of the officer's most crucial directives have not exactly failed, but have proven themselves impossible to follow "correctly." The second and main directive is, of course, that the machine works all by itself. The first, with which we will begin our analysis of Kripke's reading, is this notion of "'Sei gerecht,' heißt es" ("'Be just,' it says"). To the problems with "Sei gerecht, heißt es," we can actually find a hint of the analytic tradition in Kittler's work—for he invokes Russell's theory of nonsense via category error to argue that the problem with the machine stems from its instructions, or what it is "programmed" to do. That is, according to Kittler, the machine is programmed to carry out specific sentences ("Ehre deinen Vorgesetzten!") and has never before been asked to carry out a general one ("Sei gerecht!")—therefore, Kittler argues that the machine may simply not be programmed to function with "Be just" and, like a computer, it "crashes."[31] However, I will argue that the problem or potential problem is not with "Sei gerecht," but rather with "heißt es." Using Kripke's argument, we will be able to see that by "heißen" it is entirely possible that the officer means something entirely different than our usual notion of "to be called," and has, unbeknownst to the explorer, simply *used the word "heißt" to indicate this "other thing,"* because, there being no super-rule to control the rules of how words or other operators are used in each and every case, there is no way to stop him.

This is an adaptation of the Kripkean term "quaddition," noted with the function "quus" rather than "plus." How can we *really* say that any action may be made out to accord with a rule? Because there is no way for us to prove that the way an operation, designated by a particular mark, worked in the past will be the way it works in the future. "Quaddition," Kripke explains, works just like addition—until it ceases to, and the trouble is that there is no way for us to know or control when the operation will mutate. Take, for example, the supposedly easy computation 68 + 57. "I perform the computation, obtaining, of course, the answer '125,'" he finds, and, further, this answer, after careful review, should be

> correct both in the arithmetical sense that 125 is the sum of 68 and 57, and in the metalinguistic sense that "plus," as I intended to use

> that word in the past, denoted a function which, when applied to the numbers I called "68" and "57," yields the value 125.
>
> Now suppose I encounter a bizarre skeptic.[32]

This bizarre skeptic suggests that the answer should instead have been 5, which Kripke's fall guy first purports to be "obviously insane." But, after closer consideration of the skeptic's argument, suddenly all is not so certain: is Kripke *sure* that by "+" he meant addition in the way most of us who have completed elementary school conceive of addition? After all:

> Who is to say what function this was? In the past I gave myself only a finite number of examples instantiating this function. All, we have supposed, involved numbers smaller than 57. So perhaps in the past I used "plus" and "+" to denote a function which I will call "quus."

X "quus" y, furthermore, works exactly like addition as long as y is less than 57. But if y is over 57? X "quus" y is always 5. "Who is to say," asks Kripke, that "this is not the function I previously meant by '+'?"[33] Thus as Kripke conceives it, Wittgenstein's "new kind of rule skepticism" can be summed up as follows: if we have a rule/operator/category/signifier (counting, addition, color, etc.) and we have, until a certain moment, gone about our business applying it in our "normal" accustomed way (1 + 1 = 2; 3, 6, 9; turquoise), how can we *prove* that we were ever "really" following the rule like we believed it was written, and not, instead, doing something else—*quounting*, *quaddition*, *schmolor*, etc.—something *that can be marked by the word or expression we usually use to mark our operation* ("I'm counting," "+," "this chair's color is turquoise"), but which *really means something else*?[34]

Conventional wisdom would tell us that no normal person can read the old commandant's writing and that when it was the officer's turn to die, the machine didn't work and thus his death was, indeed, "unmittelbarer Mord." But, as Wittgenstein's §201 would have it, *there is actually no way to tell.* For how are we to know, really, for certain, that when the officer says "'Sei gerecht,' heißt es," by "heißt" he means "says" and not something else, say, "queißt," which *means* "says, *except* in this particular situation, in which case it means causes an extralinguistic epiphany on the body" and which, unfortunately, is designated in ordinary language, unbeknownst to (or forgotten by) the officer, by the word "heißt"? While this would certainly be inconvenient for many of the most compelling metaphorical or allegorical interpretations of "In the Penal Colony," and may seem a tad contrived, its is meant to convey merely the shadow of a doubt that "heißt es" means what we think it means, to show that it is hasty to assume that this phrase *can* mean in the way we expect it to in the context of a reliable narrative. Because "In the Penal Colony" is not a reliable nor particularly "successfully" executed narrative, and its climax cannot be assumed to function in the way a standard narrative climax would. Thus if we are to give credence to at least this part of Kripke's interpretation of §201 (which I do find quite helpful), we can then see that the most striking element of the officer's suicide is not simple dramatic irony. The officer's death is, instead, something far more chilling because there is simply nothing that can be done with it: the officer's suicide, rather than being the easily judged "unmittelbarer Mord," is "unmittelbar" but perhaps not as simple as "Mord": it is uninterpretable.

A Skeptical Conclusion

Here, then, we must examine the consequences—philosophical and literary—of determining the undeterminable. The good news is that the dis/solution of the rule-following paradox is not as clear as that of the paradox of ostension; this is advantageous, in the sense that it therefore cannot itself be dismantled with such ease; the less-good news is that the complexity of the rule-following passages of the *Investigations* cause their very existence to be the source of extensive debate, especially about Saul Kripke. Kripke is the foremost example of philosophers who argue that rule skepticism can be solved the same way referential skepticism can (and thus, on the literary side of things, also implying that the "problems" we encountered in both referential and metaphorical meaning can also be resolved): not simply by language's use, a so-called rule and its "Gebrauch in der Sprache," but its patterns and forms of use *within* a community of language users, as part of a "form of life" (*Lebensform*). But problems arise, just as before: first of all, the solution of a language community or *Lebensform* itself could be taken to espouse exactly the kind of superconcept or super-rule the very paradox of rule-following precludes.[35]

Secondly, and presenting vastly more far-reaching problems, Kripke's approach (along with countless others) posits that §201 has philosophical consequences because it espouses actual philosophical doctrine—and not just §201, but all of the *Investigations*. This brings us back to our original discussion of Wittgenstein's text and "the problem with [philosophical] progress," and radically skeptical approaches: as we saw before, unlike Kripke, a number of "New Wittgenstein" critics believe that the paradoxes we have just examined with great care—ostensive definition, rule-following—and the "conclusions" their three-stage arguments offer are not substantive philosophical theses at all, but rather nicely written nonsense; this is often called a Pyrrhonian view, whereas the belief that the *Investigations* do indeed perform philosophy (just *correctly*) is often called "non-Pyrrhonian" or "anti-Pyrrhonian." We will return to this debate shortly, as its importance in the late Wittgenstein canon cannot be overstated.

But first, there are also far-reaching literary consequences of a Kripkean take on the rule-following paradox as it appears in Kafka's fiction, and in his penal colony in particular: Kripke's (philosophical) solution (and he is not alone) to the rule-following paradox brings us back to the idea of a community of speakers, a *Lebensform*. For, argues Kripke, "of course" Wittgenstein wishes "to solve" the rule-following problem, because "the skeptical conclusion is insane and intolerable."[36] The way to "solve" the rule-following crisis is first—nominally—to free ourselves from "the grip of the normal presupposition that meaningful declarative sentences must purport to correspond to facts."[37] Once we have cleared ourselves of the disproven idea that (as the author of the *Tractatus* may have claimed) words and, more specifically, logical structures, correspond to facts in the world, what we have left is the idea of a language community or *Lebensform*. That is, a rule "works" or a language is "understood" when "each person who claims to be following a rule can be checked by others."[38] So by this rationale, the uninterpretability of the officer's suicide would, in Kafka's story, have been nullified if the officer had simply had colleagues.

But here is the problem with the language-community solution, which encapsulates once again the problem of philosophical or anti-philosophical doctrine in literature, which is that the clever authors of literature can very easily write a language community that is nonexistent or nonfunctional, and with that creation show exactly how fallible the language-community "solution" is, regardless of its untenability as an esoteric philosophical thesis, but rather because of the unreliability of the human members of a community. For example: what happens when a community does not comprise a *Lebensform*, a "form of life," but rather, so to speak, a *Todesform*, a form of death? The prisoners in "In the Penal Colony," all of whom are allegedly susceptible (or, at least, were susceptible) to the same "Schuld ist immer zweifellos" commandment of the officer, seem defined more than anything else by the constant threat of death that follows them around; as the officer's description or depiction of his community would have it, every resident in Kafka's penal colony (including, it turns out, the officer himself), seems defined by his death, by his method of death, or by the justification of his death; by the lost sacrificial capabilities of his death; or by the imminence of his death. And as such, the community is more than anything else defined by its proximity to death (and more so, even, after the officer has met his, as the death transitions from perceived sacrifice to "unmittelbarer Mord").

The culmination of the officer's lengthy description of how the machine works is exactly the kind of singular case of behavior (*Verhalten*) that would normally constitute a "form of life," but in this situation actually constitutes a "form of death"—an execution, *eine Exekution* (at least when the machine's work is executed properly [1:164]). And just as what the colony has in place of a *Lebensform* is, as it were, a *Todesform*, what could have been the officer's community of speakers is, instead, isolation, claimed/perceived community and, most of all, silence. This is especially evident in the silent directive on what claims to be the old commandant's gravestone, which the explorer encounters on his retreat from the colony. The stone is inscribed, and it warns of the old commandant's impending resurrection—which would introduce an actual, living community that could substantiate the officer's own claims:

> Hier ruht der alte Kommandant. Seine Anhänger, die jetzt keinen Namen tragen dürfen, haben ihm das Grab gegraben, und den Stein gesetzt. Es besteht eine Prophezeiung, daß der Kommandant nach einer bestimmten Anzahl von Jahren auferstehen und aus diesem Hause seine Anhänger zur Wiedereroberung der Kolonie führen wird. Glaubet und wartet! (194–95)

> Here lies the Old Commandant. His adherents, who now must remain nameless, have buried him here and set this gravestone. There exists a prophecy that after a set number of years the Commandant will return, and reclaim his adherents from this house and reclaim sovereignty over the Colony. Have faith, and wait!

Leaving aside the probable reality that the officer himself could easily have written that inscription with no "community" of "Anhänger" to speak of, even if said "community" did exist, their uprising has not happened yet, and the only comfort an adherent to the officer's (and old commandant's) pseudo-rules may have is that of blind faith: "Glaubet und wartet!" ("Believe and wait!"). So blind faith rather than relying upon a mode of behavior (here the "form of death," usually a "form of life") created by a language community may now be to the rule-following paradox—which is akin to the "flat-footed" response to rule skepticism: we know how to follow a rule *because we just do*. The machine malfunctioned because *it obviously did*. It was indeed "unmittelbarer Mord" because it *was*.

This mentality is in fact substantiated by Wittgenstein himself when he posits that "Wenn ich der Regel folge, wähle ich nicht. Ich folge der Regel *blind*" ("When I follow a rule, I don't choose. I follow the rule *blind*") (§219). And this "flat-footed" response to rule skepticism is put forth eloquently by Finkelstein in his reading of Crispin Wright's criticisms of Kripke (a terrific example of the forbidding web of secondary criticism about which Stern warned us): Finkelstein quotes Wright as arguing that Kripke's entire line of reasoning—How do we *know* that by "plus" Jones meant "plus" and not "quus"? How do we *know* that by "arbeiten"the officer meant "arbeiten" and not "quarbeiten"?—can and should be met with the response: *we just do* (*Glaubet*, in other words). This, however, in Finkelstein's reading, accounts (despite purported reliance on pattern) for just the kind of Platonism that Finkelstein insists is "not Wittgenstein's view" (and fealty to "Wittgenstein's view" is always paramount, though nobody seems to agree what it was). Rather:

> The Platonist who figures in Wittgenstein's texts is someone who first imagines that there's a gulf between every rule and its application, and only then thinks that somehow, mysteriously, the rule (or its meaning, or something) autonomously manages to call for one activity rather than another. Once we stop thinking of words in isolation from the human lives in which they are embedded—once we give up imagining that there's a gulf between every rule and its application—we can say, innocently, that a particular rule autonomously called for this or that.[39]

Thus the action of flat-footedness, however natural it may seem (the machine malfunctioned because *it just did*) carries with it exactly the kind of weddedness to abstract superconcepts (and thus by definition also philosophical theses) so many Wittgenstein critics—the Pyrrhonians especially, but even anti-Pyrrhonians would likely not come to a consensus about Platonism in the *Investigations*—see as exactly the wrong way to go about reading Wittgenstein.

However, while the flat-footed response against Kripke is (arguably) relatively easy to argue against, the more calmly reasoned critiques, Stern's or Goldfarb's among them, make a stronger case both against Kripke's solution and, in a broader sense, for a Pyrrhonian or at least anti-philosophy-tolerant approach. Stern, for example, acknowledges that Kripke's reading "has certainly succeeded in focusing critical attention on the central importance of Wittgenstein's treatment of meaning, rules and rule-following. But," he cautions, "as an exposition of Wittgenstein's treatment of rules and private language, it must be considered a failure."[40] The reason why, Stern reveals, has nothing at all to do with a flat-footed or "it just does" quasi-Platonism. Rather, this brings us full circle, back to the motto of (narrative *or* philosophical) "progress": the second, more pressing problem with the language-community "solution" and with many readings of the *Investigations* as a whole is that Kripke (and others), in Stern's conception, does not correctly situate §201within the *Investigations*, and that philosophers who espouse that the *Investigations* "advances" philosophical theses (undertakes the goal of philosophical progress), has misunderstood the text entirely.

Instead, Kripke and others have failed to situate the paradox of §201, and instead read it "straight," that is, as if it were Wittgenstein's "real" voice speaking, when in reality, Stern argues that

> Kripke failed to see that the paradox of section 201 is a problem for the voice the author argues with, the "interlocutor." The skeptical paradox only arises if one thinks of grasping a rule as a matter of being able to say something that explains the meaning of the words in question, for which Wittgenstein reserves the term "interpretation" ("*Deuten*"). Indeed, that is the main moral of this section of

> the *Philosophical Investigations*: the interlocutor's view is mistaken precisely because he views interpreting as essential to grasping a rule. Thus, despite the fact that Kripke makes so much of the first paragraph of section 201, where Wittgenstein sums up "our paradox" and his initial reply to it, he never quotes or even refers to the second paragraph, where Wittgenstein replies that the paradox is due to a mistaken conception of understanding or a matter of "interpreting," providing explanations where one substitutes one expression of a rule for another.[41]

The problem with Kripke's interpretation is that despite its revolutionary method and sharp identification of *some part* of §201's ability to dismantle a previously taken-for-granted semantic construct, it fails to *situate* itself correctly in the maze, as it were, of §201 (directly after the rule-following paradox comes the revelation that "Die Sprache ist ein Labyrinth von Wegen. Du kommst von einer Seite und kennst dich aus; du kommst von einer andern zur selben Stelle, und kennst dich nicht mehr aus" ["Language is a labyrinth of paths. You come from one side and don't know where you are; you come from another side to the same place, and you don't know where you are"] [§203]). Thus Kripke's conception insists, despite its best efforts, upon the presentation of a paradox that requires a reliance *on* philosophical progress. Kripke thus ends up falling into the pattern of so many other Wittgenstein readers, a pattern that "treats Wittgenstein's opposition to theses as a device that allows Wittgenstein to avoid stating the controversial theses he supposedly really believes—the theses the reader finds in Wittgenstein's writing."[42]

Wittgenstein, Stern argues, "would have regarded Kripke's skeptical thesis and paradoxical solution as equally nonsensical consequences of a mistaken conception of language and rules."[43] This realization, in turn, has tremendous bearing in Kafka's literary world as well. To Stern, it seems as if Kripke's conception of and proposed solution to the rule-following paradox is the closest the mouse of a parallel-universe "Little Fable" could ever have come to successfully switching direction, of heeding the first paradigm shift while never really "grasping" that the problem is and always was that the mouse was a mouse in a maze in the first place (so, in this situation, the problem is that Kripke is a philosopher attempting to philosophize anti-philosophy in the first place). Kripke's only possible result is to be gobbled up whole, either by critics standing in for what Wittgenstein "really" wanted or, in a more generous conception, Wittgenstein himself. Like Kafka's fable mouse's original problem, one of Wittgenstein's *Investigations* voices also claimed that a philosophical problem had the form "Ich kenne mich nicht aus" ("I don't know where I am") (§123). And that—not just the content of the "problem," but the form of "Ich kenne mich nicht aus," the presumption of the need for reorientation in the "right" direction, and the fact that it *is* a philosophical problem—is what Kripke's problem may be as well. The bearing of this idea on Kafka's "Penal Colony" is grimmer yet: if our problem was, for example, believing that any "progress" could be advanced in the penal colony at all—progress toward interpreting what the officer's suicide "means," and above all the luxury of identifying what passes for a sensical *narrative* progress(ion)—then where does that leave the story? What is the point of reading it, if our only valid result is to realize that there is no such thing as a "correct" mode or direction of advancement through it?

An Actual Conclusion

On the purely literal, textual level, the story (and what enigmatic sensical narration there remains in it) seems to leave us with a grim choice: either accept, in all of its faults and its complete narrative nonworkability, the language-community "solution" (the old commandant has adherents in the colony who can substantiate the officer's stories) or operate on blind faith (that the old commandant will somehow rise again): both choices, it turns out, are the same, as they both hinge on allowing the idea that the old commandant's adherents' return has any merit at all; they both *are* simply "Glaubet und wartet!" The only other choice seems to be a non-choice: the acceptance of uninterpretability and simple removal of oneself from the situation—which is, after all, what the explorer in the penal colony does: he simply removes himself from the situation as quickly as possible, sailing away on the boat that brought him there in the first place, shaking a knotted rope at the soldier and the prisoner so that they can't even entertain the thought of stowing away (1:195).

One glaring issue remains, however, even after the story has ended and the explorer has ceased his explorations (or at least these particular ones): if only the officer had just demonstrated an execution instead of merely describing one, if only the officer had just executed the prisoner as he originally claimed he would, then we would have had an instance of "correct" use and thus the officer's suicide—provided that the rest of the story went in exactly the same manner as it is actually written—would have the kind of concrete meaning and metaphorical "meaning" so many of us ascribe to it. But let us not forget the most confounding element of Wittgenstein's rule-following paradox: even a documented precedent, a prior behavior (*Verhalten*) is just that and nothing more. All behavior is merely singular incidents, every case (every *Lebensform*) different. Thus although the glaring absence of a "correct execution"—and we may be tempted to ask why Kafka has done this, to which there is no satisfactory answer—provides ammunition for the theory that the machine may never have worked "correctly," even a "correct" precedent does nothing, in the end, to guarantee the presence of a rule. Thus even with a small amount of narrative speculation, Kafka's provocative demonstration of the penal colony's rule-following paradox remains unsolvable.

But what about coming at both the Kafka and Wittgenstein "problems" via yet another way of looking at Wittgenstein's motto, "Überhaupt hat der Fortschritt das an sich, daß er viel größer ausschaut, als er wirklich ist" ("But overall, the thing about progress is that it always appears greater than it really is")? What of the opposite of progress, which is situation? If we remember, Wittgenstein insisted that the *Investigations* were to have been seen as a collection of landscape sketches, whose readers should have no "object" other than to recognize them as such. Using this idea, we could discover just as plausibly that in Kafka's story, the *Forschungsreisende*'s problem comes in the unfortunate presumptions of his name, which forces upon him a purpose, which we now understand could not have ended well: *forschen* (explore, research, make progress of knowledge) and *reisen* (travel, move in a particular direction). In setting up the events the way Kafka has—by placing the burden of narrative proof within an unreliable, extended description, by making the process of reading and writing of the apparatus impossible to understand without experience (*Erfahrung*), and then making said experience the uninterpretable "unmittelbarer Mord" of the officer and sudden release of the prisoner—Kafka has made sure that the entire nominal purpose of the research trip (*Forschungsreise*) is called into question; after what he has seen it is doubtful that he will have any legitimate "progress" on which to report and instead may be called into a crisis of career. What the explorer seems fated not to have recognized is the misleading pretense of his vocation—and, not coincidentally, his only identifying moniker, his entire identity within the narrative. The problem with his search for (research) "progress" was that it ended up being not nearly so great as it appeared; the problem with our expectation for narrative progress is that we failed to see exactly that expectation as the problem. By playing as he has with the entire assumption of causal narrative "reality," by sabotaging, in effect, his execution of the narrated execution, Kafka has forced us to confront what turned out to be misguided expectations of narrative "sense" or narrative "meaning." For if the officer's suicide precludes interpretation and simply just is, definitive interpretive "progress" of the story must largely halt as well. Not only, it seems, is an "ordinary language" theory of narrative meaning prohibitively problematic, but the attempt to define it is invalid. The discovery of this invalidity is, then, the only progress here.

Chapter 6

✦

The Private Language Argument and the Undermining of "Josefine the Singer"

I have just argued at length that Kafka's conception of prose narration, at least as expressed in "In the Penal Colony," is highly skeptical to the point of Pyrrhonianism: that is, the officer's act of apparent self-sabotage is *itself* unmasked as highly questionable, thus revealing that the very act of alleged narration that got us to this point has itself been sabotaged, and ultimately challenged to the point of self-immolation. Thus, though in the process I have gone to similarly great lengths to demonstrate the success with which Kafka undermines the conceit of narrative progression, I have not turned Nestroy's words into an all-encompassing epigram of my own project. That is to say, while it has primarily to do with unmasking one misconception after the next, there has been substantial progress made here in determining not what these Kafka works mean, but how they do (or, at times, and more importantly, how they undermine our notions of meaning). That said, I have left one prominent approach that may turn even my own project Pyrrhonian after all.

This is an angle with which I approach, fittingly enough, Kafka's last story, "Josefine the Singer, or the Mouse Folk" ("Josefine die Sängerin, oder das Volk der Mäuse"). In the story, a nameless first-person collective "wir" describes a mysterious singer who, rather than singing in a traditional manner, "pipes" or "squeaks," but is somehow revered as a folk hero to the "mouse people," a descriptor only provided in the title. Throughout the course of the story, it is revealed that Josefine's revered place in the community is as questionable as her singing, and the rather unsurprising revelation of her disappearance at the end hails the eventual disappearance of her legend as well:

> Vielleicht werden wir also gar nicht sehr viel entbehren, Josefine aber, erlöst von der irdischen Plage, die aber ihrer Meinung nach Auserwählten bereitet ist, wird fröhlich sich verlieren in der zahllosen Menge der Helden unseres Volkes, und bald, da wir keine Geschichte treiben, in gesteigerter Erlösung vergessen sein wie alle ihre Brüder. (*GW* 1:294)

> Perhaps we will not miss so much after all. But Josephine, delivered from the earthly troubles, which in her opinion lie in wait for the chosen ones, will happily lose herself in the numberless crowd of heroes of our people. And soon, since we are not historians, in this increased deliverance she'll be forgotten, like all her brothers.

The goal of this book's final chapter is to see why this peculiar conclusion—which also marks the conclusion of Kafka's writing life and life altogether—is of particular significance, but to do so we must first return several times to the beginning of the story and the many claims it makes that, as we will soon see, turn out to be wildly contradictory. At first glance, "Josefine" appears to be about a singer whose song is simultaneously vitally important to the culture from which it originates (and from which it distinguishes itself), and indiscernible as song to anyone except for possibly Josefine herself. It is almost as if Josefine's "singing" represents a form of sublime communication that not even she fully understands, but that only she can initiate. It is as if an alternative form of language exists, one that is both private (deliberately not understandable to its own audience) and transcendent, in that it is somehow more important than all of them. Or, at any rate, it seems that way as the story begins, as our narrator explains: "Unsere Sängerin heißt Josefine. Wer sie nicht gehört hat, kennt nicht die Macht des Gesanges" ("Our singer is named Josefine. Anyone who has not heard her does not know the power of song") (1:274).

This initial approach to "Josefine" is a major subject of the critical canon, such as David Ellison's examination of Josefine's apparent status as a "servant of the sublime." Ellison points out that the primary reason the mouse people are unable to understand Josefine is that they are either unable or unwilling to *raise themselves* (*sich erheben*) "to the level of music":

> [U]nser Leben ist schwer, wir können uns, auch wenn wir einmal alle Tagessorgen abzuschütteln versucht haben, nicht mehr zu solchen, unserem sonstigen Leben so fernen Dingen erheben, wie es die Musik ist (1:274).[1]

> Our life is hard; we are no longer able, even on occasions when we have tried to shake our daily cares, to raise ourselves to anything so high and far as music.

However, as Ellison himself points out, the story turns out to be vastly more complicated than an earth-bound people incapable of transcending to the point that would enable them to properly understand their diva, who serves the familiar Kafkan sublime that hangs permanently just out of reach.

My own final chapter explores Kafka's last story in terms of what appears at first to be Josefine's private or transcendental language, a "language" that consists of a sort of music (or the nonmusical, or even *nonverbal* gesture) her people cannot fully understand, but somehow still appreciate—until they fail to. My first goal is to integrate the field's most compelling theories about Josefine's apparent language with a final element of Wittgenstein's late work: by far the best-known and most-analyzed section of the *Investigations*, which philosophers refer to as the private language argument, and which is first introduced in §243. My second goal, which should now come as little surprise, is to demonstrate that the successful completion of this approach results in the revelation of yet another illusory foundation.

My concurrent examination of the relevance of Wittgenstein's work to Kafka's—and by extension to certain important elements of literary modernism in general—will end in this way, with a demonstration of the analytic relevance of Wittgenstein's late work with Kafka's final story, that itself concludes with the necessary unmasking of one final illusion. This final illusion is that of the formal requirements of so-called descriptive or philosophical prose (borrowing the terminology of Scherpe and Corngold, respectively). For in "Josefine," Kafka has left aside even the pretention of narration, and instead presents the story openly as a descriptive or, as Corngold has put it, "hybrid" work—and I would like to argue here that Kafka fails even at *this* subversive and borderline avant-garde form of literary prose. However, through the philosophical discussion surrounding Wittgenstein's private language argument, we will see that this alleged failure is actually one of Kafka's most notable literary (and philosophical) accomplishments.

Step 1: Introducing "Josefine" to the Private Language Argument

Kafka's final story has been called an "exceptional" work, in the literal sense of the word, just as its heroine is called an exception ("nur Josefine macht eine Ausnahme" ["Josephine alone is the exception"]), among her stubbornly unmusical people (1:274). As numerous critics have argued convincingly, there are several reasons the story—composed as the complications from Kafka's tuberculosis reached his throat and took away his own ability to speak—is an exception in his canon.[2] As Michael Minden has recently argued, the story comes to us not from the pseudo-omniscient perspective of a protagonist largely excluded from the one community he needs the most (the Law, the family, the Castle village), but, even more than in the case of the penal colony's impotent explorer, from the perspective of the "established" society itself.[3] From this perspective, the story is exceptional because it is more or less narrated from a perspective that the more canonical Kafka works strive so terribly hard to conceal. Further, as Ritchie Robertson has argued, as an example of Kafka's late work, "Josefine" is "for the most part quiet and restrained. It lacks the disturbing or disgusting images" of the early stories "and also their dramatic intensity."[4] In addition, as Ruth V. Gross has argued, "Josefine" is also a marked exception to Kafka's canon because of its choice of a female subject (I hesitate to say "protagonist" because of the narrative distance from Josefine, which we will discuss at some length later on).[5] And Doreen Densky has pointed out recently that Kafka's eerie choice to narrate the story from a first-person plural perspective makes it exceptionally difficult to grant whatever passes for a narrative voice any solidity whatsoever.[6]

What I want to argue here is that this story is actually not exceptional in the way we believe it to be—that these qualities make the story somewhat unlike Kafka's other work, but that it possesses other and more important qualities that make it far more canonical than critics such as Minden argue it is. I believe that what makes "Josefine" a canonical story—albeit an extreme example of one—is its remarkable Pyrrhonian trajectory. Not unlike the way in which Wittgenstein both appears to advance philosophy in the *Philosophical Investigations* and actually rejects the conceit of philosophical progress altogether, Kafka also appears to present a final story, but actually presents something closer to an anti-story along the lines of "In the Penal Colony."

In fact, I think of "Josefine" and "In the Penal Colony" as kindred, first of all in content: note their shared presence of questionable acolytes who are actual ignorers, their final acts of noncommunicative self-disappearance, and so on. But perhaps more importantly, the stories are connected in the way they undermine their own form. With "Josefine," Kafka finishes what "In the Penal Colony" began: a total undermining of the conceit of literary prose, of the very ability of a story to express *anything*, whether important or trivial—of, in short, the fear that gripped Kafka for most of his life and manifested itself at the end in physical form. Indeed, "Josefine" is about a songstress who is not one, a "mouse people" who are neither people nor mice, a cherished cultural icon who, it turns out, is neither cherished nor particularly iconic. And, more than that, "Josefine" is also, along the same lines as "In the Penal Colony" but to a much more extreme extent, a story that is not one.

The extent to which this is the case is only possible in light of a further exploration of Wittgenstein's private language argument, for two important reasons. First, as we will see, the argument provides a highly elucidatory apparatus to investigate what it actually is Josefine might be doing. Secondly, and more importantly, the private language argument's centrality to the Pyrrhonianism debate in Wittgenstein studies provides the final demonstration as to why "Josefine" itself is, if it can even be classified as a "story" at all, a definitive example of what I will call Kafka's Pyrrhonian literature—that is, literature whose greatest literary triumph exists in undermining its own status as literature.

As we have seen to a certain extent already, the *Investigations* are at once revelatory and enraging, in that they appear to offer important and legitimate advances in the philosophy of language and the philosophy of mind—and yet, their author insists that anyone who comes away from the work with an appreciation for the advancement of these theses is doing it wrong.

Therefore, while we may indeed extrapolate philosophical theses from the *Investigations*, in particular from the private language argument, which Ray Monk reminds us is by far the most heavily discussed of Wittgenstein's entire canon, we must have those very theses' self-immolation in front of our eyes, lest we delude ourselves further that the text is something it is not. It is my final argument in this book that Kafka, once again, accomplishes something remarkably similar in his deathbed work to what Wittgenstein accomplishes in his. That is, while we may certainly read and enjoy "Josefine" as a work of prose fiction, as a story, as a work of literature, to leave it at that is to delude ourselves about what Kafka is actually doing. It is my contention that he is, not unlike Wittgenstein, enticing us to *follow* a story, to make conclusions like we would when we read a story, even a descriptive and highly philosophical story—only to destroy the very conceit of storytelling before our eyes.

How is this destruction accomplished? In Wittgenstein's case, he appears to present a hypothesis that it is *indeed* possible to have a private language. He then quite convincingly dismantles the conceit of a private language, and in doing so seemingly decries several hundred years of philosophical inquiry. This makes it seem as if he has not only advanced a philosophical thesis, but a truly revolutionary one. However, if we have paid any attention to any part of the *Investigations*, especially its introduction, we have to remember that presupposing a dismantling of Cartesian dualism and everything that came as a result of it—dismantling the mind-body divide, dismantling the very conceit of a spiritual self that only oneself can understand—also presupposes a protracted interaction *with* the philosophical canon, and this is something Wittgenstein insisted he did not undergo, because it could not be done.

With "Josefine," Kafka accomplishes a similar movement. Although Kafka is most certainly not making an *argument* about the same thing Wittgenstein is, I will argue that he is most certainly making a *statement* about the dubious existence of a special class of communication. For while Josefine's singing language (or rather "singing" "language") is not private in the same sense, the first thing we learn about it is that nobody in her audience truly understands what makes it special—or even what makes it singing. In the end, Kafka and Wittgenstein entice us with problems to solve—in Kafka's case, it is the problem of what (and how revered) Josefine's singing really is; in Wittgenstein's it is the alleged question he himself puts forth of how a private language would work. The first step in understanding what ends up as a dramatically Pyrrhonian arc for both authors is the step wherein they create intricate and fascinating problems and tempt us to try to solve them.

For Kafka, this is the simple problem of what Josefine is actually doing, and what her place in the community of the "mouse folk" actually is—for, as should be unsurprising to any reader of Kafka, the information we are given is conflicting. Indeed, the nameless narrator, as we have just seen, begins the story with what appears to be a statement of pure adulation: "Wer sie nicht gehört hat, kennt nicht die Macht des Gesanges" ("Anyone who has not heard her does not know the power of song"). The actual ambiguity of this statement notwithstanding (and we will address this later on), the adulation is short-lived, as the narrator only a few hundred words later modifies this adulation. After admitting that "unserer Volk" is necessarily unmusical and that they actually prefer silence, he begins what turns into the story's larger trend of undermining:

> Ist es denn überhaupt Gesang? Trotz unserer Unmusikalität haben wir Gesangsüberlieferungen; in den alten Zeiten unseres Volkes gab es Gesang; Sagen erzählen davon und sogar Lieder sind erhalten, die freilich niemand mehr singen kann. Eine Ahnung dessen, was Gesang ist, haben wir also und dieser Ahnung entspricht Josefinens Kunst eigentlich nicht. Ist es denn überhapt Gesang? Ist es nicht vielleicht doch nur ein Pfeifen? (1:275)

> Is it even singing? Despite our unmusicality we have singing traditions; in the old times of our people there was singing; legends tell of it and some songs even survive, though it's true nobody can sing them anymore. So we have an idea of this, what singing is, and Josefine's art doesn't actually correspond to it. Is it then singing at all? Is it not perhaps just a piping?

And it is not just the singing that is methodically undermined to the point of total destabilization—Josefine's revered place in the community, as "die Ausnahme," is as well. For by the end of the story, Josefine, before disappearing entirely to little notice or concern, comes across as a temperamental diva—one who, for example, insists on shortening or canceling her concert altogether on account of dubious foot pain: "So behauptete sie z.B. neulich, sie habe sich bei der Arbeit eine Fußverletzung zugezogen, die ihr das Stehen während des Gesanges beschwerlich mache; da sie aber nur stehend singen könne, müsse sie jetzt sogar die Gesänge kürzen" ("Recently she claimed to have hurt her foot in the course of work, which would have made standing while singing difficult; given, then, that she could only sing standing, she would have to cut the concert short") (1:292).

The question that Kafka's narrator has presented as the main issue of the story seems at first rather simple: what is her "singing," really, and why is she deemed important? Although the critical output regarding "Josefine" is markedly less prolific than that of Kafka's middle works, there are substantial insights to be found in the work of the classic canon (Margot Norris, Ritchie Robertson, and Ellison, for example), as well as some recent inquiry by Kata Gellen that widens the scope of how, rather than what, Josefine's gestures can potentially mean. For Norris, the significance of Josefine's non-singing maintains the common critical focus on Kafka's obsession with (mis)communication, here characterized by active forgetting or significant negation, and the unique bestial conception of Josefine as a late-career figuration of this obsession, a sentiment with which Ellison agrees.[7] Similarly, Robertson focuses on Josefine's pseudo-singing as "a profound and subtle meditation on the nature and value of art," in which "conventional ideas about the autonomy and value of art, even the ideas that a distinct aesthetic realm exists, turn out to be equally illusory." Indeed, Robertson argues quite rightly that Josefine herself is under an illusion about her art, and the other mice preserve her illusion with great solicitude, but, despite her claims, her performances are simply the medium through which the individual communicates with the communal spirit of his people.[8] Gellen, on the other hand, offers a starkly original take on what it is that Josefine is doing and why it remains important despite not actually being singing. "Wherein lies her power if not in her song?" Gellen asks; the answer is that "her ability to unify the mouse folk derives from her physical position, her self-transformation into a piece of architecture."[9]

Although I largely agree with each of these theories to some extent, each curiously avoids taking into account why it is that Josefine's song as it is described *cannot* mean in the first place. Is this because it is obvious? Hardly, as the narrator's description of the "piping" is wildly inconsistent at best, and so a non-language that is impossible to characterize cannot be so easily dismissed as noncommunicative. Indeed, I believe there is a tremendous amount of insight to be gained, at least temporarily, by isolating and subjecting to rigorous language analysis what, to the best of our ability to discern it, Josefine is actually doing and how much she may or may not be able to communicate and thus have an effect on her people. This is where Wittgenstein's work in both language in use (*PI* §43) and the refutation of a private language argument come into play, for these parts of the *Investigations* address what I feel to be exactly the aspects of Josefine's peculiar exceptionalism that the critical canon has yet to examine fully.

For Wittgenstein, the original problem he appears to present seems even more straightforward than Kafka's alleged problem with Josefine: how would a "private language" work? The primary example he uses is that of the private sensation and apparently incommunicable "language" of pain. As we will see, this is quite topical to "Josefine," given that her ostensible purpose is to express without articulating, through her "song," the particular and apparently incommunicable anguish of her people. What Wittgenstein plays at wanting to know at the outset of the private language argument is: how can a person in pain truly bridge that space between the nonlinguistic sensation of pain and the expression of it? That is, "Wie kann ich denn mit der Sprache noch zwischen die Schmerzäußerung und den Schmerz treten wollen?" ("How, then, can I enter, with language, into the space between expression of pain and pain?") (§245). To see why this is both tremendously important and surprisingly relevant to "Josefine," let us first examine in more detail these aspects of Josefine's peculiar form of communication that exemplify both pain and incommunicability.

Step 2: Kafka and the Undermining of Josefine

Again, the end result of both the Kafka and Wittgenstein texts is that each, in its own way, dismantles its original conceit, but to see why this is we must backtrack considerably and treat each conceit as a legitimate concept. This will momentarily involve approaching the Wittgenstein text as if it is advancing an important philosophical thesis, and presently involve approaching the Kafka text as if it were a more traditional prose narrative with a developing, progressing story, with a plot and an arc. In the case of "Josefine," then, the first thing we will notice is the apparent rejection of exactly this protagonist-to-plot relationship, replaced instead by the complete breakdown or contradiction of nearly every characteristic attributed to Josefine in the story's opening paragraph, a phenomenon Margot Norris has aptly characterized within the larger story's status as more than anything a "gesture of retraction."[10]

As we have reviewed several times at this point, at the outset our narrator insists: "Wer sie nicht gehört hat, kennt nicht die Macht des Gesanges" ("Anyone who has not heard her does not know the power of song"). The stunning ambiguity of this sentence—*does this rightly imply its opposite, that those who have heard her do?*—will be revisited in great detail at the close of this chapter, but for now to grasp fully the extent to which the story retracts itself, let us trust its idiomatic surface. That is, at the outset of this story, we are apparently meant to assume that *because* he who has not heard Josefine knows not the power of song, Josefine *must* be a tremendously powerful singer. And this is curious, given the immediate way in which the narrator undermines the very audience that is supposed to reaffirm Josefine's greatness. This begins in the first of five consecutive sentences that, as Gross has quite rightly pointed out, "are negated or contain negations," and which Minden rightly sees as contributing to the story's "tantalising self-cancelling effect upon its readers": "Es gibt niemanden, den ihr Gesang nicht fortreißt, was umso höher zu bewerten ist, als unser Geschlecht im ganzen Musik nicht liebt" ("There is nobody who is not carried away by her singing, which makes it even more worthwhile, as we are not in general a music-loving sort") (1:274).[11] How indeed can her song fail to move its audience when that audience is by definition *unmoved* by song? But it's not just that the mouse people do not normally care for music—as what Ellison refers to the story's "narrative unweaving" continues, it emerges that this people actually prefers *silence*: "Stiller Frieden ist uns die liebste Musik" ("Silent peace is for us the dearest music") (1:274).[12]

Indeed, only Josefine is the exception to this general anguish at sound, but again, that particular podium begins to crumble almost immediately; the mouse people are "doch ganz unmusikalisch; wie kommt es, daß wir Josefines Gesang verstehn oder, da Josefine unser Verständnis leugnet, wenigstens zu verstehen glauben" ("For we are completely unmusical; how does it come to be that we understand Josephine's singing—or, since Josephine denies our understanding, at least think we can") (1:274). How, indeed, does an "unmusical" people love Josefine's music? Is it because, as Minden has argued, she "performs for the community their own vulnerability"?[13] This would lend credence to Robertson's insistence that "it is not Josefine's performance but the act of listening to it that matters"—but, again, *why*?[14] Metanarratively, it makes sense, at least if we approach it from a Corngoldian psychoanalytic perspective, wherein the subject of the story is actually Kafka's unmusicality, which "resurges in [his] late work" as a "return of the repressed in a mode in which it could be tolerated, a fusion of the *even* pleasure of writing and the *odd* pleasure of a reflection on the nature of music."[15] Narratively, however, we are still left at a loss: why, and indeed *how*, does an unmusical people (allegedly) love the (alleged) song of its (alleged) singer?

Instead of answering this question, Kafka's narrator replaces the answer, in proto-Wittgensteinian fashion, with *another* question that works to undercut it: how can an unmusical people even be *qualified* to judge something as "Gesang" in the first place? This question has, to be sure, a deceptively "simple" answer:

> Die einfachste Antwort wäre, daß die Schönheit dieses Gesanges so groß ist, daß auch der stumpfeste Sinn ihr nicht widerstehen kann, aber diese Antwort ist nicht befriedigend. Wenn es wirklich so wäre, müßte man vor diesem Gesang zunächst und immer das Gefühl des Außerordentlichen haben, das Gefühl, aus dieser Kehle erklinge etwas, was wir nie vorher gehört haben und das zu hören wir auch gar nicht die Fähigkeit haben, etwas, was zu hören uns nur diese eine Josefine und niemand sonst befähigt. Gerade das trifft aber meiner Meinung nach nicht zu, ich fühle es nicht und habe auch bei andern nichts dergleichen bemerkt. Im vertrauten Kreise gestehen wir einander offen, daß Josefinens Gesang als Gesang nichts Außerordentliches darstellt. (1:274–75)

> The simplest answer would be: the beauty of her singing is so great that even the dullest sense cannot resist it, but this answer is unsatisfactory. If it were really so, we would, before her song, have an immediate and lasting feeling of the extraordinary, a feeling that from her throat comes something we have never heard before, and which we are not even capable of hearing, something that Josephine alone and nobody else makes possible. But I don't agree with that opinion,

> I do not feel it and I've never observed it in others. In trusted circles we tell each other often that Josefine's singing, as far as singing is concerned, is nothing extraordinary.

Here the undermining gains in intensity: perhaps her singing is so spectacular even those who do not care for music love it. But this is not the case: what we learn here is that her "singing" is rather ordinary. And this question is again not answered, but instead simply leads us to the larger, central, and most severely undermining question of the story: *is what Josefine does even really singing* (as we have seen before, "Ist es denn überhaupt Gesang?" [1:275]).

This question-leads-to-worse-question-leads-to-even-worse-question structure exemplifies what Ellison has rightly characterized as the story's "highly concentrated declarative (assertive) exposition," which, as we will see both now and in harsher and more complete light later in the chapter, are also "the essential elements of the narrative's eventual undoing."[16] And the central element of this undoing is the question: is Josefine actually just whistling, or piping (*pfeifen*)? As Robertson has characterized it, "the very nature of [Josefine's] art is problematic, for she does nothing but squeak, and this is the sound made by all the mice as a matter of course."[17] And yet, the narrator initially determines that it is not, in fact, *ordinary* piping, but instead something mysterious, *something that cannot be described but which has an effect upon its audience nonetheless.*

Indeed, this indescribable greatness is great not because what Josefine does is at all extraordinary, but because of the extraordinary effect ("große Wirkung") on its audience: "Und wenn man vor ihr sitzt, versteht man sie; Opposition treibt man nur in der Ferne; wenn man vor ihr sitzt, weiß man: was sie hier pfeift, ist kein Pfeifen" ("And when we sit before her, we understand her; we can only see opposition from a distance; when we sit in front of her, we know: what she's piping here is no piping") (1:277). What we are left with mid-story is that Josefine is somehow special *and* not special, exceptional and not exceptional; as Gross has described her, a seeming contradiction—but she is more than this. For the result of this contradictory force is that Josefine's status, her very presence, the very description of who she is and what she is, seems to be completely vanishing. In fact, the truth—the "Rätsel ihrer großen Wirkung"—is that when Josefine sings, nobody understands her at all; indeed, "sie singt ja ihrer Meinung nach vor tauben Ohren; an Begeisterung und Beifall fehlt es nicht, aber auf wirkliches Verständnis, wie sie es meint, hat sie längst verzichten gelernt" ("in her opinion she's singing to deaf ears anyway; there is no lack of rapture and acclaim, but real understanding, as far as she sees it, she's learned to stop expecting") (1:278).

And yet, this does not stop her from feeling entitled to understanding, entitled, indeed, to her "große Wirkung." The narrator has her saying: "Ich pfeife auf euren Schutz" ("I pipe for your protection") while the people think privately: "Ja, ja, du pfeifst" ("Yes, yes, you pipe"). And, further, what she "pipes" is, in seeming opposition to its great effect, thin and weak, what the narrator enchantingly describes as a "Nichts an Stimme" ("nothing in voice") (1:281–83). Effectively, Josefine's allegedly enrapturing abilities also hinge on her ability to express both a completely unremarkable piping and *a nothing*—for again, silence and nothingness is the most revered "sound" of all in this community:

> Sie spricht es nicht so aus und auch nicht anders, sie spricht überhaupt wenig, sie ist schweigsam unter den Plappermäulern, aber aus ihren Augen blitzt es, von ihrem geschlossenen Mund—bei uns können nur wenige den Mund geschlossen halten, sie kann es—ist es abzulesen. (1:281)
>
> She doesn't put it in so many words, or any other words; she says very little altogether; she is silent among the blabbermouths. But from her eyes it flashes, from her closed mouth—among us few can truly shut his mouth; she can—we can read it.

But the story would be far less confounding if, even in her squeaking and her silence, Josefine actually were as revered as we were initially led to believe she is. In fact, instead she seems to have all of the behavior of a diva with none of the rapturous audience to which she feels entitled—for example, if she feels her audience is insufficient, often she initially refuses to go on at all, and requires rather extreme measures of placation:

> Man tröstet sie, umschmeichelt sie, trägt sie fast auf den schon vorher ausgesuchten Platz, wo sie singen soll. Endlich gibt sie mit undeutbaren Tränen nach, aber wie sie mit offenbar letztem Willen zu singen anfangen will, matt, die Arme nicht wie sonst ausgebreitet, sondern am Körper leblos herunterhängend, wobei man den Eindruck erhält, daß sie vielleicht ein wenig zu kurz sind—wie sie so anstimmen will, nun, da geht es doch wieder nicht, ein unwilliger Ruck des Kopfes zeigt es an und sie sinkt von unseren Augen zusammen. (293)
>
> We comfort her, flatter her, we all but carry her to the place she's meant to sing. Finally she bursts into uninterpretable tears, but when she begins, with what is obviously the end of her will, to sing—exhausted—her arms not spread out as usual but instead hanging down lifelessly next to her body, so that we get the impression that they're a little bit too short—just as she's about to start, now, she can't do it after all, an unwilling shake of her head shows us this, and she breaks down before our eyes.

What much of the finest criticism of this story attests, and not necessarily wrongly, is that what is happening here is a rather obvious but still quite moving dismantling, and not just of Josefine's status as an artist, but of her "art form" itself, which, it turns out, is both impossible to describe and surprisingly banal. Chris Danta, for example, sees both the undermining of Josefine's "art" and her disappearance as an unveiled parallel to her creator, in both his relationship to his own art and his demise, while Robertson characterizes not just "Josefine," but Kafka's late oeuvre on the whole, as focusing largely upon "the relationship between the speculatively or artistically inclined individual and the society he or she belongs to."[18] This is certainly apparent in the text itself, as the narrator insists of Josefine that "was sie anstrebt, ist also nur die öffentliche, eindeutige, die Zeiten überdauernde, über alles bisher Bekannte sich weit erhebende Anerkennung ihrer Kunst" ("what she strives for is public, unambiguous, enduring recognition of her art, one that goes farther than anything we have ever known") (1:289).

However, instead of focusing, like the vast majority of criticism of this story does, on the active *dismantling* of, or in the view of some critics, active forgetting of, a questioned art form, what if instead we, rather counterintuitively, concentrated on the structure of that art form on its own, separate from its public? While this may seem unnecessary—after all, what is Josefine without her mouse folk?—instead it is quite the opposite: in fact, by examining the difficulty (or, rather impossibility) of Josefine's singing language, we can actually see just why it must *fail* to capture the anguish of its public, and in doing so relate it to both Wittgenstein's private language argument itself, and its eventual undermining.

Step 3: Wittgenstein and the Impossibility of Private Language

Indeed, returning again to Wittgenstein, the failure of Josefine's squeaking is fascinating to investigate through a language game, one that itself introduces and elucidates the final section of the *Investigations* I investigate alongside Kafka: the private language argument. I would like to go about this by setting up a first move in the game that mirrors the first move in the private language argument: it would seem feasible that the primary reason that Josefine's squeaking *cannot*—again, not does not, but *cannot*—fully and convincingly sing the pain and vulnerability of her people is that one *cannot* actually express one's pain in a way that others can actually understand it. That is, the sensation of pain is a private sensation, and any language meant to codify, homogenize, and express that pain, be it speaking or squeaking, would simply be an unsuccessful articulation of this private sensation. In this argument, the "language" of pain is *private*. But is a private language possible? As Wittgenstein introduces the argument in §243, it seems quite possible indeed. After all, people talk to themselves in different ways all of the time:

> Ein Mensch kann sich selbst ermutigen, sich selbst befehlen, gehorchen, tadeln, bestrafen, eine Frage vorlegen und auf sie antworten. Man könnte sich also auch Menschen denken, die nur monologisch sprächen. Ihre Tätigkeiten mit Selbstsprächen begleiteten. –Einem Forscher, der sie beobachtet und ihre Reden belauscht, könnte es gelingen, ihre Sprache in die unsre zu übersetzen.

> A person can encourage himself, order himself, obey, blame, punish, put a question forth and answer it. We could even think of people who only spoke in monologue. Who accompanied their activities by talking to themselves.—An explorer who watched them and listened to their speech might be able to translate their language into ours.

But talking to oneself is not the same as a truly private language, Wittgenstein reminds us. Talking to oneself is merely using common language silently. And indeed, what Josefine is doing is not talking (squeaking) to herself; she is squeaking *from* herself in a way that is supposed to express her *own* pain and fear in a way that somehow reminds her listeners of *their* pain and their fear, while still remaining, in its inexpressiblitity, necessarily distant enough from them that her singing/squeaking/expressing is destined to fail. That would be something completely different, *a private language* spoken aloud in public, one Wittgenstein describes thusly as §243 continues: "Wäre aber auch eine Sprache denkbar, in der Einer seine inneren Erlebnisse—seine Gefühle, Stimmungen, etc.—für den eigenen Gebrauch aufschreiben, oder aussprechen könnte?" ("Would a language also be possible to imagine, in which a person could write down his inner experiences—feelings, moods, etc.—for his own use?"). The interlocutory voice asks the next feasible question about this, which is: "—Können wir denn das in unserer gewöhnlichen Sprache nicht tun?" ("—Well, can't we do that in our ordinary language?"). Wittgenstein's straw man is quick to point out that expressing inner sensation with ordinary language ("to oneself" or aloud) is not what he means: "—Aber so meine ich's nicht. Die Wörter dieser Sprache wollen sich auf das beziehen, wovon nur der Sprechende wissen kann; auf seine unmittelbaren, privaten, Empfindungen. Ein Anderer kann diese Sprache also nicht verstehen" ("—But that is not what I mean. The words of this language will refer to what can only be known to the person speaking; to his immediate, private sensations. Another person could thus not understand it").

Again, this would seem to describe rather well the predicament in which Josefine finds herself (again, assuming that in her world, squeaking is language): she is speaking using the vehicle of the mouse folk's ordinary language—squeaking—but in a way that is indescribably set apart, so that its true nature remains, as Wittgenstein has just said, incommunicable ("unmittelbar"). And again, what Josefine needs to—but cannot—express is, as Wittgenstein has just said, private sensation: fear, anguish, pain.

In Josefine's case, it does seem that her pain, her sensations, form a kind of "private language." And if this is the case—thus triggering the next phase of the language game—this would mean that her problem, and I suppose by extension the problem of all such "artists," is that they can express their anguish (or other emotions) *internally*, but only internally. In this view, the idea that there then *is* something within them that they cannot express is a foregone conclusion. This reformulation of the same language crisis that I have been discussing for much of this book is one, then, that "solves" the crisis by predicating it upon the existence of a private language—specifically, in this case, a private language of pain.

Wittgenstein posits at the private language argument's outset that there is indeed something slightly off about the way words relate to—or refer to—sensations ("Wie *beziehen* sich Wörter auf Empfindungen?" ["How do words *relate* to sensations?"] [§244]). Perhaps, he argues, we learn the meaning of the word "pain" like this: "Es werden Worte mit dem ursprünglichen, natürlichen, Ausdruck der Empfindung verbunden und an dessen Stelle gesetzt" ("Let words be connected with the original, natural, expressions of the sensation and used in their place") (§244). That is, a child is injured and cries, "und nun sprechen ihm die Erwachsenen zu und bringen ihm Ausrufe und später Sätze bei. Sie lehren das Kind ein neues Schmerzbenehmen"—and, eventually, the word "pain" does not *mean* "crying," but rather it replaces the wordless cry ("and then the adults talk to him, and teach him exclamations and later sentences. They teach the child a new behavior of pain") (§244). And yet, Wittgenstein's initial narrator is not satisfied with this relationship; he wishes to know in a more precise way how we can actually use language precisely and effectively to "get between pain and the expression of pain" (§245). Again, this is effectively the question at the heart of why, in Kafka's story, Josefine's singing fails: in what way has the narrator, and have we, and has Josefine herself, decided to get between pain and its expression?

Wittgenstein "answers" this question by rephrasing it into a more difficult problem in §246, which many philosophers believe to be the true introduction to the private language argument. In this remark, the problem is phrased as such: In what sense are sensations private, and why does it matter? (In our case, our interpretation of why Josefine's squeaking is both special and fails would lead to this: In what sense are Josefine's sensations private, and thus in what sense is her squeaking a private language?). Section 246 begins: "In wiefern sind nun meine Empfindungen privat?" ("To what extent are my sensations private?") For, after all, interjects one of Wittgenstein's interlocutory voices, another person can never really know if someone is in pain: "—Nun, nur ich kann wissen, ob ich wirklich Schmerzen habe; der Andere kann es nur vermuten" ("—Well, only I can know if I'm really in pain; another person can only guess it"). This, then, would ensure that pain—and therefore, by extension, most if not all sensation—is private; one registering one's pain to oneself would, then, be a form of private language.

Not so fast, says an interlocutor: "Das ist in einer Weise falsch, in einer anderen unsinnig" ("That is in one way false, and in another nonsensical"). Why in one way false? Because, it turns out, the interlocutor has misunderstood the use of the verb *wissen* (to know; "nur ich kann wissen"): "Wenn wir das Wort 'wissen' gebrauchen, wie es normalerweise gebraucht wird (und wie sollen wir es denn gebrauchen!) dann wissen es Andre sehr häufig, wenn ich Schmerzen habe" ("If we are using the word 'to know' as it's normally used [and how else should we use it!], then other people know quite often when I'm in pain"). The first interlocutor is not convinced: "Ja," insists the interlocutory voice, "aber nicht mit der Sicherheit, mit der ich selbst es weiß!" ("Yes, but not with the certainty with which I myself know it!"). How does this undermine the understanding of the word *wissen*? Surprisingly, Wittgenstein's problem is not with the perceived issue here of one being unable to communicate the fact of one's pain to another, with the *certainty* one can only have about her own pain. That is, the problem is about the words we use to claim that certainty in the first place:

> —Von mir kann überhaupt nicht sagen (außer etwa im Spaß) ich wisse, daß ich Schmerzen habe. Was soll es denn heißen—außer etwa, daß ich Schmerzen habe?
>
> Man kann nicht sagen, die Andern lernen meine Empfindung nur durch mein Benehmen,—denn von mir kann man nicht sagen, ich lernte sie. Ich habe sie.
>
> Das ist richtig: es hat Sinn, von Andern zu sagen, sie seien im Zweifel darüber, ob ich Schmerzen habe; aber nicht, es von mir selbst zu sagen.

> —It can't be said of me at all (except perhaps as a joke) that I know I am in pain. What, then, is that supposed to mean—except perhaps that I am in pain?
>
> Others can't be said to learn of my sensations only from my behavior—for about me one can't say: I learned them. I have them.
>
> Here is the truth: it makes sense to say about other people that they are in doubt about whether I'm in pain, but not to say it about myself.

What, after all, does it mean to say "I know I am in pain"? Though others can, *we* can't say we don't know *we're* in pain (for everyone knows her own pain!), so for Wittgenstein it is equally impossible to say we *do*. Thus, in this situation, we are misusing the verb *wissen* (to know), or at any rate we are presupposing a meaning of it that doesn't really make sense. So there *can't* be a private language of pain, because that would be tantamount to saying "I know I am in pain," in German "Ich *wisse*, daß ich Schmerz habe," a strange and intentional use of the first subjunctive, which is used exclusively for reported speech and thus almost never in the first person. Indeed, he seems to have used "ich wisse" for a very important reason, and that is to show immediately to any speaker of German that this use of *wissen* is contradictory: why would one have to report one's own speech?

In short, the presupposition of a private language of sensation actually rests upon a tremendous misunderstanding about how *all* language works, indicative in this particular misuse. Wittgenstein further attacks this misunderstanding in §247, by demonstrating that if we were to defend our (mis)use by attempting to clarify our purpose ("Absicht"), that simply demonstrates a further misunderstanding of the word *Absicht*:

> "Nur du kannst wissen, ob due die Absicht hattest." Das könnte man jemandem sagen, wenn man ihm die Bedeutung des Wortes "Absicht" erklärt. Es heißt dann nämlich: so gebrauchen wir es.
>
> (Und "wissen" heißt hier, daß der Ausdruck der Ungewißheit sinnlos ist.)
>
> "Only you can know if you had that intention." We might tell someone this when we are explaining to him the meaning of the word "intention." For then it means: that is how we use it.
>
> (And here "know" means that the expression of uncertainty is senseless.)

To summarize this extraordinarily difficult but highly relevant idea: we cannot actually say "Ich wisse, daß ich Schmerz habe," because that odd use of the self-reported word "know" is so bound together with the odd context in this situation—which is, according to one of Wittgenstein's interlocutors, the "purpose" of self-reporting our own pain, a curious and unnecessary activity. Thus, in order to *know* what "know" means in this situation, we also have to know what "purpose" means in this situation, which means all we really *know* is how "know" is used *in this particular situation*. Thus, all a sentence such as "Ich wisse, daß ich Schmerz habe" *really* means is the expression of several *grammatical* facts in a particular context: an unconventional but technically correct use of the first subjunctive followed by a dependent clause. What we have here is simply, as Monk has put it, a misunderstanding of the difference between a *grammatical* remark like this one and a material remark—that is, a remark that makes some sort of discovery rather than simply expressing preexisting facts.[19] "Ich wisse, daß ich Schmerz habe" is simply a grammatical remark we have been under the *illusion* is a material one.

Now with our new understanding of the *mis*understanding of *wissen* comes a new understanding that the sentence "Empfindungen sind privat" ("Sensations are private") is *itself* a grammatical rather than a material remark.[20] Monk further helps us to see that in §§247–49, Wittgenstein has actually cautioned us that "if we then start talking about the certainty with which we know our own pain, then we need to be shown that what prompts such talk is a confusion between a grammatical remark and a material one."[21] The point is then demonstrated in its absurd extreme in §248, when Wittgenstein compares "Empfindungen sind privat," which we mistakenly believe should denote some sort of *discovery* about the existence of private sensations (and thus the possibility of a private language), and "Patience spielt man allein" ("One plays [the solitaire game] Patience by oneself"), which is a banal and tautological remark. Thus, arguing that "sensations are private" as a meaningful sentence that actually says something about the existence of a private language is not *arguing* at all; it is simply making an obvious remark that imparts no discoveries about language, but rather perpetuates a significant *mis*understanding about the nature of language.

Perhaps our problem is not that private language itself is impossible, but that we have been approaching the problem the wrong way. Wittgenstein's straw-man narrator attempts to come up with a different and more viable way in which a private language is possible: if the statement that "Empfindungen sind privat" is not actually indicative of a private language, then what about a different sort of private language? That is, what if I were to claim that I could keep a sensation diary, so that every time I felt a certain sensation I'd name it "E" and write "E" every time I felt it? (§258). Wittgenstein's interlocutor is not buying it: how is the sign "E" *sure* to evoke that particular sensation? Easy, claims the first voice: I concentrate that way, I do it on purpose—so any "correct" use of the diary would predicate correct memory of the sensation. Aha, says the interlocutor: but there is no "Kriterium für die Richtigkeit" ("criterion for correctness") in this situation. "Man möchte hier sagen: richtig ist, was immer mir als richtig erscheinen wird. Und das heißt nur, daß hier von 'richtig' nicht geredet werden kann" ("We would like to say: right is whatever will seem right to me. And that only means that here we can't talk about 'right' ") (§258). The result is that the entire game of being able to keep a feeling diary to which one would assign a "private" sign is again illusory, for in order for a sign to be truly unintelligible to *other* users, it would also have to be unintelligible to *its* user, and thus its entire existence would be predicated on the absence of the very functionality it would have to possess in order to truly be a private sign. There is no private language—there is simply, as originally put forth in §243, ordinary language spoken to oneself.

This brings us back to square zero when attempting to determine if a private language exists, and the implication of this train of thought in Kafka's story is this: it seemed like Josefine was failing to capture her audience because her legitimate private sensations were expressible to her via squeaking, but largely incommunicable to her audience. Kafka's narrator has contradicted the exceptionalness of Josefine's squeaking while still somehow making the case for it, but seen from this angle, we have no choice but to determine that her squeaking is actually 100 percent the banal and ordinary language of her people. And thus, her people fail to respond to the squeaking *not* because the squeaking fails to be intelligible to them—but because they simply, for one reason or another, do not like it.

Step 4: A Pyrrhonian View of Kafka's Late Work

Still, Wittgenstein's dissolution of the conceit of private language may not seem tremendously important outside certain specialized philosophical discussion, but let us not forget that the stakes here are actually quite high: the ostensible foundation of all modern philosophy, Descartes's *Meditations*, hinges *directly* upon exactly the kind of mind-body duality the existence of a private language would justify. Thus, what makes the so-called private language argument the most discussed in all of Wittgenstein's philosophy is the potential implications it has for philosophical discourse altogether. That is, if a private language is impossible (because for it to be unintelligible to other users it would also have to be unintelligible to *its* user), then not just the conceit of private language is toppled, but so is the entire conceit of a purely mental and philosophical realm. This has consequences for "Josefine" as well, and these are more far-reaching than they at first appear.

The apparent relevance of the private language argument to "Josefine" is, in short, the following discovery: the common claim that Josefine is simply *incapable* of expressing to others a private anguish that is expressible to *her* is fully subverted. Instead, what she is really doing with her "Nichts an Stimme" ("nothing in voice") is, actually, nothing. Her squeaking may *appear* to have an adulated place in her people's canon of performance artists—much like, Wittgenstein implies, Cartesian dualism has in philosophy—but in actuality, occupying that place is merely the mouse folk's ordinary language of squeaking. So Josefine's status is not in peril because the public *now* fails to appreciate her (similarly to the foregone publics in the penal colony or "A Hunger Artist"); it was always and only in peril, or rather it was never special in the first place. Instead, it was ignored or mildly tolerated as the ordinary squeaking it was.

But how is this possible? Does the first paragraph of this story not introduce Josefine's character as an exception, and does it not claim that "Wer sie nicht gehört hat, kennt nicht die Macht des Gesangs" ("Anyone who has not heard her does not know the power of song")? The final step of this exploration is to return to this sentence, and bring the entirety of Wittgenstein's Pyrrhonian project together to clarify our last major misunderstandings about this story: not only have we as readers been under the mistaken impression that Josefine was ever perceived as special in the first place, but we have also been under the mistaken impression that Kafka has been telling us a story about this at all. What I would like to show here is that upon closer inspection, the story of Josefine is *not* actually a story that takes the form of a litany of contradictions—it is simply the unremarkable presentation of several grammatical facts that subvert the act of narration altogether. In this way, it is what we can call Pyrrhonian literature or Pyrrhonian storytelling.

What we have to realize is that the conclusions we have just come to regarding both Wittgenstein's private language argument *and* "Josefine," however elucidatory, are still predicated upon one grand illusion apiece. Wittgenstein *appears* very convincingly to have argued that there is no such thing as a private language; there is *language* that is spoken to oneself, but if that language can be intelligible *to oneself*, then it can be intelligible period. And as we have just seen, the consequences of his argument are potentially vast. In Kafka's case, the story also seems rather convincingly to have exposed its central artist as banal and unworthy of exceptional status. And yet, to stop at both of these "theses" would be to miss the entire point of both texts.

For what is at stake here is that, no matter how elegant and final both texts' "theses" seem to be about the nature of philosophy and art, no matter how many misunderstandings they appear to have uncovered, another and even more grievous misunderstanding prevails if we do not recognize that these "conclusions" are, in fact, not conclusions but *illusions*. Much of the philosophical criticism of Wittgenstein's private language argument addresses the problem that the argument (or alleged argument) cannot *actually* be the intense negation of—and therefore engagement *with*—the history of modern epistemology. As we have seen briefly before, philosophers refer to what Wittgenstein is doing with the private language argument—and, by extension, the entire *Investigations*—as Pyrrhonianism, as self-immolation, creation of something to show, in that creation, its assured destruction. As David Stern has succinctly pointed out, while on the surface the *Investigations* have little in common with—in fact, seem to completely destroy every thesis of—the earlier *Tractatus*, what they do have in common is perhaps the most important thing about each one: Pyrrhonianism.

Again, a unifying Pyrrhonian impulse has been discussed with respect to Wittgenstein's entire corpus at exhaustive length, and indeed there is no analyst of any aspect of the *Investigations*—and, for some critics from the "New Wittgenstein" group, of the *Tractatus* as well—that can approach anything in them without addressing at least one of two extreme cases (to borrow a term from the earlier Wittgenstein) of *Investigations* interpretation. That is, one must, to some extent, argue that *either* Wittgenstein's investigations *do* advance philosophical theses, and that Pyrrhonianism is *itself* a philosophical thesis and thus cannot be fully realized, or that the *Investigations*, like the *Tractatus* before it, is a text that offers pseudo-theses, transitional remarks, and that the full act of understanding them absolutely necessitates their self-destruction.

The problem with the first approach is that if one is to believe that Pyrrhonianism is a thesis, and a valid one, one would have to follow through on the *Investigations*' Pyrrhonian trajectory—and thus acknowledge the throwing away of yet another ladder, which leaves behind perhaps only one thesis, Pyrrhonianism (which then must throw itself away to be complete). This is intensely problematic, in that without those philosophies which the Pyrrhonian has demanded self-destruct, Pyrrhonianism does not make much sense. The problem of the second approach is that—Diamond's "transitional" thesis aside—this would mean that every discovery we have previously made about important linguistic paradoxes such as that of ostension and rule-following is not *really* a discovery. Thus, despite Wittgenstein's stark instructions regarding landscape sketches, we are left somewhat bereft of a reason to read the *Investigations* at all.

There is no answer that could possibly be satisfying or comforting enough. What we have instead is, succinctly put, a compelling *impossibility*. Unsurprisingly, I would also like to use the term "compelling impossibility" to talk about "Josefine," because I believe that the most important thing about this text is not the systemless and yet systematic takedown of its protagonist, but the fact that this takedown is only illusory. And, further, this particular illusion cements the work as an utterly defiant piece of prose, one that lures us quite convincingly into believing that we are reading a story but then, in the end, disabuses us of that notion. In short, "Josefine" is a companion piece to Wittgenstein's *Investigations* not because of its curious portrayal of a "private" language that isn't one, but because of its status as a Pyrrhonian text, one that also forces us to chose from gradients of two equally compelling but rather fatalistic approaches to it. These approaches are as follows: either "Josefine" is a story, but it is a story that destroys the act of storytelling, or "Josefine" is not a story at all. The first approach is Pyrrhonian; the second is austere. And as we now well know, these approaches parallel two major approaches to Wittgenstein's philosophy.

To see why both approaches are equally possible and equally necessary, we should examine closely both the end and the beginning of "Josefine." The story (or, more properly, pseudo-story) ends with its heroine, her reputation in shambles and her art questioned to the point of its existence, refusing to sing altogether, her "gift" and thus her own existence disappearing from the mouse people:

> So war es letzthin, das Neueste aber ist, daß sie zu einer Zeit, wo ihr Gesang erwartet wurde, verschwunden war. Nicht nur der Anhang sucht sie, viele stellen sich in den Dienst des Suchens, es ist vergeblich; Josefine ist verschwunden, sie will nicht singen, sie will nicht einmal darum gebeten werden, sie hat uns diesmal völlig verlassen. (1:293)

> That happened a while ago; but the latest news is that she has disappeared, just at a time when she was expected to sing. It is not only her followers who are looking for her; many have put themselves in the

> service of the search, but it's all to no avail; Josephine has vanished, she won't sing; she won't be begged into singing a single time; this time, she has deserted us completely.

This at first seems to solidify the nonexistence of a "private language" for Josefine—what she achieves in refusing to sing, after that very "singing" has been undermined to mere squeaking and then even worse than that, is not that she keeps her unique ability to express the mouse folk's pain to herself in a private "language," but that she achieves true privacy, total silence and isolation, necessarily *without* language. Indeed, this seems to be the inevitable conclusion of her story:

> Bald wird die Zeit kommen, wo ihr letzter Pfiff ertönt und verstummt. Sie ist eine kleine Episode in der ewigen Geschichte unseres Volkes und das Volk wird den Verlust überwinden. Leicht wird es uns ja nicht werden; wie werden die Versammlungen in völliger Stummheit möglich sein? Freilich, waren sie nicht auch mit Josefine stumm? War ihr wirkliches Pfeifen nennenswert lauter und lebendiger, als die Erinnerung daran sein wird? War es denn noch bei ihren Lebzeiten mehr als eine bloße Erinnerung? Hat nicht vielmehr das Volk in seiner Weisheit Josefinens Gesang, eben deshalb, weil er in dieser Art unverlierbar war, so hoch gestellt? (1:294)

> Soon the time will come when her last squeak sounds and falls silent. She is a small episode in the eternal history of our people, and the people will overcome the loss. It won't be easy for us; how can our gatherings be possible in total silence? Still, weren't they also silent when she was there? Was her piping actually notably louder or more alive than it will be in memory? Was it even during her lifetime more than a simple memory? Was it not, actually, because Josephine's singing was already, in this way, incapable of being lost, that our people in their wisdom prized it so highly?

In what way have Josefine's status or art form been *overcome*? Has the folk overcome the loss of Josefine due to what Ellison has termed the "general forgetfulness" that subsumes the entire story?[22] I believe it is more insidious than this. In fact, the word Kafka uses here at the end of Josefine, *überwinden*, is the same word Wittgenstein uses at the end of the *Tractatus* to call for an overcoming (or, in some translations, transcending) of the illusion of philosophical language. My view of Josefine's status supports this use of *überwinden*—the mouse people have not overcome Josefine's singing because they no longer like it (or never liked it); instead, they (and we) have simply come to view it for what it really is: nothing, really, but another ladder to be thrown away. Minden has called the "fact" of Josefine's separateness "the only certain thing about her," but I believe this to be an illusion as well.[23] Again, paralleling the earlier Wittgenstein and the end of the *Tractatus*, the final lines of "Josefine," as we now revisit them, are an acceptance of silence:

> Vielleicht werden wir also gar nicht sehr viel entbehren, Josefine aber, erlöst von der irdischen Plage, die aber ihrer Meinung nach Auserwählten bereitet ist, wird fröhlich sich verlieren in der zahllosen Menge der Helden unseres Volkes, und bald, da wir keine Geschichte treiben, in gesteigerter Erlösung vergessen sein wie alle ihre Brüder. (1:294)

> Perhaps we will not miss so much after all. But Josephine, delivered from the earthly troubles, which in her opinion lie in wait for the chosen ones, will happily lose herself in the numberless crowd of heroes of our people. And soon, since we are not historians, in this increased deliverance she'll be forgotten, like all her brothers.

But why must a fully realized understanding of Josefine's squeaking result in overcoming the illusion that it was ever special in the first place? This brings us, finally, back to the first lines of the story, to a particular sentence that I insisted some time ago was dangerously ambiguous: "Wer sie nicht gehört hat, kennt nicht die Macht des Gesangs" ("Anyone who has not heard her does not know the power of song").

The problem with this sentence is that in order to believe that "Josefine" contains contradictions and digressions—which, as Samuel Frederick has pointed out recently, would still make it a narrative, albeit a relatively plotless one—one must take the first sentence as a material remark.[24] That is, one must understand the negations in it to imply their positive counterparts: if he who has not heard her knows not the power of song, then he who *has* heard her *does*. But where in this sentence is that implied positive correlation truly demanded? Where is it proven? It is not—only in the proper context, the context in which Josefine's audience is enraptured, does this implied meaning solidify. But this context does not exist—in fact, an opposite context does—and so what we have instead is a remark in a contextual vacuum. In previous chapters we have learned that within this contextual vacuum, no unshakable ostensive reference can be pinned onto any word in this sentence, nor can its implied opposite "rule" truly be a rule. And in this chapter we have learned that the result of discovering that there is no such thing as a private language is the simultaneous discovery of the misunderstanding of the nature of our language wherein we mistake a grammatical remark for a material one. The most important aspect of "Josefine" that Wittgenstein's private language argument can teach us is that most readers mistake "Wer sie nicht gehört hat, kennt nicht die Macht des Gesangs" for a material remark that implies a positive correlation, wherein in actuality it is merely a grammatical remark that states a fact whose causality is completely indeterminate: "Wer sie nicht gehört hat, kennt nicht die Macht des Gesangs." He who has not heard her does not know the power of song. Nothing about the German language actually predicates a causal relationship between these clauses. As a grammatical remark, the sentence simply states a set of grammatical facts that are fairly redundant. He who has not heard Josefine does not know the power of song, *but the reason he does not know the power of song could be anything*. To assume otherwise would be to assume we know how the causal relationship is being used in this context, and that assumption is faulty. Thus, at no point in the story was the power of Josefine's alleged song ever even attested, and as a result it cannot really be contradicted, digressed, or forgotten. Robertson has argued that the story leaves "unsolved the question of the nature and value of Josefine's performances," but viewed as a Pyrrhonian work it does something quite different and quite remarkable: it leaves *dis*solved the question of the nature and value of Josefine's singing.[25]

A Final Conclusion

With its central problem dissolved, unmasked as an illusory problem, I believe this leaves "Josefine" vulnerable to the claim I have previously made that it is not a story per se. Minden has argued that the text has "rolled up its own meaning behind it until, most obviously, it finishes by establishing the absence of exactly that which it had set out to make present to the reader (that is, Josefine)," but again, without a positive statement about Josefine at the start, this is actually impossible.[26] Far more accurate is Robertson's characterization that in "Josefine" the act of "narrative has largely given way to reflection," but again this begs the question: reflection on what?[27] On the nature of art and the artist's place in the community? Perhaps, but we must reimagine this reflection from the perspective that no remarkable art ever existed in the first place. There is but one element left undissolved, however: what of the claim that follows shortly after "Wer sie nicht gehört hat . . ." that, in the unmusical mouse folk, "nur Josefine macht die Ausnahme" ("Josefine alone is the exception")? Critics such as Ellison believe this state of exception is one of the many things the story curiously undermines.[28] Again, I believe this sentence has been misinterpreted as a material remark, with most readers assuming a more colloquial use of the verb *machen* inside of the idiomatic expression "die Ausnahme machen." In reality, without the proper context—an adoring public that actually demonstrates this exception as meaning that Josefine is actually musical—we have instead a grammatical remark: Josefine *makes* the exception, which can literally mean that she makes it for herself, that she insists upon being viewed as an artist for no reason whatsoever. It can also mean that she is the exception to something, but what exactly that is cannot actually be determined, and to assume it can would again rest upon a serious misunderstanding of language. Thus, the understandable view that, as Robertson has put it, Kafka's narrator "unfolds a series of paradoxes" is actually mistaken as well.[29]

Ellison has asked, on behalf of all of us, "What kind of narrative progression will characterize this tale?"[30] Again, as I have argued with "In the Penal Colony," I believe this tale actually has no progression whatsoever, and is barely a tale in any sense—but that, as Nestroy has written and Wittgenstein has framed the *Investigations*, again, the problem with progress is that it always looks greater than it really is. Not unlike Wittgenstein, Kafka seemed remarkably concerned (and unimpressed) with what he perceived to be conceits about language use that didn't work (bringing us back to the spear remark from the preface to part 1 of this book). In this vein, his final story does indeed serve as an exception to his earlier work, but not only because of its use of a female central character, and not only as, in the Corngoldian view, a continuation because of its fixation on the hybrid literary and speculative text or the hybrid human and animal mode of expression. "Josefine" is exceptional literature, but not an exception to Kafka's canon. This is because of its remarkable ability to finish what "In the Penal Colony" began—a protest against, an undermining of, the tradition of prose narration, itself couched in the apparent medium of prose narration.

Robertson's theory is that from 1917 on, Kafka "abandoned an expressive view of art for a mimetic one," no longer wanting to express his own feelings but rather "die Welt ins Reine, Wahre, Unveränderliche [zu] heben" ("to lift the world into purity and inalterability").[31] In other words, Kafka wanted to express the world as all that was the case—and yet, as we have seen, he remained for his entire career doubtful that his language was in any way up to the task. In this way, Kafka's late work encapsulates the Pyrrhonian aspects of both Wittgenstein's early and later work: just as Wittgenstein's *Investigations* aimed to dismantle the conceits of philosophical language the *Tractatus* failed to, and yet still within the medium of self-immolating philosophy, "Josefine," as Kafka's last work, functions similarly as a dissolution of the conceits of prose narration, still somehow contained within that very medium.

Directly in the midst of the private language argument, Wittgenstein's narrator makes a seemingly aphoristic comment: "Der Philosoph behandelt eine Frage; wie eine Krankheit" ("The philosopher treats a problem like an illness") (§255). But this is anything but a stand-alone aphorism—this is a direct indictment of the very "argument" Wittgenstein himself is allegedly making, or rather of the very idea of philosophical argument in general. That is, the philosopher is intent on *solving* something. But what happens if we stop viewing a philosophical question like a sickness? Only when we let go of the misguided need for a "cure" can we recognize the original question's most important illusions and delusions, and then we can dissolve rather than solve it. In Kafka studies, the critic has also until now been intent on solving the problem of Josefine: *Is she singing? What is she doing, really? Was her singing ever important to her people?* But, again, if we realize that those questions are not actually sicknesses that have to be cured, and once we are freed from the pressure to find answers for them, we can truly see the actual problems they present.

Concluding Thoughts

The Problem with (Critical) Progress

In the preceding chapters we have used the laws of logic to determine why, exactly, understanding something correctly and misunderstanding it are not mutually exclusive, and why this assertion is so important to *The Trial*; later, using Wittgenstein's "say/show" distinction, we have seen our conception of metaphorical meaning transformed into a misconception through a reimagining of Gregor Samsa's form as empty metaphor in *The Metamorphosis*; then, through his dismantling of the pseudo-propositions of ethics, we have come to understand that the ineffability of ethical judgment means the titular "judgment" of Georg Bendemann wasn't one at all. Through associating Kafka with Wittgenstein's *Tractatus*, we have failed to answer—and instead rendered unaskable—the three most pressing questions about these works. In this way we began to see both the form and relevance of a "logical modernism" to Kafka's literary universe.

We have then, through Wittgenstein's later work and the introduction of an analytic skepticism, witnessed the systematic dismantling of not just three more pressing questions about his most famous works—*The Castle*, "In the Penal Colony," "Josefine the Singer"—but the total undermining of the fiction process altogether. First, we saw Wittgenstein's paradox of ostensive definition acted out in all of its absurd dramatic possibility in the confounding nonreferentiality of the word *Landvermesser*, and the equally compounding system of anti-ostension in the village of *The Castle*. Then came the unexpected but unmediateable (*unmittelbar*) murder of the alleged solution to the paradox of ostension, the idea of meaning in "use," apparent by way of the paradox of rule-following as it came to life—and then dominated a death—in "In the Penal Colony." Finally, through Wittgenstein's private language argument and the subsequent arguments it ignited about the philosophical significance of the *Investigations* altogether, we saw the entire conceit of prose narration undermined altogether.

In making each of these discoveries, we simultaneously teased out both their philosophical and literary implications, in particular their implications with respect to the analytic tradition in philosophy. This process enabled us to redraw the boundaries of the rich, varied, and complex trajectory of radical skepticism in Kafka's work to include both logical analysis and ordinary language philosophy from an analytic standpoint. Without the idea of a logical modernism, the total validity of the outcome of *The Trial* (completely regardless of Josef K.'s "guilt") would be impossible to see with as much clarity or believability; indeed, without Wittgenstein's preliminary first-order logic, the entire dismantling of the question of K.'s guilt would not be possible to such an immutable extent. Nor would it have been possible to view *The Metamorphosis* from a perspective that defines metaphorical form in such a way, which in turn allows us to let go of a question of what Gregor Samsa "means" and to focus instead on the equally interesting question of how. And in "The Judgment," what turns out to be radical skepticism of the communicability of Herr Bendemann's ethical "judgment" is highlighted in its structural similarities to the conclusions about "the limits of language" Wittgenstein reaches in the *Tractatus*.

These "limits" are themselves challenged, however, by none other than Wittgenstein himself after his return to philosophy in the 1930s and to what I term an analytic skepticism. As we saw, the first casualty of his *Investigations* was the bedrock of logical philosophy, the conceit of referentiality that made the picture theory at all possible. The dismantling of this conceit again offers unique elucidation of Kafka's work in our study of *The Castle*, specifically in an appropriately Wittgenstinian dismantling of the novel's primary question: is K. a real land surveyor or isn't he? By unmasking the impossibility of asking that question, I hope I have offered both an interesting and highly skeptical interpretation of *The Castle*, and freed the critic from the onus of answering that question at all by rendering it unaskable. The exposure of unaskable questions continued as I explored "In the Penal Colony," in which I argued that in making the officer's death fiercely uninterpretable, Kafka has unraveled the notion of narrative meaning, putting in its place an obtuse descriptive universe whose very opacity is its triumph. And finally, with "Josefine," we have, thanks to Wittgenstein's private language argument and the Pyrrhonianism debate surrounding it, the furthering of that triumph, undermining the entire notion of narration to its core, and with it the question of what Josefine is actually doing as a casualty. Six works, six questions, six ways that Wittgenstein has helped us see that they cannot actually be asked.

However, this study does not dissolve all of its relevant questions, least of all the following: what has been the *point* of such an exploration for Kafka studies? This is indeed a question that can and should be asked, and one that deserves a real answer, rather than simply undermining the question once again. I believe the point of this study, and thereby its potential relevance to the discipline, to be (quite appropriately) a proverbial double-edged sword. First of all, I hope that in examining for literary purposes sections of Wittgenstein's texts that almost never make it outside of philosophical discussions, I have helped to dismantle (or prove unnecessary) a veritable line in the sand that has been present since the analytic and Continental schism that is now nearly a century old. Analytic philosophy is often considered anathema to literature from both disciplines—philosophers often do not see the interest or point in exploring the philosophy for a sake other than its own, in "using" it, as it were, as literary theory; literary theorists, as I have discussed in previous chapters, are often eager to balk at the very pretenses of immutable concepts that underlie the analytic tradition— although in Wittgenstein's work, as we have seen, that is most certainly not the case. I would even go so far as to say that, especially given the trajectory of Wittgenstein's skepticism and the interest with which he undermines the conceits of philosophy and logic, this aspect of the analytic tradition has far more in common with, for example, the deconstructionist criticism that began to dominate literary theory shortly after Wittgenstein's death in 1951. And so (in Wittgensteinian fashion) if this book is to have had a point, it would be this: I would like to think that I have opened up a new facet of modernism studies ("new" despite its sources all being primary texts from modernism), one that I very much hope will be allowed into the greater literary discourse in a less marginal way.

On the other hand, one could argue that this opening up of Kafka studies to the analytic tradition has "succeeded" only in making Kafka's well-studied language skepticism so radically skeptical that it has defeated in advance the very act of asking the questions about it that we most want to ask. Is this book, in its own way, a vastly overreaching critical version of the *Tractatus*'s final call to silence? I certainly hope not, but I also quite enjoy the parallel structure of a philosophical approach that, in its own execution, brings about its own self-immolation, *exactly in the same way* its own content has done. In the end, I suppose it is the reader's choice: does the inclusion of Wittgenstein, and by extension the analytic tradition, present a bold new direction for Kafka studies, some excellent critical progress? Or does it, simply by being what it is and doing what it does, necessarily invalidate the entire conceit of critical progress, a conceit that was illusory to begin with? Must we simply change direction, or were we doomed all along? After all, the problem with progress is that it always appears greater than it really is.

NOTES

Introduction

1. Franz Kafka, *Gesammelte Werke in zwölf Bänden*, ed. Hans-Gerhard Koch and Malcolm Pasley, vol. 7, *Zur Frage der Gesetze* (Frankfurt am Main: Fischer, 2004), 163. This edition of Kafka's collected German works will hereafter be cited in text with the abbreviation *GW* followed by the volume number and the page number. Unless otherwise noted, all translations into English are my own.

2. Johann Nepomunk Nestroy, *Der Schützling: Posse mit Gesang in vier Akten* (Vienna: Burgtheater, 1989), 179.

3. This popular view of the relationship between Wittgenstein and Nestroy is most often attributed to the eminent Wittgenstein scholar David Stern. See specifically the first three chapters of *Wittgenstein's "Philosophical Investigations": An Introduction* (Cambridge, Eng.: Cambridge University Press, 2004).

4. Ludwig Wittgenstein, *Logisch-philosophische Abhandlung/Tractatus Logico-Philosophicus* (Frankfurt am Main: Suhrkamp, 1963). As is customary in the philosophical community, here the *Tractatus* will be abbreviated *TLP* and referenced parenthetically in text by remark number, e.g., "Was gezeigt werden kann, kann nicht gesagt werden" (*TLP* 4.1212).

5. Although the invention of first-order logic as a notational language is usually attributed to Gottlob Frege, the phrase "the New Logic" is most often attributed to the early logical philosophy of Bertrand Russell, specifically his *Principia Mathematica* (1910), coauthored with Alfred North Whitehead.

6. Hans Sluga makes the same comparison between architectural (and literary and artistic) and philosophical modernism in the *Cambridge Companion to Wittgenstein*, which he coedits with David Stern (Cambridge, Eng.: Cambridge University Press, 1996). Sluga writes that the Stonborough House is "indubitably a specimen of cultural modernism and, specifically, of the formalist modernism evident in Mondrian's paintings, in Bauhaus architecture, and in the assumptions of French structuralism" ("Ludwig Wittgenstein: Life and Work," 11). Additionally, Peter Galison's is likely the best-known critique to explore the connection between philosophical and architectural modernism, specifically the early modernism characterized by Adolf Loos or the Bauhaus group and the logical positivism that came directly out of—and, Wittgenstein insisted, as a misunderstanding of—the publication of the *Tractatus*; see Galison, "Aufbau/Bauhaus: Logical Positivism and Architectural Modernism," *Critical Inquiry* 16, no. 4 (Summer 1990): 709–52.

7. Michael LeMahieu, "Nonsense Modernism: The Limits of Modernity and the Feelings of Philosophy in Wittgenstein's *Tractatus*," in *Bad Modernisms*, ed. Douglas Mao and Rebecca L. Walkowitz (Durham, N.C.: Duke University Press, 2006), 79.

8. LeMahieu, "Nonsense Modernism," 71.

9. See again Sluga, "Ludwig Wittgenstein," in Sluga and Stern, *Cambridge Companion*: "Wittgenstein's later rejection of the Tractarian philosophy can be assimilated, for similar reasons, to the antiformalist tendencies within modernism, most notably the emergence of abstract expressionism, action painting, and informalism in postwar art whose later expression in architecture, literature, and philosophy has found recognition under the label of postmodernism" (12).

10. LeMahieu, "Nonsense Modernism," 71–74.

11. P. M. S. Hacker has attributed to the *Tractatus* nearly sole credit for "engender[ing] the 'linguistic turn' characteristic of twentieth-century analytic philosophy, directing philosophical investigation and methodology towards the study of the logic of our language and its use." See his *Wittgenstein* (New York: Routledge, 1999). See also Sluga, "Ludwig Wittgenstein," in Sluga and Stern, *Cambridge Companion*, 9.

12. For an extensive discussion on why it is permissible to perform a logical analysis on fiction, see the preface to part 1.

13. Ray Monk, *Ludwig Wittgenstein: The Duty of Genius* (New York: Penguin, 1991), 315–25.

14. Ludwig Wittgenstein, *Culture and Value*, ed. Georg Henrik von Wright and Heikki Nyman (Frankfurt am Main: Suhrkamp, 1978), 7.

15. The following characterization of the differences between the "two Wittgensteins" is my own, but in the philosophical community would be considered a "Sternian" take after the work of David G. Stern.

16. This view is heavily indebted to Stern's in *Wittgenstein on Mind and Language* (New York: Oxford University Press, 1990).

17. Ludwig Wittgenstein, *Philosophische Untersuchungen/Philosophical Investigations: Dritte Auflage mit englischem und deutschem Register*, ed. and trans. G. E. M. Anscombe (New York: Macmillan, 1968), §116. As is customary in the philosophical community, references to the *Investigations* will hereinafter be cited in text with the abbreviation *PI*, the section symbol §, and section number. Unless otherwise noted, all translations to the English are Anscombe's.

18. As I have noted before (see Schuman, "Unerschütterlich," 170), there is no record of any awareness on Kafka's part of Wittgenstein's work (unsurprising, given the *Tractatus* was published only two years before Kafka's death), and the sole mention of Kafka in Wittgenstein biographical lore comes from Ray Monk, who relates an occasion on which Wittgenstein's translator and protégé G. E. M. Anscombe recommended *Der Proceß*, and Wittgenstein dismissed it with this telling remark: "This man gives himself a great deal of trouble not writing about his trouble." Monk, *The Duty of Genius*, 498.

19. Wittgenstein, *Philosophical Investigations*, 1.

20. In large part due to this faction, Stern contends, "much of what passes for interpretation of Wittgenstein is really a discussion of other interpreters' readings, so that a forbidding and intricate secondary literature has taken on a life of its own" ("The Availability of Wittgenstein's Philosophy," in Sluga and Stern, *Cambridge Companion*, 443). This literature includes the work of non-Pyrrhonian views such as that of P. M. S. Hacker, who argues that Wittgenstein advocates the view that philosophical investigation is "a therapy for diseases of the understanding, for the conceptual entanglements to which we are prone." And, further, philosophical investigation is "a quest for a perspicuous

representation of a segment of our language that is a source of philosophical puzzlement, achievement of which is part of the method of resolution of philosophical problems. The two aspects are the two faces of the pursuit of conceptual clarity." See Hacker, "Philosophy," in *Wittgenstein: A Critical Reader*, ed. Hans-Johann Glock (Oxford: Blackwell, 2001), 324.

21. In the words of Robert Fogelin, philosophers are "led into confusion because they are antecedently disposed to view various uses of language in ways inappropriate to them." See Sluga, "Ludwig Wittgenstein," 34.

22. Ibid., 35.

Preface to Part One

1. See P. M. S. Hacker, *Wittgenstein's Place in Twentieth-Century Analytic Philosophy* (Cambridge, Mass.: Blackwell, 1997).

2. H. O. Mounce, *Wittgenstein's "Tractatus": An Introduction* (Chicago: University of Chicago Press, 1981); Stern's *Wittgenstein's "Philosophical Investigations": An Introduction*; Ray Monk, *How to Read Wittgenstein* (New York: W. W. Norton, 2005).

3. LeMahieu, "Nonsense Modernism," 68.

4. Sluga and Stern, *Cambridge Companion*, 9.

5. Monk, *The Duty of Genius*, 36–61.

6. See Bertrand Russell, *Philosophy of Logical Atomism*, ed. David Pears (Chicago: Open Court, 1985), 35–40. I am referring in particular to the assertion that "the logic which I shall advocate is atomistic, as opposed to the monistic logic of the people who more or less follow Hegel. When I say that my logic is atomistic, I mean that I share the common-sense belief that there are many separate things; I do not regard the apparent multiplicity of the world as consisting merely in phases and unreal divisions of a single indivisible Reality" (36).

7. Monk, *The Duty of Genius*, 62–104.

8. Alain Janik and Steven Toulmin, *Wittgenstein's Vienna* (New York: Simon and Schuster, 1973), 191–200.

9. Monk, *How to Read Wittgenstein*, 19.

10. My own translation; while *TLP* 1 is identical to every major English iteration, with *TLP* 7 I have chosen to translate as literally as possible, thus ending rather inelegantly with a preposition.

11. *TLP* 1.1. See Ludwig Wittgenstein, *Tractatus Logico-Philosophicus*, trans. C. K. Ogden (Minneola, N.Y.: Dover, 1999). Unless otherwise noted, all subsequent renderings of the *Tractatus* in English are Ogden's, with modifications where noted.

12. Russell, *Philosophy of Logical Atomism*, "Facts and Propositions," 35–48.

13. Stern, *Wittgenstein on Mind and Language*, 35.

14. My own translation; most English translators of Wittgenstein shy away from neologism, as he did not use any, but in English we have no equivalent for *sinnvoll* in this context, other than the neologism "sensical" (possible extant words, such as "sensible" and "meaningful," have inappropriate connotations).

15. Although I acknowledge, throughout this book, the philosophical and literary importance of the "new" or "resolute" readings of the *Tractatus* (most notably attributed to Cora Diamond and James Conant), unless otherwise identified, all exegesis of the end of the *Tractatus* will assume a mainstream or "metaphysical"

reading. Although many literary scholars who use the *Tractatus* assume the Diamond/Conant view is dominant or even well represented in philosophy, this is actually not the case. The "new" reading is a minority reading and, though quite compelling, also flawed in ways that are outside the scope of this project. Operating under the influence of the eminent philosopher and judicious Wittgenstein reader David Stern, I do not find it particularly productive to take a "stand" on "which Wittgenstein" is "correct"—I believe it is contrary to the spirit of the project, and the spirit of Wittgenstein himself, who took great pains in his entire career to dismantle the conceit of "correct."

16. See "Notes to 'Introduction,' " n18.

17. Karen Zumhagen-Yekplé, "The Everyday's Fabulous Beyond: Nonsense, Parable, and the Ethics of the Literary in Kafka and Wittgenstein," *Comparative Literature* 67, no. 3 (2012): 430.

18. Friedrich Nietzsche, *Werke in drei Bänden*, ed. Karl Schlechta (Munich: Hanser, 1960), 322.

19. Hugo von Hofmannsthal, "Ein Brief," in *Das erzählerische Werk* (Frankfurt am Main: Fischer, 1969), 106.

20. Fritz Mauthner, *Beiträge zu einer Kritik der Sprache* (Hamburg: Felix Meiner, 1967), 1:5.

21. Ibid., 54.

22. Ibid., 2.

23. Karl Kraus, *Die Fackel* 288, p. 15.

24. J. P. Stern, "Karl Kraus's Vision of Language," *Modern Language Review* 61, no. 1 (January 1966): 71.

25. Karl Kraus, *Magie der Sprache: ein Lesebuch*, ed. Heinrich Fischer (Munich: Suhrkamp, 1974), 328.

26. Ibid., 344; Stern, "Karl Kraus's Vision," 72.

27. Kraus, *Magie der Sprache*, 344.

28. Ibid.

29. Ibid.

30. Janik and Toulmin, *Wittgenstein's Vienna*, 191–93.

31. Karl Kraus, *Nachts* (Hamburg: Severus Verlag, 2013), 72.

32. Walter Sokel, *The Myth and Power of the Self: Essays on Franz Kafka* (Detroit: Wayne State University Press, 2002), 92.

33. Walter Sokel, "Language and Truth in the Two Worlds of Franz Kafka," *German Quarterly* 52, no. 3 (May 1979): 369.

34. Stanley Corngold, *Lambent Traces: Franz Kafka* (Princeton, N.J.: Princeton University Press, 2004), 123.

35. Theodor W. Adorno, "Aufzeichnungen zu Kafka," in *Prismen* (Frankfurt am Main: Suhrkamp, 1969), 303–4.

36. Zumhagen-Yekplé writes: "Our coming to understand what the parable has to teach us depends upon our ability to pay careful attention to the ways in which the *point* of the parable emerges, unstated, from a gap inhering between the two extremes of experience it depicts: that of everyday facticity on the one hand and of a fictive and fantastic pure transcendence (represented by the calls to 'cross over' to the fabulous beyond and to 'become parables') on the other." See Zumhagen-Yekplé, "The Everyday's Fabulous Beyond," 430.

37. Ibid., 431.

38. See Zumhagen-Yekplé, "The Everyday's Fabulous Beyond"; Ben Ware, "Ethics and the Literary in Wittgenstein's *Tractatus Logico-Philosophicus*," *Journal of the History of Ideas* 72, no. 4 (2011): 595–611.

39. Kai Evers, *Violent Modernists* (Evanston, Ill.: Northwestern University Press, 2013).

40. LeMahieu, "Nonsense Modernism," 68.

41. Henry Sussman, *Afterimages of Modernity: Structure and Indifference in Twentieth-Century Literature* (Baltimore: Johns Hopkins University Press, 1990), 50–59.

42. Marjorie Perloff, "But Isn't the Same At Least the Same?' Wittgenstein and the Question of Poetic Translatability," in *The Literary Wittgenstein*, ed. Wolfgang Huemer and John Gibson (London: Routledge, 2004), 34–54.

43. Monk, *The Duty of Genius*, 176–77.

44. Wittgenstein, *Culture and Value*, 24.

45. Diamond and Conant warn: "There should be no substitute for the hard task of working through the book on one's own. A resolute reading does not aim to provide a skeleton key for unlocking the secrets of the book in a manner that would transform the ladder into an elevator, so that one just has to push a button (say, one labeled 'austere nonsense') and one will immediately be caused to ascend to Tractarian heights without ever having to do any ladder-climbing on one's own." Cora Diamond and James Conant, "On Reading the Tractatus Resolutely: Reply to Meredith Williams and Peter Sullivan," in *Wittgenstein's Lasting Significance*, ed. Max Kölbel and Bernhard Weiss (London: Routledge, 2004), 47.

46. Monk, *The Duty of Genius*, 140–43.

47. Michael Riffaterre, *Fictional Truth* (Baltimore: Johns Hopkins University Press, 1990), viii; John Searle, "The Logical Status of Fictional Discourse," in *Contemporary Readings in the Philosophy of Literature: An Analytic Approach*, ed. David Davies and Carl Matheson (Toronto: Broadview, 2008), 15.

48. Searle, "Logical Status," 15.

49. Ibid., 16.

50. Ibid., 19–20.

51. Gregory Currie, "The Concept of Fiction," in Davies and Matheson, *Contemporary Readings*, 36.

52. Michael Lackey, "The Literary Modernist Assault on Philosophy," *Philosophy and Literature* 30, no. 1 (April 2006): 51–52.

53. Ibid., 52.

54. Ibid., 58.

55. I would like to "thank" the brilliant Kata Gellen, my onetime editor, fellow Kafka scholar, and friend, for bringing up this crucial question and thus forcing me to address it in print.

Chapter 1

1. An earlier draft of this chapter appeared in *The German Quarterly* 85, no. 2 (Spring 2012): 156–72. I would like to thank James Rolleston for permission to revise and republish and Kata Gellen for a tremendous job of editing.

2. Rolf J. Goebel, "The Exploration of the Modern City in *The Trial*," in *The Cambridge Companion to Kafka*, ed. Julian Preece (Cambridge, Eng.: Cambridge University Press, 2002), 45.

3. Mark Anderson, *Kafka's Clothes: Prague, Politics, and the Fin de Siècle* (Oxford: Oxford University Press, 1992), 145–55.

4. David I. Grossvogel, "*The Trial*: Structure as Mystery," in *Franz Kafka: Modern Critical Views*, ed. Harold Bloom (Philadelphia: Chelsea House, 1996), 186.

5. Sokel, *Myth and Power of the Self*, 228.

6. Ibid., 228–35.

7. Ibid., 231.

8. Ibid.

9. Ibid.

10. Gottlob Frege, *Begriffsschrift, eine der arithmetischen nachgebildete Formelsprache des reinen Denkens* (Halle: Nebert, 1879), 26–55.

11. Monk, *The Duty of Genius*, 105–37.

12. See Sussman, *Afterimages of Modernity*, 50–59; and Stephen Mulhall, *Wittgenstein's Private Language: Grammar, Nonsense, and Imagination in Philosophical Investigations §§243–315* (Oxford: Clarendon, 2007), 133–43; and *PI* §293.

13. I am deeply indebted to Waldemar Rohloff, who has discussed with me with incomparable thoroughness the nuances of both Wittgenstein's logic in the *Tractatus* and contemporary first-order logic. I would also like to thank Janek Wassermann of the University of Alabama for a patient and crucially edifying read of the original version of this chapter, which appeared as an article in the *German Quarterly*. See Schuman, "Unerschütterlich."

14. Jean-Francois Lyotard, *The Differend: Phrases in Dispute*, trans. Georges van der Abbelle (Minneapolis: University of Minnesota Press, 1988), 9.

15. *Sachverhalt*, as Wittgenstein describes it, is the logical relationship between objects in the world that create the presence of all facts, *Tatsachen*. See *TLP* 2: "Was der Fall ist, die Tatsache, ist das Bestehen von Sachverhalten" ("What is the case, the fact, is the existence of states of affairs").

16. K. has not yet maintained innocence, but Franz has maintained it for him, and in the world of the Court official articulation of any kind seems to equate proof (see, for example, Clayton Koelb's excursus on the "rhetorical gap" in the warders' "Sie sind ja gefangen." "Kafka's Rhetorical Moment," *PMLA* 98, no. 1 [1983]: 40).

17. Technically "not guilty and not not guilty," which is logically equivalent to ~(G v ~G), "not (guilty or not guilty)."

18. Max Black, *A Companion to Wittgenstein's Tractatus* (Ithaca, N.Y.: Cornell University Press, 1964), 228.

19. Two remarks from the *Tractatus* that have a markedly logocentric foundation but are often assigned metaphysical (mis-)reading are 4.1212 ("Was gezeigt werden *kann*, *kann* nicht gesagt werden" ["What *can* be shown, *cannot* be said"]) and 5.6 ("Die Grenzen meiner Sprache sind die Grenzen meiner Welt" ["The limits of my language are the limits of my world"]). In the former remark, the "was" that "gezeigt werden kann" is "die logische Form . . . der Wirklichkeit," or "the logical form . . . of reality," and in the second, the limits Wittgenstein speaks of are indeed the limits of logic (*TLP* 4.18, 5.61).

20. Goebel also has a compelling take on this contradiction, though he prefers to view it as "allegorical details" that "do not form a unified whole" rather than details that contradict each other. He also points out that the painting "eludes

the hermeneutic desire to establish a determinate coherent meaning—in other words, it says nothing," which I again argue is as a result of it containing a major contradiction. See Goebel, "Exploration," 53.

21. Sussman, "Kafka's Aesesthetics: A Primer," in Rolleston, *A Companion to the Works of Franz Kafka* (Rochester, N.Y.: Camden House, 2002), 135.

22. Jon Barwise and John Etchemendy et al., eds., *Language, Proof, and Logic* (Stanford, Calif.: CLSI Publications, 1999), 157.

23. Ibid., 155–60, with particular attention to the review of the rule "⊥ Elimination" (159).

24. Ibid., 159 (emphasis mine).

25. This example is about a logical relationship between two sentences in a larger derivation whose intricacies we do not know; therefore it is imperative that the two sentences in the example not have an obvious relationship of logical consequence to muddy the demonstration of the rule (such as the premise being "Yesterday was the thirtieth of November"). The point here is that in logic, one can indeed get from "That man is wearing shoes" to "Today is the first of December" with enough steps, some of which can indeed include a contradictory premise. In fact, many logicians will introduce a contradiction into a derivation on purpose simply to use *ex falso quodlibet* and be able to introduce something new that might help.

26. Barwise and Etchemendy, *Language, Proof, and Logic*, 41–44.

27. Sokel, *Myth and Power of the Self*, 228–35.

28. In addition to making it so that the validity of K.'s case does not make us rest any easier about it, this realization also sheds some very peculiar and Wittgenstinian light on the oft-discussed final sentence of *The Trial*, in particular the assertion that K., at least according to his own conception, dies "Wie ein Hund!" What separates man from the animals is, presumably, among other things the ability to communicate—so without the ability to communicate what is most important of all, logical structure, both K. and the Law are essentially inhuman.

Chapter 2

1. An earlier version of this chapter appeared in *Modern Austrian Literature* 44, no. 2/4 (2001): 19–32. I would like to thank Craig Decker for permission to republish.

2. Martin Greenberg, *The Terror of Art* (New York: Basic, 1968), 63.

3. Ibid., 64.

4. Friedrich Nietzsche, "Über Wahrheit und Lüge im Außermoralischen Sinn," in *Werke in drei Bänden*, ed. Karl Schlechta (Munich: Hanser, 1960), 3:1022.

5. Greenberg, *Terror of Art*, 68.

6. Ibid., 68.

7. Georg Bendemann's leap fits this classification largely thanks to Corngold's exploration of metaphor and chiasmus in "Das Urteil," wherein he sees Georg's father's condemnation of Gregor as an "innocent child" but "more actually a devilish person" as a conflation of the literal and metaphorical worlds, a chiasmus in which a literal impossibility becomes a literal occurrence out of metaphorical necessity (*GW* 1:52). See Stanley Corngold, "Metaphor and Chiasmus in Kafka," *Journal of the Kafka Society of America* 5, no. 2 (1981): 23–31.

8. Anthony Thorlby, "Kafka and Language," in *The World of Kafka*, ed. J. P. Stern (London: Weidenfeld and Nicholson, 1980), 137.

9. Corngold, *Lambent Traces*, 67–81.

10. An exception to this is Sussman's *Afterimages of Modernity*, wherein he offers an analysis of the *Tractatus*—itself as literature—alongside Kafka's work, primarily as an example of what he terms the anorexic aesthetic in both writers' work (rather than the "obese" discourse he associates with Derrida; this is discussed at greater length in my introduction). What is *unsaid* in the *Tractatus*—the "metalinguistic acts" that include "spareness of expression," "numerical code," and "unmarked transitions that undermine the numerical code"—becomes equally as important as what is said, an argument Wittgenstein made himself in regard to his own necessarily unsayable ethical corpus. For example: "In reading Wittgenstein, in the *Tractatus logico-philosophicus* and less pointedly in later works, one confronts a series of significant gestures whose place is beyond the narrative, that is, beyond the specific contemporary problems and issues within the history of philosophy that Wittgenstein is addressing." My analysis, though indebted to Sussman's, differs in that it reads the *Tractatus* in a far more philosophically standard way and seeks structural similarities in both texts on a purely textual level. See Sussman, *Afterimages of Modernity*, 50–59.

11. Gilles Deleuze and Feliz Guattari, *Kafka: Toward a Minor Literature*, trans. Dana Pollan (Minneapolis: University of Minnesota Press, 1986), 15–16.

12. A canonical example of the former is, of course, Sokel's *Myth and Power of the Self*; in terms of the latter, see Adorno, "Aufzeichnungen zu Kafka."

13. Max Brod, *Franz Kafka: Eine Biografie* (Frankfurt am Main: Fischer, 1962), 94.

14. Greenberg, *Terror of Art*, 69.

15. Adorno, "Aufzeichnungen zu Kafka," 303.

16. Sussman, "Kafka's Aesthetics," 138.

17. Thorlby, "Kafka and Language,"136.

18. Ibid., 137.

19. I. A. Richards, "Metaphor," in *The Philosophy of Rhetoric* (London: Oxford University Press, 1976), 89–114; Max Black, "Metaphor," *Proceedings of the Aristotelian Society*, n.s. 55 (1954–55): 273–94.

20. Black, "Metaphor," 274.

21. Ibid., 283.

22. Ibid., 276.

23. Ibid., 281.

24. Ibid.

25. Adorno, "Aufzeichnungen zu Kafka," 303.

26. Black, "Metaphor," 281.

27. Ibid.

28. Deleuze and Guattari, *Kafka*, 18–19.

29. Ibid., 13.

30. Black, "Metaphor," 283.

31. Ibid., 284–86.

32. Ibid., 285.

33. The fact is that it *is* an actual *Tierstimme*—this metaphor works on two levels, as both a "successful" metaphor and a collapsing one; the first level is what we are exploring currently; the second is explored at more length in section 2 of this chapter.

34. Black, "Metaphor," 289.

35. See "Ein Landarzt" ("A Country Doctor"), *GW* 1:200–204: "Ich bleibe bei Rosa" ("I'm staying with Rosa") says the amorous stableboy, giving a name that sticks to the heretofore nameless servant girl; "Rosa" is the word with which the doctor then begins to describe the boy's odd wound; "an dieser Blume," he says to the boy, "gehst du zugrunde" ("This flower will be the death of you"). The repetition and morphing of roses and flowers calls up not only the "commonplaces" of fragility and feminine beauty, but also the well-known "Rose" poems of the German canon, including Goethe's "Heidenröslein."

36. Deleuze and Guattari, *Kafka*, 14–15.

37. Black, "Metaphor," 291.

38. Although the intellectual affinity between *The Metamorphosis* and the *Tractatus* may not yet be apparent, the temporal affinity is: the *Tractatus* was composed while Wittgenstein was a soldier during World War I (though published in 1921, the bulk of it was written from 1916 to 1918), almost exactly concurrent with the composition of *The Metamorphosis* (1915).

39. This is the distilled trajectory of *TLP* 2–2.11, 3.001.

40. See note 11.

41. Black, *Companion*, 3.

42. As we will see, however, Wittgenstein's use of the word *unsinnig* (and not *sinnlos*) in 6.54 gives resolute readers ample reason to believe that "throwing away" the saying/showing distinction is not at all antithetical but instead totally faithful to the text. (Although, to be fair, the fact that Wittgenstein has provoked a difference at all between *sinnlos* and *unsinnig* belongs to the 4s, to the text of the *Tractatus*, and an employment of that distinction in order to strengthen the "resolute" reading actually destroys it. This, and many other reasons, is why the "resolute" reading remains largely contested.)

43. Cora Diamond argues quite convincingly that unlike Bertrand Russell, who places great emphasis on category error being distinguishable from pure gibberish, Wittgenstein believes all attempts at expressing philosophy in language fall, more or less, into the same category as "I am going to the readily." See Diamond, "What Nonsense Might Be," *Philosophy* 56, no. 215 (1981): 5–22.

44. Mark Anderson, "Sliding Down the Evolutionary Ladder? Aesthetic Autonomy in *The Metamorphosis*," in Franz Kafka, *The Metamorphosis: Translation, Backgrounds and Context, Criticism*, ed. and trans. Stanley Corngold (New York: W. W. Norton, 1996), 154.

45. Ibid., 155.

46. Ibid., 156.

47. Ibid.

48. Corngold, "Thirteen Ways of Looking at a Vermin," *Literary Research/Recherche litterare* 21, nos. 41–42 (2004): 61.

49. Adorno, "Aufzeichnungen zu Kafka," 305.

50. Günter Anders, *Kafka Pro und Contra: Die Proceß-Unterlagen* (Munich: C.H. Beck, 1951), 40.

51. Stanley Corngold, "Kafka's *The Metamorphosis*: Metamorphosis of the Metaphor," in Kafka, ed. Corngold, *The Metamorphosis*, 82.

52. Ibid., 84.

53. Ibid., 85.

54. Corngold, "Thirteen Ways," 65–67.

55. Günther Drosdowski, *Duden: Das große Wörterbuch der deutschen Sprache: in acht Bänden* (Mannheim: Dudenverlag, 1993), 8:4107.

56. Corngold, "Metamorphosis of Metaphor," 86.

57. Ibid.

58. Jacques Derrida, "White Mythology," trans. F. C. T. Moore, *New Literary History* 6, no. 1 (Autumn 1974): 18. (Cited parenthetically in text hereafter.)

59. Donald Davidson, "What Metaphors Mean," *Critical Inquiry* 5, no. 1 (1978): 33.

60. Ibid., 34.

61. Ibid., 43.

62. Ibid., 45.

63. Black, "Metaphor," 289.

64. Corngold, "Thirteen Ways," 79.

65. Thorlby, "Language," 136.

66. Anders, *Kafka Pro und Contra*, 42.

67. Deleuze and Guattari, *Kafka*, 14.

Chapter 3

1. Uta Degener, "What Kafka Learned from Flaubert: 'Absent-Minded Window-Gazing' and 'The Judgment,' " in *Kafka for the Twenty-First Century*, ed. Stanley Corngold and Ruth V. Gross (Rochester, N.Y.: Camden House, 2011), 81.

2. Corngold, "The Hermeneutic of 'The Judgment,' " in *The Problem of "The Judgment": Eleven Approaches to Kafka's Story*, ed. Angel Flores (New York: Dorian, 1977), 47; David Stern, "Guilt and the Feeling of Guilt," in Flores, *The Problem of "The Judgment,"* 120.

3. Russell Berman, "Tradition and Betrayal in 'Das Urteil,' " in Rolleston, *A Companion*, 87.

4. Ritchie Robertson, "Kafka as Anti-Christian," in Rolleston, *A Companion*, 104.

5. Walter Sokel, "Nietzsche and Kafka," in Corngold and Gross, *Kafka for the Twenty-First Century*, 70.

6. Stern, "Guilt," 141; Berman, "Tradition," 85.

7. Sokel, "Nietzsche and Kafka," 71.

8. Peter von Matt, "Eine Nacht verändert die Weltliteratur," in *Franz Kafka: Neue Wege der Forschung*, ed. Claudia Liebrand (Darmstadt: Wissenschaftliche Buchgesellschaft, 2006), 102.

9. Adorno, "Aufzeichnungen zu Kafka," 303–4.

10. James Phelan, "Progression, Speed, and Judgment in 'Das Urteil,' " in *Franz Kafka: Narration, Rhetoric, and Reading*, ed. Jakob Lothe, Beatrice Sandberg, and Ronald Speirs (Columbus: Ohio State University Press, 2011), 22.

11. Corngold, "Hermeneutic," 39, 40.

12. Russell, *Philosophy of Logical Atomism*, 35–40.

13. Corngold, "Hermeneutic," 59.

14. This is, interestingly, also the main characterization of how language works in one of Martin Greenberg's classic pieces of criticism of "The Judgment," although he puts it in nonlogical terms: "Language tries symbolically to bridge the split between consciousness and existence, between our thinking and

what is." Greenberg, "The Literature of Truth: Kafka's Judgment," *Salmagundi* 1, no. 1 (1965): 7.

15. According to Greenberg, we learn these "main facts" during Georg's "reverie" after sealing the letter. For James Rolleston, these same passages present "facts only slightly colored by Georg's viewpoint." And later in the story, Stern is confident that "it is a fact that Georg has been neglecting his friend." Greenberg, "Literature of Truth," 10; Rolleston, "Strategy and Language," in Flores, *The Problem of "The Judgment,"* 137; Stern, "Guilt," 125.

16. Greenberg argues: "From the 'It was a Sunday morning' of the beginning, the reader is led to expect an omniscient narrator discussing the object of the story, Georg, his subjectivity and his objective standing in the world. The first paragraph shifts quickly from the narrator's view of the row of houses to Georg's perspective, the landscape across the river. This perspectival disruption is continued, alternating between objectifying description and subjective point of view, when the narrator and the reader appear to be aligned with Georg's subjectivity itself, particularly through the use of indexical terms [such as 'here' and 'later']." Greenberg, "Literature of Truth," 9.

17. Ibid., 15.

18. Ibid., 15.

19. Berman, "Tradition and Betrayal," 92.

20. Ibid., 92–93.

21. There is of course no singular "standard" or "metaphysical" reading of the *Tractatus*, but three of the most canonical interpretations that more or less fit into that school of thought are Mounce's *Wittgenstein's "Tractatus": An Introduction*, Black's *A Companion to Wittgenstein's Tractatus*, and Hacker's *Insight and Illusion*. My summary of the "standard" reading of the *Tractatus*—as with much work that deals with Wittgenstein—is based on the broad interpretive goals of these three texts: how the picture theory is represented in language, how thoughts put into words are said to express reality, how things can be shown and not said, the importance of truth-functionality, and, most importantly, that in the penultimate remark, 6.54, the "unsinnig" to which Wittgenstein relegates the *Tractatus* does not preclude it from showing with its logical form. Specific concrete interpretations by these philosophers are cited when appropriate.

22. Cora Diamond, "Throwing Away the Ladder," *Philosophy* 63, no. 243 (1988): 8.

23. Ibid., 7.

24. Ibid., 8.

25. Ibid., 9–10. Diamond arrives at this resoluteness through a protracted interaction with Frege (and Russell), whose work Wittgenstein studied intensely in the years before he wrote the *Tractatus*. Unlike what Wittgenstein would later argue, Frege believed that sentences were "complex names" made up of a proper name and a function; the simple proper name was complete on its own (for example, *Mein Vater*), but the function (*ist immer noch ein Riese*) was not. The function needed the proper name (by proper name, *Eigenname*, Frege meant any name that signified an object) for completion. The problem was that in natural (as opposed to logically perfect) language the logical distinction between the sign for a proper name and a sign for a function was, as Diamond puts it, "not marked in a way that [was] easy to see." Frege first attempted to express the inadequacy

of describing this distinction in ordinary language (using ordinary language), and then used that very inadequacy to justify the creation of a logically perfect language (the *Begriffsschrift*) where ambiguity was no longer an issue. In the logically perfect language, there were finally distinct signs for function and object, thus making it possible to dispose of the prior complaint about the inadequacy of ordinary language to make the function/object distinction. And thus, to Diamond, "'There is a distinction between functions and objects, and it comes out in the clear difference between signs for functions and those for objects in a well-designed notation'" is "what you could call a 'transitional' remark."

26. Ibid., 22.

27. See Zumhagen-Yekplé, "The Everyday's Fabulous Beyond."

Preface to Part Two

1. See David Stern, *Wittgenstein's "Philosophical Investigations": An Introduction*, 3–5.

Chapter 4

1. John Zilcosky, "Surveying the Castle: Kafka's Colonial Visions," in Rolleston, *A Companion*, 281. Zilcosky argues very interestingly that the choice of alleged profession is actually quite important for the novel, and effectively departs from established metaphorical critiques of "land surveying" in favor of a concurrent exploration of a 1914 memoir about an actual colonialist land surveyor.

2. Mark Harman, "Making Everything 'a Little Uncanny': Kafka's Deletions in the Manuscript of *Das Schloss*," in Rolleston, *A Companion*, 329, 333. An interesting example Harman offers is that in an early draft K. had a mysterious decisive deed; in deleting these and other clues to what K. "really" wants Kafka instead "buried the workings of his hero's psyche in the interstices of his writing."

3. Elizabeth Boa, "*The Castle*," in Preece, *The Cambridge Companion to Kafka*, 62, 72. For Boa the key to the puzzle is in an exploration of the notion of *Heimat* from the perspective of exclusivity and insider-ness—evident, for example in the behavior of the village natives, in which "communal identity crystallizes around the exclusion of scapegoats," especially those, like K., perceived as "urban."

4. Sussman, "Kafka's Aesthetics," 126.

5. *PI* introduction, 1; see also this book's introduction.

6. Walter Sokel, *Tragik und Ironie: Zur Struktur seiner Kunst* (Munich: Langen, 1964), 404.

7. Stephen Dowden, *Kafka's Castle and the Critical Imagination* (Rochester, N.Y.: Camden House, 2005), 36.

8. Dowden argues: "We have reason to believe that K. may be lying about being a surveyor (he is dressed shabbily and, like a hobo, has only a knapsack and walking stick with him, no surveying equipment), so we have little ground to suppose he could have expected anything more than a night's lodging at the inn." *Kafka's Castle*, 50.

9. Ibid., 36.

10. The initial instance of alleged self-naming—"daß ich der Landvermesser bin"—is again the primary instance, and its phrasing as a subordinate clause should bring to mind two eminent critics whose conception of Kafka's writing tricks lend credence to K. being, or at any rate beginning as, an impostor, James

Rolleston and Clayton Koelb. Rolleston's early work described Kafka's characters as play-actors narrating the theater of their own destinies as they went along, whereas Koelb's previously cited concentration on the "rhetorical moment" of *The Trial* in which K.'s arrest is covertly legitimized without ever actually taking place also applies to this situation—here it is a *dass* and not a *ja* that creates the rhetorical gap, presumably leading K.'s interrogators to refute an act of engagement that has already taken place. See James Rolleston, *Kafka's Narrative Theater* (State College: Pennsylvania State University Press, 1974); Koelb, "Kafka's Rhetorical Moment."

11. As Stern points out, he will then turn around and do the same thing with logic (*PI* §§65–133). Stern, *Wittgenstein's "Philosophical Investigations": Introduction*, 108–32.

12. My own translation.

13. Mark E. Blum, *Kafka's Social Discourse: An Aesthetic Search for Community* (Bethlehem, Pa.: Lehigh University Press, 2011), 170–71. The crux of his argument is that "Kafka's intention in K.'s interactions with the Castle officials is to reveal the complexities of the societal Weberian iron cage as it conditions the character and quality of temporality imposed by public authority."

14. See Elsbeth Schmidhäuser, *Kafka über Kafka: "Der Proceß"—gelesen und gesehen*, vol. 20 (Münster: Lit Verlag, 2000).

15. See Rolleston, *Kafka's Narrative Theater.*

16. Sussman, "Kafka's Aesthetics," 133.

17. As Jacob Burnett has written: "Attempting to establish meaningful contact with the castle through modern means proves impossible. When K. does get through, the conversation is filled with contradictions and deceptions and ends with a firm and seemingly eternal rejection. Not only the modern fails to reach the center: the dubious messenger Barnabas appears the moment K. hangs up the phone, as if to insist on the point that premodern devices like letters and messengers, too, are ineffectual to reach a central grounding core of being." Burnett, "Strange Loops and the Absent Center in *The Castle*," in Corngold and Gross, *Kafka for the Twenty-First Century*, 111.

18. Although aside from Frieda, who "knows" him in the biblical sense and the landlady, who "knew" him in the same, this "knowing" consists largely of peeping at Klamm through a hole in the wall of the inn where he keeps an office–the idea of "to know" here being yet another instance of a common gesture not meaning what we think it should mean.

Chapter 5

1. Walter Benjamin, *Benjamin über Kafka: Texte, Briefzeugnisse, Aufzeichnungen*, ed. Hermann Schweppháuser (Frankfurt am Main: Suhrkamp, 1981), 88.

2. Though largely culled from each theorist's general trajectory with respect to "In the Penal Colony," specific references to the above approaches appear on the following pages of the following works: Sokel, *Myth and Power of the Self*, 22; Anderson, *Kafka's Clothes*, 174–90; Goebel, "Kafka and Postcolonial Critique: Der Verschollene, 'In der Strafkolonie,' 'Beim Bau der chinesischen Mauer,' " in Rolleston, *A Companion*, 187; Danielle Allen, "Sounding Silence," *Modernism/modernity* 8, no. 2 (2001): 325; Andreas Gailus, "Lessons of the Cryptograph: Revelation and the Mechanical in Kafka's 'In the Penal Colony,' " *Modernism/*

Modernity 8, no. 2 (2001): 296; Richard Jayne, "Kafka's 'In der Strafkolonie' and the Aporias of Textual Interpretation," *Deutsche Vierteljahresschrift für Literaturwissenschaft und Geistesgeschichte* 66, no. 1 (1992): 96; Wolf Kittler and Gehrhard Neumann, eds., *Franz Kafka: Schriftverkehr* (Freiburg: Rohmbach, 1990), 117; Koelb, "Kafka's Rhetorical Moment," 67; Stanley Corngold, *The Necessity of Form* (Ithaca, N.Y.: Cornell University Press, 1988), 229; Heinz Politzer, *Franz Kafka: Parable and Paradox* (Ithaca, N.Y.: Cornell University Press, 1974), 99.

3. Anderson, *Kafka's Clothes*, 174.

4. Klaus Scherpe, *Beschreiben, nicht Erzählen!: Beispiele zu einer ästhetischen Opposition: Von Döblin und Musil bis zu Darstellungen des Holocaust* (Berlin: Humboldt-Universität zu Berlin, Philosophische Fakultät II, Institut für deutsche Literatur, 1995), 4.

5. Georg Lukács, "Franz Kafka oder Thomas Mann?" in *Werke*, vol. 5, *Probleme des Realismus II: Der russische Realismus in der Weltliteratur* (Neuwied am Rhein: Luchterland, 1962), 4:500.

6. Scherpe, *Beschreiben*, 5.

7. Ibid., 6.

8. Scherpe, "Kafkas Poetik des Beschreibens," in *Kontinent Kafka: Mosse-Lectures an der Humboldt-Universität zu Berlin*, ed. Klaus Scherpe and Elisabeth Wagner (Berlin: Vorwerk 8, 2000), 99.

9. Ibid., 90.

10. Kittler and Neumann, *Franz Kafka: Schriftverkehr*, 131.

11. Gailus, "Cryptograph," 298, 299.

12. Allen, "Sounding Silence," 330.

13. Koelb, "Kafka's Rhetoric," 68.

14. Ibid., 68–69.

15. Ibid., 67.

16. Sokel, *Myth and Power of the Self*, 22–23.

17. Stern, *Wittgenstein's "Philosophical Investigations": An Introduction*, 146–49.

18. Ibid., 140–50.

19. Ibid., 146.

20. Goebel, "Postcolonial Discourse," in Rolleston, *A Companion*, 187.

21. Politzer, *Parable and Paradox*, 104.

22. Margot Norris, "Sadism and Masochism in Two Kafka Stories: 'Ein Hungerkünstler' and 'In der Strafkolonie,' " *Modern Langauge Notes* 93, no. 3 (1978): 430, 432.

23. Ibid., 434.

24. Koelb, *Kafka's Rhetoric*, 69.

25. Jacques Derrida, *Writing and Difference*, trans. Alan Bass (Chicago: University of Chicago Press, 1978), 227.

26. Koelb, *Kafka's Rhetoric*, 83–84.

27. Robert J. Fogelin, "Wittgenstein's Critique of Philosophy," in Sluga and Stern, *Cambridge Companion*, 56.

28. David H. Finkelstein, "Wittgenstein on Rules and Platonism," in *The New Wittgenstein*, ed. Alice Crary and Rupert Read (London: Routledge, 2000), 53, 55.

29. Ibid., 55.
30. Ibid., 61.
31. Kittler and Neumann, *Franz Kafka: Schriftverkehr*, 136.
32. Saul Kripke, *Wittgenstein on Rules and Private Language: An Elementary Exposition* (Cambridge, Mass.: Harvard University Press, 1982), 8.
33. Ibid., 8–9.
34. Ibid., 9–20, 60.
35. David Stern, *Wittgenstein's "Philosophical Invesigations": An Introduction*, 3.
36. Kripke, *Wittgenstein on Rules and Private Language*, 60.
37. Ibid., 78–79.
38. Ibid., 101.
39. Finkelstein, "Rules and Platonism," 68.
40. David Stern, *Wittgenstein's "Philosophical Investigations": An Introduction*, 208.
41. David Stern, *Wittgenstein on Mind and Language*, 178.
42. Kripke, *Wittgenstein on Rules and Private Language*, 178.
43. Ibid., 179.

Chapter 6

1. David R. Ellison, "Narrative and Music in Kafka and Blanchot: The 'Singing' of Josefine," *Yale French Studies* 93 (1988): 199.
2. Chris Danta posits that the story is in fact about "the artist's own fatal descent into silence," about "the death of the artist—the real rather than the metaphorical death." See Danta, "Kafka's Mousetrap: The Fable of the Dying Voice," *SubStance* 37, no. 3 (2008): 152.
3. Michael Minden, "Kafka's 'Josefine die Sängerin, oder das Volk der Mäuse,' " *German Life and Letters* 62, no. 3 (July 2009): 298.
4. Ritchie Robertson, *Kafka: Judaism, Politics, and Literature* (Oxford: Clarendon, 1985), 273.
5. Gross has argued that Josefine's musicality represents a femaleness in opposition to the maleness of Kafka's writing, and that in the story Josefine "has no defenses, and her name, as we have seen, is merely a patriarchal trope. She is not more, not less than her song. When she sings, she sings herself: When she ceases to sing, she must herself disappear." Further, Kafka's narrator comes in the form of the "paternal care" of someone who understands Josefine well enough to explain her ineffability properly. Ruth V. Gross, "Of Mice and Women: Reflections on a Discourse in Kafka's 'Josefine die Sängerin, oder das Volk der Mäuse,' " *The Germanic Review* 60, no. 2 (1985): 61–65.
6. Doreen Densky, "Proxies in Kafka: *Koncipist* FK and *Prokurist* Josef K," in *Kafka for the Twenty-First Century*, 120–35.
7. Robertson, *Kafka*, 367; Ellison, "Narrative and Music," 197.
8. Robertson, *Kafka*, 281.
9. Kata Gellen, "Hearing Spaces: Architecture and Acoustic Experience in Modernist German Literature," *Modernism/modernity* 17, no. 4 (November 2010): 814.
10. Margot Norris, "Kafka's Josefine: The Animal as the Negative Site of Narration," *Modern Language Notes* 98, no. 3 (April 1983): 366.

11. Gross, "Of Mice and Women," 61; Minden, "Kafka's 'Josefine,'" 303.
12. Ellison, "Narrative and Music," 198.
13. Minden, "Kafka's 'Josefine,'" 356.
14. Robertson, *Kafka*, 280–81.
15. Corngold, "Musical Indirection in Kafka's 'Forschungen eines Hundes,'" in Lothe, Sandberg, and Speirs, *Franz Kafka*, 189.
16. Ellison, "Narrative and Music," 198.
17. Robertson, *Kafka*, 279.
18. Danta, "Mousetrap," 153; Robertson, *Kafka*, 275.
19. Monk, *How to Read Wittgenstein*, 92.
20. Ibid.
21. Ibid.
22. Ellison, "Narrative and Music," 202.
23. Minden, "Kafka's 'Josefine,'" 299.
24. Samuel Frederick, *Narratives Unsettled: Digression in Robert Walser, Thomas Bernhard, and Adalbert Stifter* (Evanston, Ill.: Northwestern University Press, 2012).
25. Robertson, *Kafka*, 279.
26. Minden, "Kafka's 'Josefine,'" 303.
27. Robertson, *Kafka*, 273.
28. Ellison argues: "From the very beginning of the story there is a fundamental narrative skepticism about music—about its 'essence'—as well as an interesting indifference to the efforts of Josefine, which tends to complicate the assertive tone of the remainder of the paragraph." On one hand she's the exception; on the other hand "it is not clear from the first paragraph whether the mouse folk has enough interest in music or in the performance activities of Josefine to accept or receive this potentially mediated song." Ellison, "Narrative and Music," 200–201.
29. Robertson, *Kafka*, 279.
30. Ellison, "Narrative and Music," 202, my emphasis.
31. Robertson, *Kafka*, 280; Franz Kafka, *Tagebücher, 1910–1923* (Frankfurt am Main: Fischer, 1949), 534.

WORKS CITED

Adorno, Theodor W. "Aufzeichnungen zu Kafka." In *Prismen*, 302–43. Frankfurt am Main: Suhrkamp, 1969.

Anders, Günther. *Kafka Pro und Contra: Die Proceß-Ungerlagen*. Munich: C. H. Beck, 1951.

Anderson, Mark. *Kafka's Clothes: Prague, Politics, and the Fin de Siècle*. Oxford: Oxford University Press, 1992.

———, ed. *Reading Kafka: Prague, Politics, and the Fin de Siècle*. New York: Schocken, 1989.

———. "Sliding Down the Evolutionary Ladder? Aesthetic Autonomy in *The Metamorphosis*." In Franz Kafka, *The Metamorphosis*, edited by Stanley Corngold, 154–71. New York: Norton, 1996.

Austin, J. L. *How to Do Things with Words*. Cambridge, Mass.: Harvard University Press, 1975.

Benjamin, Walter. *Benjamin über Kafka: Texte, Briefzeugnisse, Aufzeichnungen*. Edited by Hermann Schweppenhäuser. Frankfurt am Main: Suhrkamp, 1981.

Binder, Hartmut. *Kafka-Kommentar zu den Romanen, Rezensionen, Aphorismen, und zum Brief an den Vater*. Munich: Winkler, 1976.

———. *Kafkas "Verwandlung": Entstehung, Deutung, Wirkung*. Frankfurt am Main: Stroemfeld, 2004.

Black, Max. *A Companion to Wittgenstein's "Tractatus."* Ithaca, N.Y.: Cornell University Press, 1964.

———. "Metaphor." *Proceedings of the Aristotelian Society*, n.s. 55 (1954–55): 273–94.

Bloom, Harold, ed. *Franz Kafka: Modern Critical Views*. Philadelphia: Chelsea House, 1996.

Blum, Mark E. *Kafka's Social Discourse: An Aesthetic Search for Community*. Bethlehem, Pa.: Lehigh University Press, 2011.

Blumenberg, Hans. *Paradigmen zu einer Metaphorologie*. Frankfurt am Main: Suhrkamp, 2005.

Boa, Elizabeth. "The Castle." In Preece, *Cambridge Companion to Kafka*, 61–79.

Bodine, Jay F. "Karl Kraus, Ludwig Wittgenstein and 'Poststructural' Paradigms of Textual Understanding." *Modern Austrian Literature* 22, no. 3 (1989): 143–85.

Brod, Max. *Franz Kafka: Eine Biographie*. Frankfurt am Main: Fischer, 1962.

Burnett, Jacob. "Strange Loops and the Absent Center in *The Castle*." In Corngold and Gross, *Kafka*, 105–20.

Canning, Peter M. "Kafka's Heirogram: The Trauma of the 'Landarzt.' " *The German Quarterly* 57, no. 2 (1984): 197–212.

Conant, James. "Elucidation and Nonsense in Frege and Early Wittgenstein." In Crary and Read, *The New Wittgenstein*, 174–217.

Constantine, David. "Kafka's Writing and Our Reading." In Preece, *Cambridge Companion to Kafka*, 9–24.

Corngold, Stanley. *Franz Kafka: The Necessity of Form.* Ithaca, N.Y.: Cornell University Press, 1988.

———. "Introduction." *Monatshefte* 103, no. 3 (2011): 339–43.

———. *Lambent Traces: Franz Kafka.* Princeton, N.J.: Princeton University Press, 2004.

———. "Medial Allusions at the Outset of *Der Proceß*; or, Res in Media." In Rolleston, *A Companion*, 149–70.

———. "Metaphor and Chiasmus in Kafka." *Newsletter of the Kafka Society of America* 5, no. 2 (1981): 23–31.

———. "Thirteen Ways of Looking at a Vermin: Metaphor and Chiasmus in Kafka's *Die Verwandlung*." *Literary Research/Recherche litterare* 21, no. 41–42 (2004): 59–85.

Corngold, Stanley, and Ruth V. Gross, eds. *Kafka for the Twenty-First Century.* Rochester, N.Y.: Camden House, 2011.

Crary, Alice, and Rupert Read, eds. *The New Wittgenstein.* London: Routledge, 2000.

Curie, Gregory. "The Concept of Fiction." In Davies and Matheson, *Contemporary Readings.*

Davidson, Donald. "What Metaphors Mean." *Critical Inquiry* 5, no. 1 (1978): 31–47.

Davies, David, and Carl Matheson, eds. *Contemporary Readings in the Philosophy of Literature: An Analytic Approach.* Toronto: Broadview, 2008.

Degener, Uta. "What Kafka Learned from Flaubert: 'Absent-Minded Window-Gazing' and 'The Judgment.' " In Corngold and Gross, *Kafka.*

Deleuze, Gilles. *The Logic of Sense.* Edited by Constantine V. Boundas. Translated by Mark Lester and Charles Stivale. New York: Columbia University Press, 1990.

Deleuze, Gilles, and Felix Guattari. *Kafka: Toward a Minor Literature.* Translated by Danna Pollan. Minneapolis: University of Minnesota Press, 1986.

Derrida, Jacques. "Justices." *Critical Inquiry* 31, no. 3 (Spring 2005): 689–721.

———. "White Mythology: Metaphor in the Text of Philosophy." Translated by F. C. T. Moore. *New Literary History* 6, no. 1 (Autumn 1974): 5–74.

Diamond, Cora. "Throwing Away the Ladder." *Philosophy* 63, no. 243 (1988): 5–27.

———. "What Nonsense Might Mean." *Philosophy* 56, no. 215 (1981): 5–22.

Dodd, William J. "Kafka and Freud: A Note on 'In der Strafkolonie.' " *Monatshefte* 70, no. 2 (1978): 129–37.

Dowden, Stephen D. *Kafka's Castle and the Critical Imagination.* Rochester, N.Y.: Camden House, 1995.

Drosdowski, Günther. *Duden: Das große Wörterbuch der deutschen Sprache: in acht Bänden.* Vol. 8. 8 vols. Mannheim: Dudenverlag, 1993.

Finkelstein, David H. "Wittgenstein on Rules and Platonism." In Crary and Read, *The New Wittgenstein*, 53–73.

Fleming, Richard. *First Word Philosophy: Wittgenstein-Austin-Cavell, Writings on Ordinary Language Philosophy.* Lewisburg, Pa.: Bucknell University Press, 1994.

Fogelin, Robert J. "Wittgenstein's Critique of Philosophy." In Sluga and Stern, *Cambridge Companion to Wittgenstein*, 34–58.

Frege, Gottlob. *Begriffsschrift, eine aer Arithmetischen nachgebildete Formelsprache des reinen Denkens*. Halle: Nebert, 1879.

———. "Über Sinn und Bedeutung." *Zeitschrift für Philosophie und philosophishe Kritik* 100 (1892): 25–50.

Gilman, Sander L. "A View of Kafka's Treatment of Actuality in *Die Verwandlung*." *Germanic Notes* 2 (1971): 26–30.

Goebel, Rolf J. "The Exploration of the Modern City in *The Trial*." In Preece, *Cambridge Companion to Kafka*, 42–61.

———. "Kafka and Postcolonial Critique: Der Verschollene, 'In der Strafkolonie,' 'Beim Bau der chinesischen Mauer.' " In Rolleston, *A Companion*, 190–212.

Gray, Richard T. "Disjunctive Signs: Semiotics, Aesthetics, and Failed Mediation in 'In the Penal Colony.' " In Rolleston, *A Companion*, 211–45.

Greenberg, Martin. *The Terror of Art: Kafka and Modern Literature*. New York: Basic, 1968.

Grossvogel, David I. "*The Trial*: Structure as Mystery." In *Franz Kafka: Modern Critical Views*, edited by Harold Bloom. Philadelphia: Chelsea House, 1996.

Hacker, P. M. S. "Philosophy." In *Wittgenstein: A Critical Reader*, edited by Hans-Johann Glock, 322–47. London: Blackwell, 2001.

———. "Was He Trying to Whistle It?" In Crary and Read, *The New Wittgenstein*, 353–88.

Hagberg, Gary. "Wittgenstein Underground." *Philosophy and Literature* 28, no. 2 (2004): 379–92.

Hamann, Johann Georg. *Aesthetica in Nuce*. In *Sämtliche Werke*, 2:197–217. Vienna: Herder, 1949.

Harman, Mark. "Making Everything 'a Little Uncanny': Kafka's Deletions in the Manuscript of *Das Schloss*." In Rolleston, *A Companion*, 325–46.

Hegel, G. W. F. *Phänomenologie des Geistes*. Edited by Johannes Hoffmeister. Hamburg: Felix Meiner, 1952.

Heidegger, Martin. *Beiträge zur Philosophie (vom Ereignis)*. Edited by Friedrich-Wilhelm v. Hermann. Frankfurt am Main: Klostermann, 1989.

Heidsieck, Arnold. *The Intellectual Contexts of Kafka's Fiction: Philosophy, Law, Religion*. Columbia, S.C.: Camden House, 1994.

Heller, Erich. *Franz Kafka*. Edited by Frank Kermode. New York: Viking, 1974.

Hofmannsthal, Hugo von. "Ein Brief." In *Das erzählerische Werk*, 102–33. Frankfurt am Main: Fischer, 1969.

Huemer, Wolfgang, and John Gibson, eds. *The Literary Wittgenstein*. London: Routledge, 2004.

Huyssen, Andreas, and David Bathrick, eds. *Modernity and the Text*. New York: Columbia University Press, 1989.

Janik, Allan, and Stephen Toulmin. *Wittgenstein's Vienna*. New York: Simon and Schuster, 1973.

Jayne, Richard. "Kafka's 'In der Strafkolonie' and the Aporias of Textual Interpretation." *Deutsche Vierteljahresschrift für Literaturwissenschaft und Geistesgeschichte* 66, no. 1 (1992): 92–128.

Johnston, William M. *The Austrian Mind: An Intellectual and Social History, 1848–1938*. Berkeley: University of California Press, 1972.

Kafka, Franz. *Gesammelte Werke in Zwölf Bänden.* Edited by Hans-Gerhard Koch and Malcolm Pasley. 12 vols. Frankfurt am Main: Fischer, 1994.

———. *The Metamorphosis: Translation, Backgrounds, Contexts, Criticisms.* Edited and translated by Stanley Corngold. New York: W. W. Norton, 1996.

———. *Tagebücher, 1910–1923.* Frankfurt am Main: Fischer, 1949.

Kittler, Wolf, and Gerhard Neumann, eds. *Franz Kafka: Schriftverkehr.* Freiburg: Rombach, 1990.

Koelb, Clayton. "Critical Editions II: Will the Real Franz Kafka Please Stand Up?" In Rolleston, *A Companion*, 28–32.

———. *Kafka's Rhetoric: The Passion of Reading.* Ithaca, N.Y.: Cornell University Press, 1989.

———. "Kafka's Rhetorical Moment." *PMLA* 98, no. 1 (1983): 37–46.

Kraus, Karl. *Magie der Sprache: Ein Lesebuch.* Edited by Heinrich Fischer. Munich: Suhrkamp, 1974.

Kripke, Saul. *Wittgenstein on Rules and Private Language: An Elementary Exposition.* Cambridge, Mass.: Harvard University Press, 1982.

Lackey, Michael. "The Literary Modernist Assault on Philosophy." *Philosophy and Literature* 30, no. 1 (April 2006): 50–60.

LeMahieu, "Nonsense Modernism: The Limits of Modernity and the Feelings of Philosophy in Wittgenstein's *Tractatus*." In *Bad Modernisms*, edited by Douglas Mao and Rebecca L. Walkowitz, 68–93. Durham, N.C.: Duke University Press, 2006.

Lewis, David. "Truth in Fiction." In Davies and Matheson, *An Analytic Approach*, 83–98.

Lukács, Georg. *Wieder den missverstandenen Realismus.* Hamburg: Classen, 1958.

Lyotard, Jean-Francois. *The Differend: Phrases in Dispute.* Translated by Georges van der Abbelle. Minneapolis: University of Minnesota Press, 1988.

Mauthner, Fritz. *Beiträge zu einer Kritik der Sprache.* 3 vols. Hamburg: Felix Meiner, 1967.

Miller, J. Hillis. *Speech Acts in Literature.* Stanford, Calif.: Stanford University Press, 2001.

Monk, Ray. *How to Read Wittgenstein.* New York: Norton, 2005.

———. *Ludwig Wittgenstein: The Duty of Genius.* New York: Penguin, 1991.

Mounce, H. O. *Wittgenstein's "Tractatus": An Introduction.* Chicago: University of Chicago Press, 1981.

Mulhall, Stephen. *Wittgenstein's Private Language: Grammar, Nonsense, and Imagination in Philosophical Investigations §§243–315.* Oxford: Clarendon, 2007.

Nietzsche, Friedrich. *Jenseits von Gut und Böse.* Stuttgart: Kröner, 1921.

———. *Über Wahrheit und Lüge im Außermoralischen Sinn.* In *Werke in drei Bänden*, edited by Karl Schlecta, 3:309–22. Munich: Hanser, 1981–82.

Perloff, Marjorie. "'But Isn't the Same at Least the Same?' Wittgenstein and the Question of Poetic Translatability." In *The Literary Wittgenstein*, edited by Wolfgang Huemer and John Gibson, 34–54. London: Routledge, 2004.

———. "Toward a Wittgenstinian Poetics." *Contemporary Literature* 33, no. 2 (1992): 191–213.

Politzer, Heinz. *Franz Kafka: Parable and Paradox.* Ithaca, N.Y.: Cornell University Press, 1962.

Preece, Julian, ed. *The Cambridge Companion to Kafka.* Cambridge, Eng.: Cambridge University Press, 2002.

Richards, Ivor A. *The Philosophy of Rhetoric.* London: Oxford University Press, 1976.

Ricketts, Thomas, and James Levine. "Logic and Truth in Frege." *Proceedings of the Aristotelian Society, Supplementary Volumes* 70 (1996): 121–75.

Riffaterre, Michael. *Fictional Truth.* Baltimore: Johns Hopkins University Press, 1990.

Rilke, Rainer Maria. *Duineser Elegien.* Vol. 1 of *Gedicht-Zyklen: Werke in drei Bänden.* Frankfurt am Main: Insel, 1966.

Robertson, Ritchie. "Myth vs. Enlightenment in Kafka's *Das Schloß.*" *Monatshefte* 103, no. 3 (2011): 385–95.

Rolleston, James, ed. *A Companion to the Works of Franz Kafka.* Rochester, N.Y.: Camden House, 2002.

Rorty, Richard, ed. *The Linguistic Turn: Recent Essays in Philosophical Method.* Chicago: University of Chicago Press, 1967.

Scherpe, Klaus. *Beschreiben, nicht Erzählen!: Beispiele zu einer ästhetischen Opposition: Von Döblin und Musil bis zu Darstellungen des Hoocaust.* Berlin: Humboldt-Universität zu Berlin, Philosophische Fakultät II, Institut für deutsche Literatur, 1995.

Scherpe, Klaus, and Elizabeth Wagner. *Kontinent Kafka: Mosse-Lectures an der Humboldt-Universität zu Berlin.* Berlin: Vorwerk 8, 2006.

Schuman, Rebecca. "Kafka's *Verwandlung*, Wittgenstein's *Tractatus*, and the Limits of Metaphorical Language." *Modern Austrian Literature* 44, no. 2/4 (2001): 19–32.

———. "'Unerschütterlich': Kafka's *Proceß*, Wittgenstein's *Tractatus*, and the Law of Logic." *The German Quarterly* 85, no. 2 (Spring 2012): 156–72.

Searle, John. "The Logical Status of Fictional Discourse." In Davies and Matheson, *Contemporary Readings*, 9–21.

Sluga, Hans D. "Ludwig Wittgenstein: Life and Work." In Sluga and Stern, *Cambridge Companion to Wittgenstein*, 1–33.

Sluga, Hans D., and David G. Stern, eds. *The Cambridge Companion to Wittgenstein.* Cambridge, Eng.: Cambridge University Press, 1996.

Sokel, Walter. "Beyond Self-Assertion: A Life of Reading Kafka." In Rolleston, *A Companion.*

———. "Frozen Sea and River of Narration: The Poetics Behind Kafka's 'Breakthrough.'" *New Literary History* 17, no. 2 (Winter 1986): 351–63.

———. "Language and Truth in the Two Worlds of Franz Kafka." *German Quarterly* 52, no. 3 (May 1979): 364–84.

———. *The Myth of Power and the Self: Essays on Franz Kafka.* Detroit: Wayne State University Press, 2002.

Stern, David G. "The Availability of Wittgenstein's Philosophy." In Sluga and Stern, *Cambridge Companion to Wittgenstein*, 442–76.

———. *Wittgenstein on Mind and Language.* New York: Oxford University Press, 1995.

———. *Wittgenstein's "Philosophical Investigations": An Introduction.* Cambridge, Eng.: Cambridge University Press, 2004.

Stern, J. P. "Karl Kraus's Vision of Language." *Modern Language Review* 61, no. 1 (January 1966): 71–84.

———. "Words Are Also Deeds: Some Observations on Austrian Language Consciousness." *New Literary History* 12, no. 3 (Spring 1981): 509–21.

———, ed. *The World of Franz Kafka.* London: Weidenfeld and Nicholson, 1980.

Sussman, Henry. *Afterimages of Modernity: Structure and Indifference in Twentieth-Century Literature.* Baltimore: Johns Hopkins University Press, 1990.

———. "Kafka's Aesthetics: A Primer: From the Fragments to the Novels." In Rolleston, *A Companion*, 123–48.

———. *"The Trial": Kafka's Unholy Trinity.* New York: Twayne, 1993.

Thorlby, Anthony. "Kafka and Language." In Stern, *The World of Franz Kafka*, 133–45.

Weiler, Gershon. "On Fritz Mauthner's Critique of Language." *Mind* 67, no. 265 (1958): 80–87.

Wittgenstein, Ludwig. *Culture and Value.* Edited by Georg Henrik von Wright and Heikki Nyman. Frankfurt am Main: Suhrkamp, 1978.

———. *Philosophische Untersuchungen: Dritte Auflage, mit englischem und deutschem Register.* Edited and translated by G. E. M. Anscombe. New York: Macmillan, 1968.

———. *Tractatus Logico-Philosophicus/Logisch-philosophische Abhandlung.* Frankfurt am Main: Suhrkamp, 1963.

———. *Tractatus Logico-Philosophicus.* Translated by C. K. Ogden. Minneola, N.Y.: Dover, 1999.

———. *Vermischte Bemerkungen: Eine Auswahl aus dem Nachlass.* Edited by Georg Henrik von Wright and Heikki Nyman. Frankfurt am Main: Suhrkamp, 1978.

Zilcosky, John. "Surveying the Castle: Kafka's Colonial Visions." In Rolleston, *A Companion*, 281–324.

INDEX

References to numbered sections of works by Ludwig Wittgenstein are given in italics.

Adorno, Theodor W., 29, 61, 87

Black, Max, 44, 62–65

Corngold, Stanley, 75–81

Davidson, Donald, 62, 79–80
Derrida, Jacques, 78–79
Descartes, Rene, 184

Frege, Gottlob, 16, 40, 100–102
Freud, Sigmund, 27

Hofmannsthal, Hugo von, 23, 28

Jesenská, Milena, 129

Kafka, Franz: aphorisms, 28–29; "The Burrow" ("Der Bau"), 56; "A Country Doctor" ("Ein Landarzt"), 56, 66; "Description of a Struggle" ("Beschreibung eines Kampfes"), 58; diaries, 27–28, 86; "A Hunger-Artist" ("Ein Hungerkünstler"), 66, 184; "Jackals and Arabs" ("Schackale und Araber"), 56; *Octavo Notebooks*, 57; parables, 29–31; "Report for an Academy" ("Ein Bericht für eine Akademie"), 56
  "In the Penal Colony" ("In der Strafkolonie"): Designer (*Zeichner*), 141
  "The Judgment" ("Das Urteil"): *Verkehr* (sexual meaning), 90, 105
  The Metamorphosis (*Die Verwandlung*): aphasia, 82–83; apple thrown at Gregor Samsa, 68–69; Samsa's body, 75; Samsa's voice, 65–66; portrait of lady in fur, 66–67; *Ungeziefer*, 76–79
  The Trial: "Before the Law" ("Vor dem Gesetz"), 46–47; pornography in, 43; contradictions in, 45–46
Kraus, Karl, 23–27
Kripke, Saul, 158–59

language crisis (*Sprachkrise*), 23
logic, first-order: contradiction, 44–49, 71; *ex falso quodlibet*, 49–50; tautology, 44–45, 71; truth-table method, 48–50

Mauthner, Fritz, 23–25
metaphorical form, 62–66

Nestroy, Johann Nepomuk, 5
Nietzsche, Friedrich, 23, 57

Richards, I. A., 63–66
Russell, Bertrand, 16, 88, 206n12

Schiller, Friedrich, 57

Trakl, Georg, 16

Vienna Circle, 9, 22

Wittgenstein, Ludwig: as architect, 7–9; *Culture and Value* (*Vermischte Bemerkungen*), 9, 33; "late" Wittgenstein," 8; military service, 16; "two Wittgensteins," 6–7, 10; personal opinion of Franz Kafka, 10, 23

Wittgenstein, Ludwig, *continued*
Philosophical Investigations (*Philosophische Untersuchungen*): *§1*, 116–17; *§2–7*, 118; *§9–10*, 119; *§28*, 120; *§30*, 121; *§31*, 124; *§32*, 122; *§43*, 134; *§84*, 154; *§136–37*, 150; *§157*, 152; *§182*, 151; *§199*, 156; *§203*, 164; *§201*, 137, 149; *§216*, 153; *§243*, 169, 178; *§244*, 180; *§245*, 173, 180; *§246*, 180; *§247*, 182; *§255*, 190; *§258*, 183; family resemblance (*Familienähnlichkeit*), 128; form of life (*Lebensform*), 160–61; language game (*Sprachspiel*), 117; rule-following, 143–49
Tractatus Logico-Philosophicus: aesthetics, 95; as literature, 32–36; ethics, 97–98; format of, 15; introduction, 100; logical form, 90; pictorial form, 90; picture theory of language, 19, 43; "resolute reading," 103–4; riddle and enigma (*Rätsel)*, 94. PROPOSITIONS: *TLP 1*, 17, 32; *TLP 1.1, 1.13*, 17; *TLP 2*, 88; *TLP 2.01–2.18*, 18, 72, 89; *TLP 2.17*, 89; *TLP 2.18*, 90; *TLP 3–3.01,* 19; *TLP 3.14*, 72; *TLP 4–4.055*, 19, 72, 90; *TLP 4.0031*, 24; *TLP 4.063*, 100–101; *TLP 4.064*, 102; *TLP 4.1212*, 20, 51, 55, 72, 73; *TLP 4.18*, 49–50; *TLP 4.31*, 20, 81; *TLP 4.41*, 42; *TLP 4.442–4.46*, 71; *TLP 4.461, 4.462*, 41–50; *TLP 5.12*, 49–50; *TLP 5.143*, 50; *TLP 5.5422*, 102; *TLP 5.6*, 20, 97; *TLP 5.61*, 51–52, 92; *TLP 6*, 20; *TLP 6.41*, 98; *TLP 6.42–6.43*, 21, 35, 98; *TLP 6.44*, 105; *TLP 6.5–6.53*, 21, 94, 99; *TLP 6.54*, 22; *TLP 6.573*, 47; *TLP 7*, 22, 85

Zweig, Stefan, 16